JRE STUDIES IN RELIGIOUS ETHICS 1

Love and Society:

Essays in the Ethics of Paul Ramsey

Edited by

James T. Johnson
David H. Smith

American Academy of Religion

and

SCHOLARS PRESS

Distributed by

SCHOLARS PRESS
University of Montana
Missoula, Montana 59801

LOVE AND SOCIETY

ISBN: 0-88420-123-6
Library of Congress Catalog Card Number: 74-19665

Printed in the United States of America

Printing Department
University of Montana
Missoula, Montana 59801

Contents

Preface

The subtitle of this volume hides a story: "Essays *in* the Ethics of Paul Ramsey," not "Essays *on* the Ethics of Paul Ramsey." From the earliest planning stages of this volume the editors intended that it not be a *Festschrift* in one narrow meaning of that term. *Festschriften* often only include essays which interpret or directly build on the thought of the honoree. We believed (and believe) that a wider scope was appropriate in this case.

Paul Ramsey was born in Mississippi in 1913, graduated from Millsaps College in 1935, and received B.D. (1940) and Ph.D. (1943) degrees from Yale University. After brief teaching stints at Millsaps, Garrett Theological Seminary and Yale he joined the faculty of Princeton University in 1944. Throughout his professional career Ramsey has continued to learn; the extensive bibliography which concludes this volume represents only one index of his intellectual vitality.

This intellectual growth and change has come through dialogue: with other academics, with professionals in the military, and with physicians. Our aim, therefore, was to produce a book which would both *criticize* Ramsey's own developing thought and *embody* the principles of creative independent reflection for which he has stood. To that end we include three different types of essays in the volume: some analyze, interpret, or otherwise directly criticize Ramsey's work; others are more constructive but build on Ramsey's thought in a more or less direct way; still others simply advance the state of knowledge in areas opened up by Ramsey. Specifically, the essays by Donald Evans, Paul Camenisch, Charles Curran, David Little and David Smith fall into the first group, those by William V. O'Brien, Richard McCormick and James Johnson are in the second; the third type is represented by the contributions of LeRoy Walters, Gene Outka and William F. May.

I

All of the essays in Part I are of the exegetical/interpretive type. Too few scholars have viewed Ramsey's work with an eye to fair judgments about his exact meaning, clear delineation of developments in his ideas, or the relationship between his views and other parallel streams of thought.

Donald Evans' paper is an inquiry into Ramsey's contention that there should be exceptionless rules in Christian ethics. He notes various problems of ambiguity and imprecision in Ramsey's defense of this position. While it is logically possible to formulate an exceptionless moral rule, Ramsey has failed to show that rules with universalizable exceptions are *il*logical. And his attempts to formulate exceptionless rules make use of "elastic" or "plastic" terms with the result that these rules are only apparently exceptionless. Although they are "verbally unrevisable" Ramsey's rules are "not genuinely exceptionless." Further, it is in no way clear that either rule-utilitarian, deontological, or fidelity-obligation considerations require the statement of anything beyond "virtually" exceptionless rules; nor do theological arguments suggest a different result.

Paul Camenisch agrees with Evans that Ramsey has stressed too much the importance of exceptionless rules. But Camenisch argues that the root of this error is important. Ramsey has held that persons now live in an ethos which separates and alienates them from each other and from their individual and collective past; in this situation preservation of some form of continuity in the moral life becomes imperative. Moreover, according to Ramsey, Christian ethics as a discipline has a definite task: creation of an ethos in which the rights and integrity of individuals are protected. Camenisch thinks that Ramsey has too hastily and uncritically embraced exceptionless moral rules as a way of providing the needed continuity, but a vigorous attack on the problem of continuity was inevitable given Ramsey's perception of our time and understanding of Christian ethics.

In fact, the whole point of Camenisch's essay is that many of Ramsey's polemical and controversial forays make much more sense if his constant commitment to the protection of individual persons is kept in mind. This commitment explains Ramsey's changing (and at crucial points vague) use of covenant terminology, his complex attitude toward the role of consequences in moral reflection, and his unwillingness to tolerate moral theories which are callous about the suffering caused to persons through inattentiveness to the morality of means. Finally, Camenisch sees this same commitment to personal integrity behind Ramsey's restriction on the social role of church and moralists. (David Little, in Part II, has much less sympathy with Ramsey's views on this last point.)

Charles Curran concerns himself with another question: to what extent has Ramsey's thought been influenced by "traditional" Roman Catholic natural law theory? Curran's answer is: not as much as is often supposed.

Ramsey himself has sometimes exaggerated the similarities between his own views and those of Jacques Maritain; his use of such traditional natural law principles as the "rule of double effect" is not consistent with much of Catholic tradition. Although Ramsey has occasionally appealed to a "sense of injustice," he has neither developed this concept nor elaborated a doctrine of creation to give it theological backing. Finally, his apparently traditional defense of exceptionless rules rests on theological and philosophical foundations which are quite different from those of his conservative allies.

Thus, according to Curran, Ramsey has never developed the ontology which is a necessary component in traditional natural law theory. The starting point for his reflections is, instead, the idea of covenant love. David Smith claims that this starting point has influenced and limited Ramsey's discussions of the morality of killing. His characteristic interpretation of agape and its demands differentiates his views from those of such other theologians as Thomas Aquinas and Reinhold Niebuhr. Further, Smith agrees with Evans and Curran that Ramsey has not yet satisfactorily explained how, in his view, moral acts should be described. He has been hard pressed to use terms like *intention* and *direct doing* in ways which are both consistent and clear.

II

Paul Ramsey's writings on war might best be understood as part of his attempt to frame a Christian political ethics. Christian just war theory, he has argued, was once historically a valid political and moral doctrine; it showed how the power of the state ought to be employed. Nevertheless, Ramsey's focus has been chiefly on problems related to war and its conduct; we hope that Part II of this volume ("War and Political Ethics") reflects this duality of concern.

Both James Johnson and LeRoy Walters are concerned with "the just war tradition" in which Ramsey has claimed to anchor his political ethics. Walters' essay seeks to shed light on the functioning of just war theory by investigating four case studies in terms of the social, political and historical context in which certain selected just war theorists thought and wrote. Ramsey, Walters notes, concentrated almost exclusively on the *intellectual* history to which the theorists he treats contributed. Walters suggests both the great diversity of that tradition, on the level of conceptual development, and the ambiguous role that just war concepts have had when used as criteria to evaluate particular situations. General appeals to "the tradition" and its implications are evidently simplistic.

On the other hand, Walters does not deny the existence of a common vocabulary and set of criteria which most just war theorists could accept as normative. Johnson traces the complex religious and secular origins of these ideas and raises the question of Ramsey's relation to the historical just war tradition. The conclusion is that though Ramsey, like the tradition, begins with the thought of such seminal figures as Augustine and Aquinas, he moves from them in a way distinctive and different from that taken by historical just war thought. This is particularly apparent, Johnson argues, in two concerns central to Ramsey's thought on war, the norm of charity and the implications of his theory for strategy, both of which are entirely absent from the just war theory as it came into being.

David Little and William V. O'Brien are more concerned with the evaluation of Ramsey's political ethics as a proposed contemporary political philosophy. Little raises two major questions: (a) how does Ramsey reason about political matters and (b) to what authorities does he appeal in this reasoning? In the course of his discussion of these topics Little suggests that Ramsey defines politics "persuasively" (as he wishes it were) rather than reportively (as it is). Little is troubled by this, as well as by Ramsey's deemphasis of consequences and restrictions on the legitimate role of religious communities and spokesmen.

O'Brien shares some of these views. Ramsey, he thinks, has placed much too much weight on the principle of discrimination and not enough on the requirements of proportion and prudence. Although O'Brien is obviously sympathetic with Ramsey's attempt to formulate a non-pacifist political ethic, he (as Curran) notes the difference between Ramsey's views and "traditional" Catholic thought. Finally, O'Brien insists that Ramsey's political ethic is problematical precisely because it unrealistically restricts military policy. Of what import is an ethic which *cannot* be used?

Throughout this section, as in the first, there is recurrent reference to the problem of the basis or warrant for Ramsey's views. Smith seems to assume that these warrants are essentially theological, yet Ramsey certainly has addressed arguments to a secular audience in terms devoid of overt theological reference. What, for Ramsey, is the status of non-confessionally based ethical principles? Little seems to suggest that Ramsey's overt "natural law" arguments are really disguised religious appeals; that is part of the problem with Ramsey's "persuasive" definitions.

Charles Curran, in contrast, seems to take seriously Ramsey's appeals to a common human sense of injustice, even if he feels that Ramsey has provided an inadequate theological rationale for this appeal. James Johnson suggests a middle ground. Ramsey's thought may, in a rough way, be analogous to that of the sixteenth century Spanish theologian Francis de Vitoria. Vitoria appealed to the "secular" sensibility of his time, a sensibility which he knew to be colored and informed by Christian tradition. Just so, Ramsey self-consciously writes from and to a culture affected or tutored by Christian faith and ethics. A "natural" principle or norm for Ramsey, then, is one which can be defended without explicitly theological warrant *in this culture.* It is culture bound, but not exactly confessional.

III

Richard McCormick's essay in Part III provides an example of one type of natural law reasoning. McCormick is unabashed and straightforward in his assumption that there are commonly-held moral values to which we can all refer. The existence of these objective values means that it is plausible to speak about licit proxy consent in a somewhat broader way than Ramsey is willing to do. Whereas Ramsey is forced to oppose any non-therapeutic experimentation on children, McCormick holds that, *if the risk is negligible*, a parent may consistently give proxy consent for his/her child's involvement in some non-therapeutic procedures. The reason this is true is that the child has an interest in other values besides self-preservation; the parents are the child's moral guardians as well as his biological protectors. McCormick writes: "Why would the child so wish [to consent to the non-therapeutic procedure]? The answer seems to be that he would choose this were he capable of choice because he *ought* to do so."

The other essays in this Part use Ramsey's thought as a jumping-off place for constructive statements. Gene Outka discusses the question of the just distribution of medical resources, a topic Ramsey has approached from a different tack in *The Patient as Person.* Outka suggests that "to each according to his real needs" is a better theory of justice than others, when the resource to be justly distributed is medical care. This principle should be supplemented by a notion of similar treatment for similar cases. The effect of the argumentation is the production of a standard against which various reforms of health care delivery, as well as the present system of delivery, can be evaluated. Incidentally, this same standard is quite congruent with Ramsey's deontological theory of agape.

In the final essay William F. May, once an undergraduate student of Ramsey's, offers a theological analysis of the various ways in which society might use cadaver organs. Drawing on a wealth of anthropological, psychological and theological materials, May goes well beyond Ramsey's treatment of this same topic. He suggests that the modern hospital would be forced into a demonic social role were the routine salvaging of cadaver organs to be practiced; routine salvaging would also violate the complex and ambivalent relationship between the family of one newly dead and his body. Indeed, correct and meaningful ritual treatment of a dead body provides a basis from which ethical and social norms can be inferred.

IV

The editors wish to express their appreciation to *The American Journal of Jurisprudence, The Hastings Center Report, The Journal of Religious Ethics*, and *Perspectives in Biology and Medicine* for permission to reprint essays that originally appeared in their pages. More particularly we are most grateful to the several contributors, whose work and cooperation have made this volume possible and editing it a pleasure. The support and enthusiasm of the editors of *The Journal of Religious Ethics* during the formative stages of the volume are also deeply appreciated. Of course, the very definition of this project reveals our greatest indebtedness.

Finally, we wish to express our gratitude to Mrs. Jeanne Heffernan (secretary of the Department of Religion, Douglass College, Rutgers University) and Ms. Marlene Rodenbeck (secretary, Kennedy Center for Bioethics, Georgetown University), whose work beyond the call of duty in preparing this manuscript has been a great help to us. David Smith's writing and editorial work would have been impossible without a sabbatical leave grant from Indiana University and additional support both from the Kennedy Center for Bioethics and the Society for Religion in Higher Education. We share editorial responsibility for the volume as a whole with the exception of the Bibliography.

New Brunswick and Bloomington .... August, 1974

PART ONE

FOUNDATIONS

CHAPTER I

Paul Ramsey, Love and Killing[1]

DAVID H. SMITH

Sometimes situations arise in which a person's actions determine which of two other persons will live. Many subdivisions within this class of cases are possible, but the major one with which I shall be concerned divides the set into two groups: (A) those situations in which the persons have no prior involvement with each other (whether of competition or interdependence) and (B) those situations in which the persons are so involved. In this latter kind of case one person may be threatening the other (e.g., military conflict) or may, by virtue of his very existence, present serious dangers to the other's life (as, *e.g.*, a fetus may endanger a mother in some tragic pregnancies). I am primarily concerned with this second (B) type of case and, for the sake of convenience, will call them "conflict" cases. In these cases one of the two related parties must die and, in this sense, their lives conflict.

In the course of a professional career of some thirty years Paul Ramsey has felt obliged to address both kinds of cases. Roughly put, his contention has been that type (A) cases (in which there is no possibility of assessing a relation between the parties) are not susceptible to differential moral analysis. A "decision" between unrelated lives is best made in a "random" way so as to preserve the equal dignity of the persons involved (1970B:239-276). In contrast, type (B) or "conflict" cases have a preferential moral resolution. Ramsey holds that one must act to save a threatened party, even if the consequence of this action is the death of the threatener.

The paper which follows contains comments on two aspects of Ramsey's treatment of conflict cases: the understanding of love which is the foundation of Ramsey's ethic and his understanding of the analysis of human action. I shall comment on these topics in an attempt to show how various facets of Ramsey's work focus on a central theme, a theme which has been repeated in both bass and treble clefs throughout Ramsey's career. As the discussion proceeds I shall note some problems and alternatives.

I

The first step in assessing Paul Ramsey's discussions of conflict cases is to notice that his moral theory is controlled and informed by prior faith commitments: specifically, it is covenant centered. Its basis is the assumption that God has made a covenant with mankind and that, therefore, the chosen people have an obligation to be faithful to the covenant. There are two ingredients in this assumption. The first of these is the establishment by God of a bond between Himself and persons. The second ingredient we might call a principle of replication. As God has committed Himself to persons, so they ought to commit themselves to each other. The God-person relationship establishes a standard or norm for the believer's person-person relationships.

Ramsey's most thorough development of these ideas is still *Basic Christian Ethics* (1950A) which began with a discussion of the Christian idea of justice. Christians must define justice in terms of God's prior righteous action (1950A:12-15). Fidelity to the action of God requires congruent fidelity between persons. Therefore, Christian moral reflection always includes a referent to the past and consists of an attempt to spell out norms of conduct which are appropriate to the divine precedent: "Christian ethics is a deontological ethics" and "neighbor love is not good, it is obligatory" (1950A:115f). Faithful relations between persons are all important. In 1967 he wrote: "The Christian understanding of righteousness is . . . radically non-teleological. It means ready obedience to the present reign of God, the alignment of the human will with the Divine will that men should live together in covenant-love no matter what the morrow brings, even if it brings nothing" (1967A:108f). God requires total concern with neighbor need: "The biblical notion of justice may be summed up in the principle: To each according to the measure of his real need, not because of anything human reason can discern inherent in the needy, but because his need alone is the measure of God's righteousness towards him" (1950A:14).

For Ramsey this is the core of the Old Testament ethic, but the basic idea is continued in the New Testament. Early Christians regarded Jesus as the "righteousness of God." For them the center of the covenant was Jesus who both embodied and taught the importance of love (1950A:14-24). The love commandment, therefore, is the basic rule or principle of *Christian* morality. "Everything is lawful, *absolutely everything* is permitted which love permits, everything without a single exception" and "*absolutely everything* is commanded which love requires, absolutely everything without the slightest exception or softening" (1950A:89).

Use of the word *absolutely* is significant; it is Ramsey's way of specifying the intensity of commitment to neighbor need which love requires. The intense commitment, moreover, is not simply to general benevolence, but is directed to specifiable concrete individuals. The root of Ramsey's argument on this point is his view of the relationship between eschatology and ethics in the teachings of Jesus. His basic idea is that the message and ethic of Jesus were apocalyptic which means that they were directed to the one-to-one situation, the relationship between only two individuals. Jesus' commandment to love was concerned only with the proper form of this bipolar relationship.

According to Ramsey, Jesus expected an immediate transformation of the world by God, a transformation which would establish an historical reign of absolute justice. Thus, when Jesus commanded his followers to love, he did not expect love "to be able to deal with every form of evil" and he assigned to it a "limited but positive function" (1950A:37-39). Jesus' eschatology limited the sphere of his ethical concern. Does this invalidate the ethic in an age which does not share the eschatological views of the teacher? No, because we too can focus on bipolar relationships and strip away concern for the future, as Jesus did. For us, as for him, the eschatological and crucial situation is the relation with one particular other person. Jesus' commandment to love provides us with a norm for the one-to-one relationship. It shows me how I ought to be related to each one of the many other persons with whom I come in contact.

Therefore, the "apocalyptic" element which appeared to be a liability in the teaching of Jesus turns out to be its strongest asset. Of course we live in a world of many personal relationships, but we "need to see more clearly how we should be obliged to behave toward one neighbor . . . if there were no other claims upon us at all" (1950A:44). The relevance of Christian ethics today arises from the fact that "its standard . . . is not accommodated to man's continuing life in normal historical relationships; and this in turn is true in point of origin precisely because of Jesus' apocalyptic view of the kingdom of God" (1950A:44). Jesus demanded total concern with the needs of each particular neighbor; the Christian can abstract himself from the plurality of relationships in which he lives and measure each relationship by the "eschatological" standard. Thus the love commandment provides a kind of heuristic norm which impinges on each bipolar human relationship.

To see the relevance of this theological ethic for conflict cases we should note that Ramsey's first discussions of killing began with an analysis of the ethic of Jesus on the question of violence. Jesus taught, Ramsey holds, an ethic of absolute non-resistance. "Neither active resistance nor passive non-cooperation are identical with Jesus' strenuous ethic of non-resistance, and neither one approximates closer to it than the other" (1950A:69). If the only parties to a conflict situation are the Christian and someone who threatens his life, the Christian would be obliged to die rather than to kill. But such situations are atypical. There is almost always more than one "other," more than one relationship, to consider. Therefore, the important issue is not self-defense but proper behavior towards other persons in conflict.

Ramsey's way of resolving the conflict problem, in other words, depends on his interpretation of Jesus' ethic as "apocalyptic" or "eschatological" and, therefore, referring directly to the one-to-one relationship. Since *our* forms of responsibility involve many relationships, *we* must ask about the implications of full fidelity when *another* party's life is threatened:

> Jesus dealt only with the simplest moral situation in which blows may be struck, the case of one person in relation to but one other. He does not . . . undertake to say how men . . . ought to act in more complex cases where non-resistance would in practice mean turning *another person's face* to the blows of an oppressor (1950A:167, emphasis added).

The Christian therefore faces a problem that Jesus did not face:

> The Christian . . . must adjudicate and decide one way or another among the claims and needs of neighbors he is to serve. In doing so, he at least omits to serve some, and in this sense he wades through blood and suffering. If such a one is forced for the sake of his neighbors visibly to step over a corpse, he can . . . find within himself in his Christian conscience, a sanction which depends on a proper reading of his actual situation and the needs of neighbors determining his vocation (1950A:180).

Ramsey's inference is that love for one neighbor may require me to resist or be violent to another one. I am to love person X; he is attacked by person Y; the love for X which requires me to protect him, therefore, may require me to do violence to Y.

Ramsey has utilized this basic paradigm (that my love for one neighbor may require me to kill another who threatens him) as the core of his discussions of war and abortion. Before proceeding further we should note some important characteristics of the skeleton of the argument.

First, Ramsey's central moral argument involves work on a fairly high level of generality. He has abstracted from particulars of two different sorts. On the one hand, he has never, so far as I know, engaged in an extensive discussion of different kinds of violence. The important issue in his mind is the one which the protection paradigm enables him to resolve, the gulf between resistance and non-resistance. The distinction between various forms of violence, e.g., lethal vs. non-lethal, is of much less importance to him. Thus, once he has shown that love and coercion are occasionally compatible, Ramsey is not systematically interested in haggling over the relative *degree* of congruity which might be found between love, on one side, and psychological, socio-political, economic, legal and military forms of coercion. This is not to say that Ramsey justifies the indiscriminate use of any one of these kinds of force; it is to say that his tendency to think in terms of the paradigm has meant that he has not raised the question of the relative moral validity of various forms of power or force. (Curran, 1973:40 makes a parallel point.)

On the other hand, it is important that Ramsey's handling of conflict cases proceeds in great remove from his starting point, the Christian scriptures. Particular texts which bear on the morality of killing are never seriously considered. Equation of the eschatological demand with the one-to-one situation may be even more problematical. Further, various theological doctrines which Ramsey elsewhere uses to good purpose and which have an obvious scriptural basis are not related integrally to what Ramsey would call the "ground floor" of this discussion. Thus he never bases his argument for killing on the requirements of natural justice as a strong doctrine of creation would allow him to do.

The failure to utilize a theological anthropology may be even more striking, given the historical context in which Ramsey has written. Reinhold Niebuhr's way of handling conflict cases was to say that their origin was inevitable human sinfulness. His argument against pacifism was to concede (as Ramsey does) that love requires non-resistance, but Niebuhr then denied the applicability of love in a real world of sinners. The applicability of love to any relation in the world was established through a set of intermediate concepts (the "love-justice dialectic"). Conflict cases were then weighed relative to equality ("love in terms of logic") rather than love.

This whole mode of reasoning is not only missing from Ramsey's approach to this issue, it is antithetical to it, a fact which is obscured by Ramsey's occasional invocations of Niebuhrian realism. Anthropology, and the doctrine of sin in particular, play a very small part in Ramsey's handling of conflict situations. He never explicitly says that sin *causes* conflict. More generally one can note Ramsey's relative lack of concern with social equality. Although he is very concerned with what Gene Outka has called "equal consideration" (1972:19-21), the very concept which Niebuhr's approach pushed to the forefront is a second order matter for Ramsey.

In contrast with Reinhold Niebuhr, Ramsey's less sweeping doctrine of sin has meant that the irrelevance of love to any human decision is the one thing that can never be assumed. Rather than implying the irrelevance of love, conflict situations put love to the test. The depth of my commitment to the neighbor is, in a way, revealed in what I am willing to do for him. What kind of love do I have for someone if I am unwilling to get my hands dirty in protecting him from harm? "Participation in regrettable conflict falls among distasteful tasks which sometimes become imperative for Christian vocation. Only one thing is necessary: for love's sake it must be done" (Ramsey, 1950A:184). The justification of protective killing has nothing to do with the "superiority" of the Christian; it has everything to do with the concrete needs of a particular neighbor (Ramsey, 1950A:179f.).

Second, it is obvious that Ramsey's treatment of conflict cases reflects not only an abstraction from social and theological particulars, it is also decisively influenced by the definition of love he adopted early in his career. This radically altruistic definition is certainly open to question on both theological and psychological grounds. One historically important alternative would be to define love as friendship. This definition, often utilized in Catholic literature, might lead to a differing set of convictions about the implications of love in the conflict situation. The reciprocal sharing and affectional bond "friendship" connotes might not involve doing *everything* that the other needs. If love were understood as something other than absolute covenant fidelity to the neighbor, it would be less plausible that *love* could require killing on his behalf. That plausibility arises, at least in part, from the intensity of the agapeic bond.

A brief illustration may help. Thomas Aquinas defined charity as man's friendship for God based on God's communication of His happiness to man (1947: Q. 23, A. 1). This charity is "the fellowship of the spiritual life" (1947: Q. 23, A. 2). It is primarily love for God as the cause of happiness; persons are loved because they "partake" of happiness (1947:Q. 25, A. 12). "God is to be loved chiefly and before all out of charity: for He is loved as the cause of happiness, whereas our neighbor is loved as receiving together with us a share of happiness from Him" (1947:Q. 26, A. 2).

A consequence of this idea is that there is an "order in charity," an order which Aquinas discusses especially in *Summa Theologica* II/II Q. 26. The general thesis is that although we are to wish the same generic good (everlasting life) to all men, this does not settle the question of what benevolence for individuals may require (1947:Q. 26, A. 6). Our specific obligations based on charity are, instead, a function of persons' "character of more excellent good" and of their "closer connection" to us. Thus we are to love good persons more than bad and members of our families more than others, all other things being equal. Of course, all other things are not always equal and Aquinas must explain the relative importance of these criteria. Roughly, he holds that one should "wish a greater good to one who is nearer God" while he "loves those who are more closely united to him with more intense affection" (1947:Q. 26, A. 7).

The last point is the most relevant to our limited concerns. Consistent with it and the foregoing general theory, Aquinas holds that "man's love for himself is the model of his love for another," that "the model exceeds the copy," and that charity, therefore, requires a person to "love himself more than his neighbor" (1947:Q. 26, A. 4). One should love his neighbor more than his own body (1947:Q. 26, A. 5) but one may not compromise his friendship with God in order to care for the neighbor. His own "share of the Divine good is a more potent reason for loving than that another should be partner with him in that share." In particular, one "ought not to give way to any evil of sin, which counteracts his share of happiness, not even that he may free his neighbor from sin" (1947:Q. 26, A. 4). This last point takes on especial force when we recall that Aquinas would regard freeing the neighbor from sin as a more important obligation in charity than protecting that same neighbor's body (cf. 1947:Q. 25, A. 2).

The contrasts with Ramsey's views are interesting. While it is clear that Aquinas reconciles charity and war (1947:Q. 40), he in no way bases his reconciliation on a claim that love should provide "everything" which the other needs. The neighbor's physical needs are subordinate to his spiritual ones. More to the point, however, is Aquinas' clear view that there are obligations to self and God which may override even the most pressing obligations to one's neighbor. It would make sense for Aquinas to describe a case of a neighbor who "needed" saving, yet whom one could not save as an act of charity, since the saving act was sinful. For Ramsey the total commitment to neighbor entailed by agape makes such a limitation of the requirements of love a contradiction in terms. For Aquinas the God-relation produces obligations prior to and distinguishable from those arising from agapeic concern for neighbor. For Ramsey this does not seem to be true and the possibility of this *kind of* conflict of obligations does not seem possible.[2]

Finally, there is another and less obvious sense in which Ramsey's convictions about love affect his handling of conflict cases. While he admits that the alternative is logically consistent (1968A:501, cf. Curran, 1973:60), Ramsey himself has held for at least twenty-five years that conflicts should be resolved in favor of the physically threatened other. This victim's need for life rather than some need of the threatener is decisive. Ramsey has never systematically defended this association of agape with active physical protection. In fact, he has tended to adopt Kierkegaard's idea that love "begins with the first neighbor it sees" (1950A:95) and to minimize the problem of choice among neighbors to be loved. To do otherwise and raise questions about the relative worthiness of various neighbors as recipients of love probably seems to him inconsistent with an understanding of agape as immediately relevant to *each* human relationship.

In sum, Ramsey's discussion of conflict cases is controlled by his use of the ultimate norm of agape, understood as the obligation to do everything possible for the needs of particular neighbors. It becomes clear that agape leads to active physical protection. The centrality of this idea in Ramsey's work is seen when we remember his judgment about cases in which no "conflict" relation is present. Agape is unable to suggest a preferential resolution of such cases (1970B:239-276, cf. 1973a:220, n. 25). An asymmetric relationship of conflict in which a life is threatened provides the agapist with the paradigm situation in which killing may be required by love.

II

Were his analysis to go no further than the rough paradigm, however, Ramsey's criteria for killing would remain too vague. An appeal to the protective rationale might conceivably be too restrictive since morally culpable threats may be rare; on the other extreme, the mere insistence that killing is justified so long as the Christian has a virtuous protective motive puts no practical limit on the amount of justifiable killing. Aware of both these dangers, Ramsey has adopted, with modifications, a Thomistic theory of human action. Love is to rule not only our hearts but each of our deeds. And each deed, not simply its consequences, must be loving.

As in the case of love, thorough discussion of the sophisticated theory of action is beyond our purposes here. Nor shall I attempt to assess the accuracy of Ramsey's interpretations of various writers. Rather I shall report what I take to be Ramsey's views and suggest some difficulties with them.

It is convenient to begin with Ramsey's interpretation of Thomas Aquinas' discussion of the killing of an unjust aggressor. According to Ramsey, Augustine had held that a Christian in his private capacity ought to allow himself to be killed rather than kill the unjust threatener of his life (1950A:173-176, 1961B:35-39). Aquinas analysed the problem in a more subtle manner (1947:Q. 64, A. 7) and held that the killing of an unjust aggressor was compatible with charity since the intention of the act was life saving. Intentionality was not, for Aquinas, identified with either motive or conspicuous consequence. Rather it referred, in part, to a "reasonable" interpretation of the nature of the voluntary human act (cf. e.g., 1947:Q. 18, AA. 5,8). Not all acts killing someone have a charitable intention, but those killing *unjust* aggressors may reasonably be so described, even if the threatened person is the self.

Ramsey's writings contain no lengthy discussion of Aquinas' concept of intention, a complex if not ambiguous concept. But it is clear that Ramsey has thought that Thomas failed to provide clear criteria from which one could infer the intentionality of human behavior. Ramsey claims that it was the necessities of penitential discipline within the medieval church which forced later moralists to develop such criteria (1961B:43-58). The traditional criterion which is of most interest to him is the identification of the "intended" act with the "directly done" deed. He seems to understand "direct doing" to connote immediacy and unity of action.

Ramsey's attitude toward this identification of intention and direct doing has always been equivocal. One can see the changes of attitude on various pages of *War and the Christian Conscience.* The developments after Thomas represented a victory for "natural justice . . . over love in Christian ethical theory." Identification of the intentional with the directly done leads to difficulties in some hard cases of self-destruction. In altruistic self-destruction the self is "directly" killed, yet Ramsey felt it was very misleading to condemn such an act as suicide. If a general swallows a suicide pill to avoid giving information to the enemy, his action is one of directly killing, but his intention seems different and distinguishable from that of other less justified "suicides" (1961B:46f., 57, 185).

On the other hand, against Protestant moralists who seemed to him to be unconcerned with the nature of human actions, Ramsey described this correlation of intention and direct doing as an "improvement" because it made clear that the stress on intention did not state conditions satisfiable in terms of mere inwardness. "There is," he wrote, "need for a decisive objective reference to what is done directly, or *in fact* only indirectly permitted." "Intentions alone are always open to suspicion, unless they are also controlled by some more objective determination of right action" (1961B:50f., 55, 58).

As Charles Curran notes elsewhere in this volume, this same ambiguity has marked Ramsey's subsequent discussions of conflict cases. He has tended to adopt a tight intention/direct-doing correlation in his writings on war, since his major opponents in that context have been writers who seemed to want to reduce morality to either good motives or cost/benefit calculations. Against both, Ramsey has insisted that there is an important third level: assessment of the morality of individual acts or policies of war. Thus the predictable and inevitable collateral damage following justified acts of war raises an important issue, but a different one from the problem of the justifiability of the act in the first place. Similarly, Ramsey's later discussions of the morality of deterrence (1968A:281-366) seem to presuppose a narrow understanding of what is intended and a correspondingly tight correlation between the intended and the directly done.

On the other hand, there is another theme in these discussions (e.g., 1968A:471) which comes out even more clearly in Ramsey's discussions of abortion. The first significant discussion of abortion is in *War and the Christian Conscience.* Ramsey describes what he takes to be the traditional Roman Catholic position on the issue: direct killing is always wrong; surgery which directly kills a fetus is prohibited. If fetal life and maternal life conflict, and if the only way to save the mother is by directly killing the fetus, then there is nothing which may be done. It is better to let both die than to directly kill.

The substance of Ramsey's response to this position has never changed, but his language has. In *War and the Christian Conscience* his major concern was with the morality of war and he was therefore committed to equating the intentional with the directly done. Consistently, he thought that in order to justify abortions in cases where fetal and maternal life conflicted he had to allow an exception to the prohibition on *direct* killing. The problem with the Catholic alternative was that it failed "to allow charity any vital role in the matter of morality." Therefore, "it would be *wrong* . . . for a physican to stand by and, by failing to take indirect or if need be, *direct* action, for him to allow both to die" (1961B:176, second emphasis added). When he thought he had to choose between agapism and the tight correlation of direct-doing with intention, Ramsey clearly preferred the agapaic judgment for the protection of life:

> By the absolutely supreme end of *agape*, not every means, not even every indispensable means, is justified, but surely every means to save life the only alternative to which is . . . death . . . To make this choice, on behalf of life and *against death and inaction*, is not to do wrong but to do what we know to be right (1961B:186, emphasis added).

The admitted directness of the killing is overridden by the demands of agape.

In Ramsey's subsequent discussions of abortion he has not changed his mind about the circumstances which will justify an abortion, but he has developed a form of words which allows him to suggest that the killings involved are only *direct* in an odd sense. A physically direct abortion may be an indirect killing and therefore unintentional.

In "The Morality of Abortion" (1968g) Ramsey claimed that the salutary thing about the Catholic analysis was its distinction between "direct and indirect" abortion. Not all surgical procedures that terminate in fetal death have the same moral character. Moral character involves the intention of the action or its "primary thrust" as well as an assessment of consequences (1968g:78-84). We should note that abortions have as their objective the physical termination of life. Moral reflection on the issue cannot gloss over this.

Ramsey then goes on to say that in some circumstances a "direct" abortion may be justified. This is the same claim he had made in *War and the Christian Conscience* (1961B) but here there are additional qualifications. In the case of a justified abortion, Ramsey writes, "the intention of the action, and *in this sense its direction*, is not upon the death of the foetus . . . [but is] directed toward the incapacitation of the foetus from doing what it is doing to the life of the mother." The fetus, like many a soldier who may justifiably be killed, is personally innocent, yet he is functioning as a killer. Therefore the intention of the act which ends in his death is not killing but "incapacitation" (1968g:84, emphasis added). As Ramsey later wrote, the crucial fact is "the child's functional relation to its mother's death" (1973a:222). This relation produces a situation in which "an *observable, physically direct killing* of an unborn child should be understood to have the function of *stopping* its lethal action upon its mother's life and not to have the objective of killing that child as such apart from its fatal function" (1973a:220f., first emphasis added).

If these actions are better described as incapacitation than killing, Ramsey will have gone a long way to solving the problem that led him to adopt and adapt the Catholic terminology. For if justified abortions and acts of war are not actions of killing, morally speaking, it is much easier to say that they are acts of love. Agapism is preserved and can apply, perhaps without exception, to the most tragic conflict situations.

The problem is whether the redescription is plausible so long as intention and direct doing, understood as Ramsey seems to understand it, are identified. To say that fetal deaths and combatant casualties are not directly physically done strains our ordinary usage of words. Ramsey is aware of the problem. "The intention . . . and in this sense direction" of justified abortion is on incapacitation rather than fetal death. In *what* sense? Ramsey is here distinguishing intending from physical doing and then trying to use intentionality as a criterion for establishment of the direction of the action. But it is unclear that he succeeds, and the attempt may be doomed to failure since, on Ramsey's own account, the preoccupation with direct action arose precisely as a way of specifying intentionality.

The result of this discussion is to suggest that the analysis of action into which his treatment of conflict cases forces him represents a continuing locus of problems and development in Ramsey's thought. It seems fair to ask him to use crucial terms, such as direct doing, unequivocally, not with one meaning in one context and another meaning in another.

My sympathies lie with the looser correlation which appears most frequently in the abortion essays. There are various reasons for this. First, and most generally, moral description can, in theory, be distinguished from physical description, and it is the former that is at issue. Second, it is by no means clear that Ramsey's interpretation of the "traditional" Catholic idea of direct doing is correct. Richard A. McCormick, S.J. (1968:139f.) and Charles Curran (1973:125f.) have pointed out that the abortions Ramsey has described as "direct" yet justified would not be so described by all traditional Catholic writers. According to McCormick and Curran that tradition has not been as physicalistic as Ramsey assumes; from Thomas on its spokesmen have been concerned with moral rather than physical description. Thus to speak of an abortion as simultaneously "incapacitating" and "direct" would be a contradiction in terms. The tendency to make the terms "direct" and "indirect" attributes of the observable act rather than characteristics of the human will is not found in all Catholic literature. That literature provides, at best, a dubious precedent for Ramsey's early and tighter theory of direct doing.

Third, the real cause of this problem is conflict between two of Ramsey's objectives. His *polemical* and *controversialist* side, in high profile in the 1960's, forced him to oppose a "Gesinnungsethik," "contextualism" and some political "realism," all of which seemed to involve a tendency to gloss over the importance of fidelity in individual actions. The stress on direct doing was a useful weapon in these skirmishes. But Ramsey's consistent *systematic* concern has been the relevance of love to every human action. Yet the only way it is remotely possible to show this relevance is on the assumption of a clear distinction between the immediately identifiable event and the intentionally done act. It is inevitable that justifiable acts of love will not appear to be so. Ramsey is well aware of this fact but his sensibility is concealed by the direct doing terminology which inevitably suggests the transparency of individual actions.

Fourth, there is no reason Ramsey's theory requires the formulation of a criterion through which intentionality can be specified *post factum*. Statement of such a juridical set of criteria may be necessary in a forensic context, but it is unnecessary for a moralist, especially one who understands his role as Ramsey does. His primary concern is action guidance, not second-guessing.

Briefly put, Ramsey must choose between continuing use of vague "direct doing" terminology and presenting a coherent ethic of agapism. Should he fail to drop or define "direct doing" he will obscure his real reasons for justifying killing in some conflict situations and not others.

On the other hand, I do not think that Ramsey can avoid this complex of issues without completely reworking his theological ethic. At this point a loose contrast with one of his contemporaries may be instructive. The importance of the concept of intention and its meaning have been hotly debated among contemporary Roman Catholic moralists all of whom want to break with a physicalist tradition. The most important and forceful contributor to that discussion has been Richard A. McCormick, S.J., whose monograph *Ambiguity in Moral Choice* (1973) both summarizes and contributes to the ongoing Catholic discussion.

Following Bruno Schüller, S.J., McCormick begins by making a distinction between doing non-moral evil and doing something morally evil. Doing a moral evil means causing another person or persons to sin. To intend such an evil is intrinsically wrong. On the other hand, our assessment of the doing of a non-moral evil, such as causing a death, is less clear (1973:55, 67). Where non-moral evils conflict we can distinguish an "intending" from a "permitting" will since the former is "more closely associated with the existence of evil" (1973:72). Whether the evil is intended or permitted affects both the immediate meaning and the broad social impact of an act (1973:71). Nevertheless, and that complication taken into account, conflict of non-moral evil situations are always to be resolved by choosing the lesser evil (1973:76). Both the intending and the permitting will are to be assessed teleologically (1973:82f.). Thus, whether non-moral evil is intended or not is only relevant insofar as intentions have consequences. The consequences envisioned are not gross, but it is nevertheless with reference to them that the importance of intentionality is established. Were the distinction between permitting and intending non-moral evil without effect in a particular case, McCormick would have to say it was unimportant.

Ramsey's starting point and theoretical conclusions are totally different. His theory of obligation is deontological which means that the morality of an action is assessed not only with reference to magnitude of good or harm done but, primarily, with reference to the conformity of the action in question to agape. This question of relative conformity can be raised of any action, whatever its effects. Thus the question of *which* specimens or instances of human behavior are to be measured cannot be avoided. One extreme view would be to assess the morality of every self-conscious movement; another would be to consider only the basic intentions and goals which can be seen to govern an entire life-span. The results would be paranoid scrupulosity, in the first case; and vague generality, in the second.

In order to avoid these problems Ramsey must explain how, with reference to what, one singles out units for measurement and judgment. His answer has been to say that we should judge those things which persons *intend* to do. The trouble is that he has never defined intention or explained the criteria with reference to which it can be specified. Ramsey began a new tack in his work on this problem with his use of Eric D'Arcy's book in *Deeds and Rules in Christian Ethics* (1967A:192-225), although the thrust of that discussion is toward the assertion *that* correct description is important; we do not receive an explanation of *how* questions about proper description are to be resolved. Furthermore, this new approach has not altered Ramsey's terminology or analysis on matters of martial or foetal killing.[3]

In any event, Ramsey's commitment to a deontological ethic makes it essential for him to explain how one specifies the units of action which are appropriate subjects of moral judgment, for central to deontology is the conviction that one cannot arrive at adequate moral assessments simply by totaling up the sum of good and bad effects. Thus, insofar as Ramsey's concepts of intention and direct doing (or their equivalents) remain vague, that far will his analyses of conflict situations appear arbitrary. It will be unclear why one aspect of a given action is decisive and another is secondary. His prior theological commitments mean that McCormick's way of analysing these issues is closed to him.

Thus, the differences between McCormick and Ramsey do not lie primarily on the level of practical conclusions, or even on the level of the analysis of moral experience. At these points they are in remarkable agreement. The basic difference between them is theological, involving differing conceptions of salvation, human nature, and—especially—of love. Unless this comes out into the open we can expect that this ongoing discussion will be another misplaced debate.

III

In summary, we can say that Ramsey's discussions of conflict cases have the following characteristics. They presuppose the God-person covenant and involve the notion that we should bind ourselves to particular others as God bound himself to us. We should not consider the relative worth of persons, only their needs. Our bond to individual persons is so strong that we may kill when it is necessary in order to *protect* them. Since such actions appear ambiguous, they must be analysed. Ramsey claims that it is the intentionality of the act, what is "directly done," that is decisive amid the ambiguity.

Thus Ramsey's discussion of conflict cases is influenced in many ways by his theory of love and his theory of action. The strengths and weaknesses of his thought on killing are functions of his basic ethical method. We have noted that the theological resources he utilizes are the product of considerable abstraction from scripture. On the other hand, his failure to develop the concept of intention independently of its application arises from the controversial and common-sensical character of his mode of work. Thus he will assert the defective notion of intention adopted by another writer (1970g: 90, n. 35) or ask the reader to agree with his interpretation of a "prismatic case" through which a plausible meaning of the concept emerges (1968A:322/328).

There can be no denying that this mode of work has serious limitations. We have already noted that it may lead to a foreshortening of theological and empirical analysis. Also that it can lead to inconsistency. On the other hand, the limitations may be the inevitable price paid for profundity. Ramsey's reasoning has a much higher degree of accessibility to the modern sensibility than that of such German writers as Barth and Thielicke, both of whom deal at length with conflict cases. If Ramsey's paradigm finally settles few issues, there are even fewer conflict situations to which it does not bring light.

FOOTNOTES

[1] An earlier version of this essay was read at the American Academy of Religion Meeting in Chicago, November, 1973. I am most grateful for the suggestions made then and since by Roy Branson, Frederick Carney, Charles Curran, Stanley Hauerwas, James T. Johnson, Richard McCormick, S.J., Paul Ramsey and LeRoy Walters. None of these men, of course, can be held accountable for problems which remain.

[2] Incidentally, this may be related to Ramsey's difficulty in distinguishing the obligations of true justice from those of agape. Aquinas can not only make the distinction, he can use it to limit the number of beings who are to be loved (cf. II/II Q. 25, A. 11).

[3] How much effect the broader Anglo-American philosophical discussion of intentionality and theory of action will have on Ramsey's work remains to be seen. For one suggestive appropriation by a theological ethicist see a recent essay by Stanley Hauerwas (1973).

REFERENCES

Aquinas, Thomas

1947 *Summa Theologica: Second Part of the Second Part* (translated by Fathers of the English Dominican Province). New York: Benzinger Brothers.

Curran, Charles E.

1973 *Politics, Medicine, and Christian Ethics: A Dialogue with Paul Ramsey.* Philadelphia: Fortress Press.

Hauerwas, Stanley
1973 "The self as story: religion and morality from the agent's perspective." *The Journal of Religious Ethics* I (Fall): 73-86.
McCormick, Richard A., S.J.
1968 "Past church teaching on abortion." Pp. 131-151 in *Proceedings of the Twenty-Third Annual Convention of The Catholic Theological Society of America* (June 17-20, 1968). Yonkers: Saint Joseph's Seminary.
1973 *Ambiguity in Moral Choice.* Marquette University: The 1973 Pere Marquette Theology Lecture.
Outka, Gene H.
1972 *Agape: An Ethical Analysis.* New Haven: Yale University Press.
Ramsey, Paul
See the bibliography of Ramsey's works in this volume. Capital letters (e.g. 1950A) denote books and occasional papers; lower case letters (e.g. 1968a) denote articles.

CHAPTER II

Paul Ramsey on Exceptionless Moral Rules[1]

DONALD EVANS

Some moral philosophers and theologians, including this writer (Evans, 1968), have claimed that there cannot be an exceptionless moral rule. In a recent article, Paul Ramsey (1968a) insists that there can be. He supports his position by a series of complex arguments. His lengthy discussion deserves very careful study, for he probes with great clarity many of the most fundamental issues in ethics, both secular and Christian. I shall try to show that some of his arguments are dubious, whereas others, though not conclusive, are powerful and illuminating. (Indeed, he forces me to concede that some moral rules are "virtually" exceptionless.) Whether readers agree with him or with me, they will find his essay interesting and important. I have selected seven of his main arguments for consideration.

I

His first main argument depends on a distinction between *singular* exceptions to moral rules and *universal* exceptions, so our first step is to clarify this distinction. Suppose that "Never do X" is a moral rule.[2] ("X" is a *kind* of action such as lying, adultery, stealing, etc.) A singular or particular exception to the rule has the form ". . . except in *this* situation S1." A universal exception has the form ". . . except in this *kind* of situation S." A singular exception is a violation of a moral rule. A universal exception is a revision of a moral rule. Hence, if someone talks about an "exceptionless" moral rule, he may mean one of two very different things. He may mean a rule which cannot be violated, or he may mean a rule which cannot be revised.

Another distinction which needs to be noted immediately is one between two senses of "can": the logical and the moral (or, more generally, the normative). The question, "*Can* there be an exceptionless moral rule?" may mean "Is it logically possible for there to be an exceptionless moral rule?" Or the question may mean, "Assuming that it is logically possible for there to be an exceptionless moral rule, can there ever be an adequate moral justification (or, more generally, an adequate normative justification) for holding that any moral rule is exceptionless?"

Ramsey's first attack is on two forms of singular exceptionism which some theologians espouse. These may be called "calculative" exceptionism and "creative" exceptionism. The calculative exceptionist holds that a calculation of the beneficial consequences of violating a moral rule in situation S1 may morally justify a violation. What counts as "beneficial" depends directly on an ultimate moral norm: happiness, love, self-realization or whatever it may be. "Creative" exceptionists, according to Ramsey, "seem to speak in more intuitive terms of actions that are 'unique' and in their uniqueness 'creative' of new moral departures. They seem to regard moral action as an unrepeatable spiritual venture that alone can be truly sensitive to the demands of the hour and fully open to the needs of other persons" (1968a: 68). Hence a creative exceptionist will violate a moral rule in a particular situation S1 on the ground that S1 is unique and unrepeatable and that his own moral insight into S1 leads him to do something which happens to violate the rule.

Ramsey's attack on calculative and creative exceptionists involves two steps. The first step, which I go along with, is to show that any moral exception to a moral rule must be, in principle, universal rather than merely singular. This step depends on a definition of the word "moral" such that any moral judgment must, as a logically necessary condition, be universalizable. That is, if a man judges that he ought to do X in situation S1, he implies that anyone (that is, anyone similar in the morally relevant respects)[3] ought to do X in situations which are similar to S1 in the morally relevant respects—that is, in situations of *kind* S. Thus no judgment can be a moral judgment unless it implies a moral rule. And no judgment concerning an exception to a moral rule can be moral unless it implies that the exception applies in all similar cases. Any singular exception to a moral rule, if moral, must imply a universal exception. Thus if moral judgments are by definition universalizable, singular exceptionism involves a logical contradiction: a moral exception which is merely singular and hence not moral.

If a calculative or creative exceptionist is committed to singular exceptionism, he is involved in logical contradiction unless he rejects the universalizability requirement for moral judgments—a requirement which seems to me to be part of morality as conceived in Judaeo-Christian and Western secular moral traditions. But a calculative or creative exceptionist can retain the substance of his position without being committed to singular exceptionism. He can concede that any moral exception to a moral rule has to be universal, and hold his ground against the second step in Ramsey's attack, which we shall now consider.

According to Ramsey, "A principle or moral rule cannot be challenged without confirming its validity—'*except . . .*'—then must follow good moral reasons for the exception. Without these, no exception; with these, a class of right actions will have been defined within or beside the rule" (1968a: 72). That is, an exception to a moral rule is not morally justified unless the agent is able to "characterize" (1968a: 68) the action, stating what features of situation S1 constitute the reason for the exception. The calculative and creative exceptionists thus fail to justify their exceptions. The calculative exceptionist merely states that a *quantity* of benefits will result from violation of the rule; he does not refer to special qualitative *features* of situation and of consequences. The creative exceptionist merely claims that situation S1 is unique, and *refuses to state* a list of features which, if repeated, would justify an exception again; perhaps God or an Ideal Observer could state the list, but it would be a useless labor, for the situation is repeatable only in theory, not in reality.

According to Ramsey, neither form of exceptionism can morally justify its exceptions. Let us consider calculative exceptionism first. Ramsey draws a legitimate distinction between two broad kinds of universal exception: (a) where we give a description of the exception-making features of the situation and of the consequences of the exceptional action; (b) where we give a quantitative estimate of the beneficial consequences of the exceptional action. Consider these two examples:

(a) Never lie except to save life, as is the case in situation S1.
(b) Never lie except when lying, as compared with not lying, will promote at least quantity Q of benefit, as it does in this situation S1. (If the comparative benefit of lying is less than Q, don't lie.)

Note that the exception in (b) is not singular but universal. The calculative exceptionist need not deny that if any agent were in a situation similar in morally relevant respects, the exception would apply.[4] Where he differs from Ramsey is in his designation of morally relevant respects. The universal reason which he gives for making an exception is not expressed as a description of qualitative features of the action in the situation as it is in (a): "to save life"; rather, it is expressed in a quantitative estimate of comparative benefits. The term "benefits" is used to refer to a balance of non-moral good over evil. In some cases the main good consists in the prevention of an evil or harm. In such cases (b) could be revised so as to read, "Never lie except when lying, as compared with not lying, will prevent as much harm as lying does in this situation S1."

Example (b), then, involves a universal exception. It designates a class of situations in which an exception is morally justified. In showing that singular exceptionism is self-contradictory if any moral judgment is by definition universalizable, Ramsey has not shown that a universal exception must be stated in terms of qualitative features rather than quantitative benefits. As we shall see, there are serious problems raised by quantitative-benefit (QB) exception clauses: whether the benefits are always morally relevant, how we weigh quantity in relation to qualitative features, etc. But QB clauses cannot be prohibited merely by an appeal to the universalizability requirement.

What about creative exceptionism? As Ramsey presents it for consideration, it is not an "exceptionism" at all, for there are not explicit moral rules, and thus no exceptions are logically possible. But in order to have a creative exceptionism to consider, let us consider the following position: there are some moral rules, for example, rules concerning lying. Any particular moral judgment, qua moral—including a judgment concerning an exception to a moral rule—implies a universal judgment. But this universal judgment need not be formulated, for the universalizability requirement is purely *formal* (Evans, 1968: 405-408). The creative exceptionist concedes that if any agent and situation were to be similar in all the morally relevant respects, then the same kind of action ought to be done; but these respects are too complex or too elusive to be stated in a formulated rule; and even if they could be formulated, the rule would in fact apply only to this one case. Though repeatable in theory, the case is unrepeatable in practice. Hence an exception to a moral rule, though formally or theoretically universal, is morally justifiable even though the universal exception is not *stated* (and cannot be stated, except by an Ideal Observer). Hence our creative exceptionist might hold the following, for example:

(c) Never tell a lie except when in a situation S1 or in any situation S which resembles this situation S1 in all the morally relevant respects. And don't ask me to state specifically what these respects are, or expect that any such situation will ever occur again!

The universalizability requirement for moral judgments does not commit us to stating in each case a universal rule or universal exception to a rule. Perhaps we should do this sometimes, but on other occasions we would surely be wiser to follow the advice of a creative exceptionist and refuse to do so. On the one hand, there is the problem of sheer *complexity*. What I have in mind here is not merely the number and variety of the moral considerations which are weighed, but also the fact that their *relative weight* cannot be schematized so as to have a rule which would apply with precision to any situation other than S1. On the other hand, there is the *elusiveness* of many of the elements in some situations of moral choice, especially those which involve intimate human relations and personal life style. Especially here there are elements which elude definite conceptualization: feelings and attitudes and influences and idiosyncratic ways of viewing oneself and others. Even a very articulate and sensitive novelist or poet can only sketch and suggest some of these, and they are often unrepeatable in practice; yet they rightly enter into the heart of some moral decision-making. Along these lines Iris Murdoch in her novel, *The Bell* (1958),[5] vividly (and, I think, deliberately) illustrates the sheer irrelevance of a formulated-rule morality in much of our moral life.

To sum up. Ramsey has shown that there can be no singular exceptions to moral rules. But he has failed to show that there can be no universal quantity-of-benefit exceptions or that there can be no universal unformulated unrepeatable-in-practice exceptions. Now let us consider a new point. If such exceptions are made, they weaken or undermine the moral rules. Ramsey rightly holds that universal exceptions do not weaken or undermine moral rules, but he has in mind cases where the rule-revision is formulated in qualitative-feature descriptions, for example, "Never lie *except to save life.*" But if a moral rule is open to exception whenever a similar quantity of benefit would result, or whenever a creative moral agent judges in favor of an exception, the rule is less firm and strong.

II

Indeed, Ramsey's next claim is that a calculative exceptionism *destroys* any moral rule to which it is applied by turning the moral rule into a mere maxim or summary concerning past cases. Each case is then to be decided as it arises by direct appeal to an ultimate norm, such as utility. For example, Ramsey claims (1968a: 84-85) that if a moral rule is modified in the following way, it is destroyed:

(d) We should not commit adultery except when it would do more good on the whole to do so.

I agree with Ramsey that the most plausible way to interpret this is as the replacement of a moral rule ("We should not commit adultery") by a maxim. The maxim would be elaborated as follows:

(d)A Usually adultery results in less good than non-adultery (since it usually causes considerable evil), so usually it is wrong to commit adultery; but in each and every case we have to decide solely on the basis of which alternative will, in the particular case, produce more overall good.

I have called the example "(d)A" because it interprets (d) in an *Act*-Utilitarian way. An Act-Utilitarian appeals only to his ultimate norm in each particular case. His maxim is merely a guide, based on a summary of judgments concerning previous cases. The maxim does not provide a distinct and independent consideration alongside the application of the ultimate norm.

But we have seen that a calculative exceptionist could say something very different:

(e) We should not commit adultery except when adultery, as compared with non-adultery, will promote at least quantity Q of benefit, as it does in this situation S1.

This is best elaborated in a Rule-Utilitarian way:

(e)R The rule "We ought not to commit adultery" is a good moral rule, whose general observance produces great overall good in society. Therefore the rule should be followed except when breaking it will promote at least quantity Q of benefit, when compared with the benefit of not breaking it. Anything less than quantity Q is insufficient to outweigh the fact that one is breaking this good rule.

Here the rule provides a moral consideration which is distinct from, and independent of, any calculation of the good and evil consequences of following or breaking the rule in a particular case. The rule is weakened, of course; but it is not destroyed. In (d)A, as Ramsey rightly claims, a quantitative-benefit (QB) exception-clause destroys a moral rule, turning it into an Act-Utilitarian maxim. But if a moral rule is understood in a Rule-Utilitarian way as in (e)R (or, indeed, in a deontological way), it is not turned into an Act-Utilitarian maxim. It still has an independent weight, so that an agent follows it in some cases where breaking it would produce more benefit than following it—that is, in cases where the comparative benefit of breaking the rule is less than quantity Q.

The position set forth in (e)R involves various difficulties, some of which I shall soon note. Here I want merely to refute Ramsey's objection. If Ramsey were correct, a Rule-Utilitarian could never appeal directly to his ultimate norm to justify a universal exception to a moral rule, for he would thereby have changed the moral rule into an Act-Utilitarian maxim. If Ramsey were correct, any such direct appeal to an ultimate norm would destroy the moral rule; that is, it would be logically impossible for a moral rule to have a QB exception-clause. Thus, if Ramsey were correct, one of the main arguments against exceptionless moral rules would have been disqualified before it could enter the fray, namely the argument that we should add a QB exception-clause to many moral rules: ". . . except when following the rule would cause great harm to others." But Ramsey is not correct. His argument only holds if any QB exception has to be like (d)A rather than (e)R. When we consider (e)R we see that it is logically possible for a moral rule to have a QB exception-clause. Of course, we still have to ask, "*Should* all moral rules have a QB exception-clause?" for perhaps some moral rules should not. This is a normative issue, which we shall consider later in relation to some of Ramsey's later normative arguments.

An exception-clause to a Rule-Utilitarian rule or to a deontological rule often refers not to quantitative benefits but to definite qualitative features, for example, ". . . except to save life." Such a qualitative exemption-condition is sometimes preferred because of the notorious difficulties involved in trying to calculate quantitative benefits. I merely note these difficulties here, without pursuing them. Instead, I want to draw attention to a further difficulty which arises for (e)R, even if quantitative benefits can be calculated satisfactorily. According to (e)R, we judge that the rule can outweigh a quantity of benefit (namely, any less than Q) which might be produced by breaking it. On what basis do we decide that the rule has *this* weight, no more, no less? One way of deciding avoids the problem of weighing incommensurables, though the procedure suggested is sometimes difficult to use. On this procedure, a QB exception-clause is itself appraised in a Rule-Utilitarian way. That is, we estimate that the general observance of the modified rule (with its specific QB exception-clause) will produce more overall good in society than the general observance of the unmodified rule, or of a modified rule in which the quantity is greater or less than Q. An alternative way of deciding involves a weighing of incommensurables, yet the procedure is somehow frequently used in practice. On this procedure, the QB exception-clause is appraised in an Act-Utilitarian way (without asking "What if most people observed the modified rule?"), while the unmodified rule is appraised in a Rule-Utilitarian way. Somehow, due weight is given to both approaches and a compromise decision is made. Similarly, there is sometimes a compromise worked out between the moral weight of a deontological rule and the moral weight of an Act-Utilitarian concern to avoid serious harm where this would be caused by following the rule in some situations. Such compromises are part of everyday morality, but they raise serious problems for ethical theory, for their logic or rationale is obscure. I should note that these problems exist, without trying to solve them here.

Perhaps I should also draw attention to an assumption which is crucial in my distinction between (d)A and (e)R, the assumption that Rule-Utilitarianism is not reduceable to Act-Utilitarianism, the assumption that moral rules can have independent weight for a utilitarian. It has been challenged by some able philosophers (Lyons, 1965; Narveson, 1967: Chapter 5), but I am not convinced by their arguments and hope to show why in another article.

In this section I have attacked Ramsey's claim that a calculative exceptionist's QB exception-clause destroys any moral rule to which it is attached. In the next section I shall support his attack on one position which, if tenable, would exclude the possibility of any exceptionless moral rules.

III

Ramsey's argument is directed against the following position:

> There *cannot* be any exceptionless moral rules because, so far as human moral judgment alone is concerned, we cannot know and we cannot formulate rules of conduct that are both certain in their determination of wrongfulness or praiseworthiness and certain as to

> the description of the actions to which these verdicts apply. This point of view holds that if we are certain that a sort of action is wrong we are uncertain about the actions to which to apply this judgment, and if we are certain about the action we are talking about we remain uncertain whether it should be judged to be wrong or praiseworthy (Ramsey, 1968a: 93-94).

A philosopher or theologian who supports such a position may point to the fact that, for many moral agents, the only exceptionless moral rules are those which are "elastic" in the meaning of their descriptive terms, so that the agent is free to make a moral judgment as to whether or not the description applies. Thus a moral agent may agree that cruelty or murder is always wrong, but he has to judge what is to count as cruelty or murder. Not all infliction of pain is cruelty, and not all killing is murder. For such a moral agent, there might be a moral rule which describes a prohibited kind of action in a neutral and definite way so that there is no doubt as to what the rule applies to; but such a rule would probably have some exceptions built into it and, more important, it should be held open to further exceptions. Such a moral agent might agree that it is wrong to tell someone something which one believes to be false, intending to get him to believe this, except in such-and-such kinds of situation; but the rule would have to be revisable in relation to new or unmentioned kinds of situations.

It is a fact, then, that for some moral agents, moral rules must be either elastic in meaning or open to further exceptions. But this fact does not prove that there *cannot* be an exceptionless definite-action moral rule. As Ramsey points out, the description of a prohibited kind of action can be as definite as any other descriptions which we give of things or events; the only element of judgment which is necessary is one which is involved in *any* application of universals to particulars. And the description can be expressed in morally neutral terms so that the identification of an action as one which falls under the description does not depend on one's moral stance at all. What counts as "cruelty" depends on one's moral stance, but what counts as "telling someone something which one believes to be false, intending to get him to believe this" does not depend on one's moral stance.

There *can* be an exceptionless definite-action moral rule. Indeed, the position which Ramsey attacks, though it sometimes seems to imply that such a rule is logically impossible, is mainly concerned with denying that such a rule would be prudent or moral in view of the limitations of our human wisdom. So the real question is, "*Should* anyone accept such a rule?" We shall consider this question later. We will be in a better position to do so when we have considered a fourth argument in Ramsey.

IV

This argument is best understood in terms of the distinction, which we have just been considering, between two kinds of moral rule. The rules differ in the type of description given of the kind of action which is prohibited. One rule has a neutral and relatively definite description, the other a non-neutral and relatively indefinite description. A traditional moral rule, such as the prohibition of adultery, can be interpreted in either of these two ways. On the one hand, "adultery" may be defined as "sexual intercourse between two people, one or both of whom is married to someone else." The expression "sexual intercourse" can be more precisely defined in bodily and physiological terms, and a more precise definition can also be given to the expression "married." Then whether or not anyone approves or disapproves of an action to which the definite description applies, he has no room for doubt as to whether or not it does apply. On the other hand, "adultery" may be understood as "unfaithfulness to the marriage bond" or "marital infidelity." This is a far less definite description of a species of action, and it is non-neutral. It does not necessarily exclude every case of "adultery" in the neutral, precise sense of the word. Rather, it excludes whatever violates the mutual fidelity which is intrinsic to marriage. In order to understand what adultery is, one has to understand what marriage is. The meaning of "adultery," though not completely vague, is elastic, open to interpretation on the basis of insight. Though marital infidelity is not the same as infidelity in general, what *counts* as marital infidelity cannot always be determined in advance.

Similarly, "lying" may be defined as "telling someone something which one believes to be false, intending to get him to believe it" or, in an elastic way, as "withholding the truth from someone to whom truth is *due*." And "stealing" may be defined as "taking something which by positive law belongs to someone else, without his permission," or, in an elastic way, as "taking, without permission, something which by positive law belongs to someone else, and to which one has no *moral* right in relation to the purposes of the institution of private property."

Ramsey notes that the way in which putative exceptions are considered varies in accordance with whether the key descriptive term—"adultery," "lying," "stealing"—is understood in a precise or in an elastic way. On the one hand, there may be a universal exemption because of *exempting-conditions* (which I shall call an "E-approach"). On the other hand, there may be no exception at all but, instead, a qualification or explication or extension of the *meaning* of the rule in relation to a new or unmentioned kind of situation (I shall call this an "M-approach"). With reference to the rule against adultery, Ramsey asks us to consider roughly the following alternatives as possible justifications of the action of a Mrs. Bergmeier (in a case made famous by Joseph Fletcher, 1966: 164-165):

(f)E We should not commit adultery (i.e., sexual intercourse where one or both parties are married to another) unless a married woman is in a concentration camp whose regulations are that only pregnant women are let go, where her husband and family imperatively need her, and where there is no other recourse. (*exempting*-condition exception) (f)M We should not commit adultery (i.e., marital infidelity). The implicit meaning of marital "fidelity" and "infidelity," understood more explicitly, and qualified in relation to the woman in the concentration camp, shows us that her action was not adulterous, for it expressed and reinforced her fidelity to her husband and family. (qualified-*meaning*)

Ramsey prefers (f)M to (f)E as a justification. Similarly he prefers an M-version to an E-version in the following examples:

(g)E Lying is telling someone something one believes to be false, intending to get him to believe it. We should not lie, except when this would gravely endanger life, for example, revealing the whereabouts of a Jew to the Gestapo.

(g)M Lying is withholding the truth from someone to whom the truth is due. We should not lie. The meaning of "lying" does not, on reflection, exclude saying something false so as not to endanger life, for example, saying something false to the Gestapo who ask the whereabouts of a Jew.

(h)E Stealing is taking, without permission, something belonging by positive law to someone else. We ought not to steal, except when our family is starving and we have no other recourse but to steal some food from someone who has plenty.

(h)M Stealing is taking, without permission, something belonging by positive law to someone else, to which we have no moral right in relation to the purposes of the institution of private property. We ought not to steal. The meaning of "stealing" does not, on reflection, exclude taking food from someone who has plenty, if one's family is starving and one has no other recourse.

Are the E-versions and the M-versions of (f), (g) and (h) exceptionless? Let us consider the E-versions first. The fact that an E-version moral rule already has universal exceptions built into it does not show that it is, or that it is not, "exceptionless" in the sense of "closed to any *further* universal exceptions." An E-approach, by itself, does not settle the matter; additional reasons would have to be given if someone holds that an E-version moral rule is "exceptionless." At first sight, however, it seems that an M-approach, by itself, closes a rule to any genuine revision. No universal exception-clauses are allowed. All that is permitted is a deeper understanding of the implicit meaning of "adultery," "lying," or "stealing" in relation to new experience. Thus when Ramsey gives reasons for holding that an M-version of some moral rules is superior to an E-version, he might be interpreted as if he were thereby giving reasons for holding that these rules are exceptionless. We shall see later, however, that whether or not M-approach rules are *genuinely* exceptionless depends on whether or not they are interpreted narrowly or liberally; and Ramsey's interpretation tends to be liberal. Meanwhile it is important to consider the three reasons which Ramsey gives for the superiority of an M-approach over an E-approach.

First, an M-approach is superior in some cases because this approach has been a necessary part of civilized life as such:

> Judgments within the ethico-legal system and within the ethico-political system and within the moral constitution are always of this order. For example, the whole history of Anglo-American liberties can be written as a history of the meaning of one verdict contained in Magna Carta: "No freeman shall. . . ." That is, the history of our liberties can be written as the history of the deepening and broadening of the meaning of being a "freeman," its qualification, extension, application, the defined-features relevant to a judgment falling under it, etc. (Ramsey, 1968a:97).

Similarly there has been agreement that murder is always wrong, and the *meaning* of the offense-term "murder" has been gradually clarified and refined in our legal tradition. "The wrongfulness of it does not infect or inhibit its being of fairly definite sort. There is no circularity here, and certainly not emptiness. One is simply accumulating the feature-relevant meaning of the offense-term and out of the relevant and ruling moral principles themselves elaborating more narrowly defined discriminations of right from wrong killings" (Ramsey, 1968a:97). If we had merely a neutral description of prohibited kinds of killing, this would not, Ramsey implies, have allowed for such a developing legal and moral code. Thus Ramsey's first reason for supporting an M-approach to some moral rules is an appeal to an allegedly necessary constituent in *moral tradition.*

His second reason is an appeal to what I shall call a "*moral a priori.*"[6] He says that we can and should *bring* to situations a moral framework rather than being totally *dependent* on situations in making moral judgments. He insists on the "power of morality itself to make an imprint upon human life, the capacity of moral principle to mold and shape our lives and to specify out of its own nature the moral terrain" (1968a:90). He says that if the substantive moral relations of a covenantal morality are to survive, they "must shape the future and not be shaped indefinitely by an expectation of future morally significant revision of our fidelities by consequences to come" (1968a: 134). A further *meaning* of a moral principle "may be brought to light by experience; it certainly 'arises with' experience. But it does not 'arise from' conditioning experiences. It 'arises from' the implied meaning of principles as stipulations within these principles or terms" (1968a:91). Thus a new situation is an occasion for reflection concerning a moral principle, but it is viewed through the conceptual framework provided by that principle. For example, Mrs. Bergmeier's problem is seen in terms of marital fidelity as a loyalty to her husband and family, and not merely in terms of an exempting-condition or of a QB calculation.

Ramsey's third reason for supporting an M-approach to some moral rules is one which gives a specifically *Christian* backing and interpretation to his stress on moral *tradition* and moral *a priorism.* I shall consider this separately, later on. At the moment, I should make some comments on his first two reasons.

My first comment is that if the M-version is liberal, if it involves a very "elastic" meaning for the key moral terms—as it does in (f)M, (g)M and (h)M—it generally leads to exactly the same moral decisions as an E-version, and it is in practice also as open to revision as an E-version. The possible further revision is called a "deeper understanding of the meaning" rather than an "exception," but if in practice the two approaches have the same openness towards revision, they equally deny that the rule is genuinely exceptionless. If an M-approach is liberal throughout, then none of its rules are genuinely exceptionless, even if the wording of the rules cannot be changed. If not only the meaning of the word, but the wording itself can be changed, then of course the approach is even more liberal. But the main point to an M-approach in contrast with an E-approach is that on an M-approach one does not change the wording by adding clauses concerning exemptions, restrictions of scope, etc.; instead, on a liberal M-approach, one changes (or "interprets") the meaning of the wording.

My second comment is that although a *non*-liberal M-approach does propose genuinely exceptionless moral rules, it does so because it is really a disguised E-approach in its understanding of the rules. For example, if Mrs. Bergmeier's decision is said to be morally wrong, this judgment presupposes that "no adultery" is a verbally unrevisable rule and that "adultery" has an E-version meaning ("sexual intercourse where one or both are married to another"). So we must ask whether there *should* be an unrevisable E-version moral rule? This is still our unresolved question. It remains for us in this form because a non-liberal M-approach amounts to an E-approach plus a denial of revisability.

My third comment does not bear so directly on the possibility of unrevisable moral rules. Rather, I shall express a reservation concerning the alleged superiority of an M-approach to moral rules. Consider, for example, Ramsey's claim that "there could be no good charitable reason for saying that picking someone else's apples to save life belongs among the meanings of 'theft,' or for saying that mere verbal inaccuracies of speech to save life belong among the meanings of 'lying.' These were extensions and explanatory principles 'conditioned' by principle itself" (1968a:91-92). I agree that it would be uncharitable to use the words "theft" and "lying" in this way if we think that our moral (legal, religious) tradition forces us to hold that theft and lying are exceptionless (unrevisable in their wording). But if we do not think this about our tradition, or have no such tradition, if we do not hold an exceptionless rule in these matters, then charity does not require us to give such an elastic meaning to "theft" or "lying." And the demands of clarity, rather than charity, would be operative—in the reverse direction. The clear and straightforward thing to say is that theft and lying are prohibited *except to save life* (E-approach). Nor is it plausible to claim that an exception-clause "except to save life" is best understood, not as expressing an E-approach exemption condition, but as an alleged extension or explanation of what the rules "No theft" or "No lying" *mean.* The search for alleged implicit meanings in an exceptionless moral rule can become a fantastic exercise in ingenuity, excusable only because of its charitable motivation. The real reason for the search is that a moral rule *conflicts*, in some situations, with another moral rule such as "Preserve life" or with a QB humanitarian calculation concerning serious harm. Hence the real moral reasons are set forth by adding an E-approach exception clause or a QB exception-clause. Ramsey's liberal M-approach to the rules "No theft" and "No lying" obscures rather than enlightens.

Ramsey's account of theft and lying may be an aberration. Certainly it is clear that he does not, in general, exclude the possibility of E-approach verbal changes, or of verbal changes which arise partly from reflection on the meaning of a rule. But we should note the dangers of a liberal M-approach if verbal changes are not allowed. A casuist may then hide the moral reasoning not only from the masses but also from himself.

Does this force us to reject all moral reflection concerning a possible deeper meaning of traditional moral rules? Not at all. The pressure towards fantasy and self-deception comes from an initial commitment to verbal unrevisability. Once we grant the possibility of a revision of the moral rule, we are free to revise it in contexts where an alleged extension of meaning is implausible. But in some other contexts we may probe the meaning of the rule, rather than jump in with a revision. There can be rational respect for tradition and continuity, and a flexible imposition of moral concepts from that tradition, without a commitment to unrevisable moral rules. It seems to me that a great deal of moral reflection rightly starts from an accepted moral rule and involves an extension by analogy from standard cases to more problematic ones. For example, it seems to me that the interpretation of the meaning of "No adultery" given in (e)M is illuminating, for the very rule that might seem to preclude Mrs. Bergmeier's action is seen to justify it. In her case, an E-approach or a quantitative-benefit approach would be less illuminating. But if her problem had been whether or not to have sexual intercourse with a guard as the price for his not killing another prisoner, it would surely be more illuminating to think of it as a problem of marital fidelity *versus* preservation of life. (Ramsey tends to interpret most moral obligations as forms of fidelity, but even if the preservation of a person's life is a form of "fidelity" to him, this fidelity is in conflict with the *marital* form of fidelity in my hypothetical case.)

My main point is that it is possible to make considerable use of an M-approach, with its stress on traditional and *a priori* elements in morality, without being committed to exceptionless moral rules. Ramsey does not explicitly deny this possibility, and insofar as his own M-approach is liberal, it allows for what amounts to future exceptions to a rule as the meaning is reinterpreted in new situations. But his extensive *discussion and defense* of an M-approach seem to be part of his overall argument in favor of holding some moral rules to be exceptionless. A reader who rejects this conclusion may mistakenly think that he also has to reject all moral casuistry which focuses on the deeper meaning of traditional moral rules. There is surely a legitimate place for such reflection, especially in Christian moral thought. We may differ as to how big a place it should have, and as to which elements in a tradition should be selected for such reflection. But insofar as Ramsey reminds us that it does have a place, he is surely right.

V

In this section I shall try to clarify our basic question, "Can there be an exceptionless moral rule?" The two key words are "can" and "exceptionless." I shall examine "exceptionless" at length, and then consider "can."

We have seen that it is logically impossible for there to be a singular moral exception to a moral rule, since any moral exception, like any moral judgment, must be universalizable. Any moral exception must be universal in form, though the exception-clause does not have to be explicitly formulated.

We have also seen that it is logically impossible for there to be a strictly Act-Utilitarian "exception" to a moral rule, since such an "exception" changes the moral rule into a maxim. A moral rule provides an independent and distinct moral consideration alongside the calculation of benefits in a particular case; a maxim does not do this.

We have seen that an exceptionless moral rule can have some universal exceptions built into it, specifying the features of situations which constitute exempting-conditions, for example, ". . . except to save life." Such a moral rule is exceptionless if it is not open to any *further* feature-dependent universal exceptions. An exceptionless rule can be defined as an *unrevisable* rule. This definition, however, needs to be interpreted carefully, or it can be misleading. There are two kinds of moral rule which are held to be unrevisable in their wording, and which are nevertheless not genuinely "exceptionless."

One such verbally unrevisable moral rule, as we have seen, is a traditional moral rule in a liberal M-approach. The elastic meaning of the rule may allow not only for many of the exceptions already built into the rule on an E-approach but also for an openness which is in practice the same as that of an E-approach, where the E-approach allows that a rule is open to revision by future addition of further feature-dependent exception-clauses. What an M-approach calls "being open to a deeper understanding of the implicit meaning of the rule" can be the same in practice as what an E-approach calls "being open to possible revision of the rule in which a new exception-clause will be added." Although the M-approach moral rule is not verbally revisable, it is not exceptionless, for it is open in a way which amounts to the same thing as a revisable E-approach moral rule.

Another verbally unrevisable moral rule which is not really exceptionless would be a rule with a built-in quantitative-benefit (QB) exception-clause, where this rule is held to be closed to any further QB (or E-approach) revision. Consider an earlier example (b): "Never lie except when lying, as compared with not lying, will promote at least quantity Q of benefit." What if this rule, with its universal QB exception-clause, could not be changed? It would still not be "exceptionless" in the relevant sense of the word. The QB exception-clause does not specify the *features* of S1 which constitute an exemption-condition, and thus rule (b) provides a *qualitatively* unspecified class of exceptions. Even if rule (b) is not open to change in its QB exception-clause, this clause itself already allows the moral agent to make exceptions to the rule "Never lie" in a range of situations which are qualitatively open. Even if it were possible to give a list of all the qualitatively specified situations which, to one's knowledge, have fulfilled the QB exception-clause, such a list would be open-ended. Thus the moral rule is open in a way which, on a qualitative-exception, feature-dependent E-approach, would amount to a limitless revisability. Whether or not a QB exception-clause in a moral rule is revisable, such a clause renders the moral rule open rather than exceptionless, in the relevant sense of "exceptionless."

Thus an "exceptionless" moral rule is best understood as an E-approach definite-action moral rule which cannot be revised by the addition of further feature-dependent universal exceptions. Any rule which, in practice, allows what amounts to the same thing as such a further revision is not an exceptionless moral rule. Neither a liberal M-approach unrevisable moral rule nor a moral rule with an unrevisable QB exception-clause is "exceptionless." If there is to be an exceptionless moral rule, it must fulfill three conditions: (x) It must be stated or understood without the plastic meaning of an M-approach; (y) It must not allow any QB exception-clause; and (z) It must not be open to any further feature-dependent exception-clause if it includes any such clause now, and it must not be open to any such clause at all if it includes none now. Hence, if "No adultery" is an exceptionless moral rule it must fulfill three conditions: (x) "Adultery" has a definite, non-plastic meaning such that what *counts* as adultery does not depend on one's moral judgment. (y) "No adultery" holds, whatever the QB calculations in particular situations; no QB exception-clause is permitted. (z) The rule is not open to any feature-dependent exception-clause.

What about the rule "No adultery except to save human life"? This is exceptionless if (x) and (y) are fulfilled and if (z) prohibits any *further* feature-dependent exception-clauses.

Our question is, "Can there be an exceptionless moral rule?" Having clarified the meaning of "exceptionless," let us look at "can." At the beginning of this essay I noted two senses of "can," the logical and the moral. When we were considering the universalizability of moral judgments, the distinction was dissolved, for we saw that there cannot, logically, be a singular moral exception to a moral rule because there cannot, morally, in view of the very definition of the word "moral." This claim seemed reasonable, but it is not reasonable to define "moral" so as to make the expression "exceptionless moral rule" a contradiction; so the distinction between logical "can" and moral "can" does not dissolve here. Clearly it is logically possible for there to be an exceptionless moral rule. The question is whether there can ever be an adequate moral justification for holding that a moral rule is exceptionless. Ramsey rightly points out that the justification need not be moral, though it must be *normative.* That is, the reasons might be prudential or theological or methodological as well as moral. I agree, but I shall not try to identify the different kinds of reasons. Instead, I shall merely note here that our question is normative rather than logical or empirical.[7]

Ramsey rightly insists that the question is one of *normative metaethics.* His opponent lays down a meta-rule concerning moral rules: "No exceptionless moral rules." For the opponent, this is an exceptionless meta-rule which prohibits exceptionless moral rules! Ramsey presents arguments against this meta-rule. His arguments are also arguments in support of some meta-claims which have the form, "The moral rule 'Never do X' is exceptionless." To these arguments we now turn.

VI

Ramsey presents a variety of subtle and interrelated arguments, but I think it is possible to single out three main lines of argument without misrepresenting him. (In addition to these three, there are also some distinctively Christian considerations; but we will consider these separately in section 7.) All three lines of argument converge on some rules, but we shall consider the three separately. I shall label them the "Utilitarian," "Deontological" and "Fidelity-Obligation" arguments.

A. The main Utilitarian argument depends on a Rule-Utilitarian approach, in which a rule is justified by noting the overall good consequences for society if the rule is usually or always observed, as compared with the overall bad consequences for society if the rule is usually or always violated. For *some* rules, this is the *only* justification (e.g., a rule against leaving a cigarette carton on a public beach); but such rules are not usually called "moral" rules. Most moral rules also are justified in an Act-Utilitarian way *(usually* the prohibited kind of action produces bad effects in each particular case), and sometimes in a Deontological way (the prohibited kind of action by its very nature is usually or always wrong). But the Rule-Utilitarian justification is relevant even though *other* justifications are available. And the *main* justification for some rules—which Ramsey calls "rules of practice"—is Rule-Utilitarian. Concerning some of these rules of practice, there might be a Rule-Utilitarian justification for a *meta*-rule: "The rule prohibiting X is exceptionless." The justification would point to the overall social utility of making the rule exceptionless, rather than leaving it open to further feature-dependent exception clauses or open by virtue of a QB exception-clause.

Ramsey's view of this Rule-Utilitarian argument is not entirely clear. At one point, he seems to give it great weight: "I conclude, therefore, that there is no rational argument that can exclude the possibility that there are exceptionless moral rules, in some moral matters. The case for this seems especially strong in regard to *rules of practice*, whether these are warranted by *agapeic* or rule-utilitarian or other normative appeals" (1968a: 112). Ramsey's conclusion, however, depends mainly on his discussion of rules of practice which are not justified solely in a Rule-Utilitarian way. And later on, discussing the possibility of future revision of rules, he says this:

> The case for exceptions in our future is especially strong in all cases where *consequence* features are overriding. Perhaps in regard to all *purely* societal *rules of practice*, or rule-utilitarian rules, these should never be held closed against future further morally significant exceptions. This would hold open progressive refinements and future admissible alterations in the accepted practice, and hold open also the possibility that in certain sorts of cases unforeseen consequences of the practice upon individual persons can be taken significantly into account as a reason for violating societal rules (1968a: 118-119).

This is a neat summary of two main reasons *against* making any Rule-Utilitarian rules exceptionless: the fact that society changes so that rules may need to be changed accordingly, and the fact that a rule which promotes an overall balance of good over evil in society may produce grave evil to individuals in particular, often unforeseeable, cases—unless exceptions can be made.

On balance, I do not see how a Rule-Utilitarian consideration for an exceptionless moral rule can be adequate in the case of a purely Rule-Utilitarian rule, nor how these considerations will reinforce other arguments in the case of other rules. But note that I am talking about genuinely exceptionless moral rules, which can never be open to revision or subject to a QB exception-clause. I am not denying the possibility of strong arguments concerning some moral rules, similar to arguments concerning most *laws*, that any new exceptions ought not to be decided by interested parties, but rather by an authority which represents the interests of society as a whole and of individuals who may be harmed by such exceptions.

Before we leave Utilitarianism, I should briefly note an Act-Utilitarian argument which Ramsey also considers (1968a: 108):[8] If in this situation S1, *I* regard the moral rule prohibiting X as a rule open to revision and act accordingly, this action will influence *others* to regard the rule as being open to revision in situations *different* from S1, where no revision can be justified. My revision of the rule (adding a new feature-dependent exception clause, or applying a QB exception-clause) may be the thin edge of the wedge; thus even if my revision can have a Rule-Utilitarian justification (since the overall consequences would be good if everyone or most people were to do strictly likewise), the revision is wrong in Act-Utilitarian terms.

Note that this "wedge argument" does not show that the rule in question should be exceptionless. It does not show that the rule should never be revised, for presumably there could be circumstances in which the revision would not influence anyone else, or would not influence others in a bad way. Nevertheless the wedge argument can, in some situations, reinforce other arguments in favor of not revising a moral rule.

B. What I am calling the "Deontological" argument in support of the meta-claim " 'Don't do X' is an exceptionless moral rule" depends on the conviction that "X" specifies a kind of action which is wrong by its very *nature*, apart from its consequences. On one version of this argument, nothing more needs to be said. If doing X is inherently wrong, then it is always wrong, regardless of consequences. And it will always be wrong. The moral rule is clearly exceptionless. Just as each biological species has its own nature, which a biological science discovers, so there are (allegedly) species of human actions which moral science discovers.

This conviction, most evident in traditional Roman Catholic moral theology (e.g., McFadden, 1967: 73-77), requires no additional justification for the meta-rule. "All adultery is wrong," like "All men are rational" or "All swans are white," is allegedly not open to any possible disconfirmation by further experience; and this is not because men have decided to define "adultery," "men" and "swans" so as to make the statements analytic rather than empirical. It is because men have come to know the *nature* of adultery, men and swans.

There are some indications that Ramsey is sympathetic to this conviction, especially in his zeal for what I have called the M-approach. But insofar as his M-approach is liberal, with a plastic meaning for the terms describing prohibited kinds of acts, Ramsey's ethic allows in practice for what amounts to a revision of the moral rules. And in presenting his main deontological argument (1968a: 108-109, 114-118),[9] he assumes or postulates the empirical possibility that, in a particular case, the consequence of following a rule might be so bad as to warrant breaking (or revising) the rule. He then argues that this possibility is less likely than the possibility of making a moral mistake if one regards the rule as revisable. The possibility of error is considerable, both because of one's possible ignorance of relevant facts and, more important, because one's own self-interest or passions may lead to self-deception. Such an argument would be irrelevant if the prohibited kind of action were inherently wrong, wrong whatever the consequences. The argument depends on a conviction (cf. D'Arcy, 1963: 1-39), which seems to me very reasonable, that certain species of action have an inherent moral relevance, weight or significance, quite apart from their consequences. (This conviction has affinities with the claim that we have *prima facie* obligations, where this claim does not depend solely on Rule-Utilitarian considerations.) The greater the importance of the fact that what one is doing is adultery or lying or stealing, the less the weight given to beneficial consequences of the action. And perhaps, in the case of some moral rules, the weight which should be given to consequences is so relatively minimal that it does not merely verge on zero but disappears. Such, at any rate, is the general line of Ramsey's argument insofar as I understand it. He asks us to consider some very challenging examples:

(i) Never experiment medically on a human being without his informed consent.

(j) Never punish a man whom one knows to be innocent of that for which he would be punished.

(k) Never rape (i.e., force sexual intercourse on someone who is totally unwilling).

With regard to (i) and (j) it is clear that we do in fact try to devise a *law* which has as few loopholes as possible, and we require that any new interpretation of the law will fulfill two conditions: (1) it will be made by some socially authorized group or individual, not an interested party, and (2) it will not involve any rejection of the fundamental moral significance of the prohibited species of action. Similarly, insofar as a *moral* rule as well as a law is involved, the same restraints on individual decision-making are reasonable. Anyone who, as an interested party, tries to revise the rule in his own case, is rightly subject to the sanction of moral disapproval from society. Yet there is surely a place for individual moral autonomy even here. A conscientious moral agent may sometimes defy a law because disobedience in a very special situation, and there only, is in his eyes justified; such a moral agent would accept the legal penalties graciously, since the particular law is just and good. Similarly he might defy a moral rule upheld by society—even (i), (j) or (k), in some very special situations, and there only, and graciously accept moral disapproval although he believes that he has acted rightly. The very special situation, though conceivable, is very, very unlikely. But, since the restriction on medical experimentation and on punishment of the innocent is stringent because of the possible pressure arising from beneficial social consequences (and not merely because of the dangers of self-interested claims), it is possible that in some situations these beneficial consequences might rightly override the rule. I personally can imagine such a situation, though it is a very unlikely one. Similarly I can imagine a situation in a concentration camp where refusal to rape might produce horrendous consequences for others and where one could not convey[10] to the unwilling victim any indications of one's reasons or intentions.

The role of individual moral autonomy in relation to (i), (j) and (k) is so minimal and so restricted in scope that I would describe the rule as "virtually exceptionless." That is, I think the rule should be held to be virtually closed to future exceptions, since the theoretically possible exceptional cases are virtually zero in their practical probability. Here my position seems to be very close to Ramsey's. He speaks about rules being held to be "*significantly* closed to future exceptions" or "closed to *significant* future exceptions." But when we consider another moral rule for which he presents a similar anti-revisability argument, the importance of moral autonomy becomes more evident. As an example (1968a: 116-117; the context for the example is set in 115-116) of an allegedly exceptionless moral rule, significantly closed to future exceptions, he proposes "No premarital intercourse." In support of this, Ramsey legitimately stresses the way in which self-interest and passions can produce moral error and may lead to a failure to consider the responsibilities involved in the possibility of parenthood as a consequence of the intercourse. This line of argument does give some support for a moral rule prohibiting pre-marital intercourse, but not for making the rule exceptionless. I do not think it even shows that if there are to be any revisions, these should be done by an authority appointed by society, though it does point to the wisdom of consulting a disinterested and wise third pary in order to minimize self-deception.

In his argument Ramsey does not consider the most plausible case for breaking the rule. He assumes that the couple have not thoroughly searched their own motives and biases and possible self-deceptions and that they have not accepted in advance the responsibility for a child if contraception should fail. But what if they have? And what if they also consider good reasons for postponing marriage unless pregnancy comes—for example, there is a university regulation which would prevent the girl from completing her undergraduate studies if married. Unless pre-marital intercourse is, as such, inherently wrong, it seems to be grossly implausible to claim that a rule prohibiting it should be exceptionless; but if it *is* inherently wrong, no further argument about *possibilities* of moral error are needed.

In the preceding two paragraphs I have been discussing what I took to be Ramsey's argument. In correspondence, however, he has explained that the rule "No premarital intercourse" is understood by him according to a liberal M-approach in which marriage consists in the mutual commitment, not in the ceremony, so that the rule does not prohibit absolutely all intercourse before the wedding night, for one can get married pre-ceremonially. This view, which he had set forth in an earlier article (1965a: 112-113 especially), makes my above objections irrelevant, for the couple are not engaged in what Ramsey would call "pre-marital" intercourse. But if the rule is understood according to such a liberal M-approach, it is not *genuinely* exceptionless, and there is considerable scope for individual autonomy in interpreting the rule. If the meaning of "marital" is plastic, the rule is not genuinely exceptionless. How plastic can this meaning be? For example, what if a young man has realistic fears of impotency, is firmly committed to marry (ceremonially) the girl *if* he is not impotent, and out of concern for both her and himself seeks intercourse? If the meaning of the "marital" commitment which is pre-ceremonial is understood very broadly as a commitment to the other's fundamental well-being, even this act would not be prohibited by the rule against pre-marital intercourse. I do not know whether Ramsey would allow that such an act would be morally justifiable, though I hope so. My point is that on a liberal M-approach, the meaning of "marital" is plastic.

A rule against pre-marital sex is thus either implausibly exceptionless if interpreted on an E-approach where "marriage" means "the marriage ceremony" or it is not genuinely exceptionless if interpreted according to a liberal M-approach. Nevertheless we should recognize that Ramsey has shown that *some* moral rules should be regarded as being what I have called "virtually" exceptionless. Alongside the rules in examples (i), (j) and (k) consider another: "Never torture your wife to death, giving her to believe that you hate her." This rule, with its reference to a combination of torture, unfaithfulness, murder and heinous deceit, strains the imagination if one tries to conceive a situation so horrendous that an exception would be justified. If I were to insist on saying that even this rule is only "virtually" exceptionless, this may seem like saying that the series "1 plus $\frac{1}{2}$ plus $\frac{1}{2}^{2}$ plus $\frac{1}{2}^{3}$ plus . . . $\frac{1}{2}^{1000}$" is only "virtually" 2. Yet there is a point in saying "virtually." Moral rules form a continuum: some are open to very extensive revision, some are much less open, and some are in varying degrees virtually exceptionless. Some moralists, such as Ramsey, are concerned about "creeping exceptionism," which shifts rules which should be virtually exceptionless back among wide-open rules. Other moralists are concerned about "creeping legalism," which extends the range of allegedly exceptionless rules down among rules which should be held fairly open, and even in situations where the role of rules should be minimal. Some of the moral passion expressed in the debate arises from reasonable convictions that both creeping exceptionism and creeping legalism are, and have been, menaces to morality. Though Ramsey's article sometimes makes me worry about a tendency towards creeping legalism, it is mainly a salutary reminder of the dangers of creeping exceptionism. Concerning some moral rules, the onus is on the exceptionist to show why the rule should *not* be held as virtually exceptionless. Yet since Ramsey's argument assumes an empirical possibility that in a particular case the consequences of following the rule could be so bad as to warrant a revision of the rule, it is important to insist on the word "virtually." The insistence is a check on creeping legalism.

C. Ramsey's third main argument is specially illuminating because of the way in which it puts the onus on the exceptionist. He considers *fidelity*-obligations which arise from explicit or implicit promises. Insofar as a moral rule sets forth a fidelity-obligation, this counts against keeping the rule open to further revision in relation to unforeseen future circumstances. For example, the point of a marriage vow is that one is making a commitment of fidelity which will be binding *in spite of* unforeseen future conditions which otherwise might justify a termination of a relation of cohabitation. If there are to be exception-clauses in a promise, these should be included when the promise is made; after that, the moral obligation is not open *indefinitely* to *further* revisions, for this would destroy the point of the promise.

Some moral rules are linked with explicit promises. For example, the prohibition of adultery is linked with the marriage vows. But many other moral rules are linked with promises which are implicit. The notion of an implicit promise is a tricky one, but surely it is clear that there can be fidelity obligations, say, of friendship, even though no one has said, "I'll stand by you" or anything similarly explicit. And many of our institutional obligations arise because we voluntarily accept a job or a role and thereby implicitly accept responsibilities to individuals or groups. So the range of fidelity-obligations is quite wide. (As we shall see in section 7, Ramsey tends to interpret almost all obligations as fidelity-obligations.)

Fidelity can, of course, be considered in both a Rule-Utilitarian way and a Deontological way. A Rule-Utilitarian can justify moral rules which depend on promises by pointing to the overall social utility of these rules. And a Deontologist can justify such rules by discerning an inherent rightness in fidelity and an inherent wrongness in infidelity. Ramsey's *special* emphasis on fidelity is justified, however, because the special point to promises and to fidelity is to reduce the dependence of one's moral decisions on future circumstances and on consequences in general.

I agree with Ramsey that fidelity-obligations have this distinctive and important feature, and that, insofar as an ethical view stresses the fidelity-bonds of human life, it will give proportionately less weight to concern about future circumstances and beneficial or harmful consequences. But I do not think that he shows that any fidelity-rules are genuinely exceptionless, even if we add the word "virtually" or "significantly." It is obvious that most promises do not create such a weighty moral obligation that the related moral rule is a serious candidate for exceptionlessness. My moral obligation to return a book today as I promised, or to prepare the minutes of the club as its secretary in time for the meeting, can be overridden by a host of other obligations. Only a few kinds of promises, specially designed for the purpose, are so worded that they apparently subordinate all other moral obligations to themselves. The range of possibly exceptionless fidelity-rules narrows to a few: fidelity to one's spouse or to one's country or to one's church. If the "fidelity" is understood in a liberal M-approach way, then in each case there can be a moral rule which is verbally unrevisable. But the rule is then not genuinely exceptionless. Mrs. Bergmeier can be faithful to her husband while having intercourse with the camp guard. Bonhoeffer can be faithful to Germany while plotting Hitler's death. Charles Davis can be faithful to the Roman Catholic church while leaving it. If, on the other hand, "fidelity" is understood in a more definite way, the possibility of its being overridden by other obligations should, it seems to me, be left open. And there should be a QB exception-clause written into it: "except where following the rule would cause such great harm as to outweigh the moral obligation not to break it." Here I have merely expressed a moral conviction without argument. Support for the claim would have to take the form of a detailed description of cases where a failure to acknowledge the need for openness in a fidelity-rule has led to morally disastrous consequences. It seems to me that the likelihood of such an outcome in the future is greater than the likelihood of morally disastrous consequences if the need for openness is acknowledged. It seems to me that this is specially obvious in the case of loyalty to one's country.

I do not deny that if we keep fidelity-bonds open this can involve difficulties and dangers. For one thing there is a *psychological* problem which gives weight to a moralist's fear of morally disastrous consequences if the need for openness is acknowledged. It is difficult to grant the possibility that in some remote and undesignated circumstances a moral rule would not apply, while at the same time giving tremendous weight now to this moral rule. Certainly there is a danger that an intense preoccupation with remote contingencies can undermine one's moral commitment in the present. A person who is already wondering about what he would do if his wife becomes incurably insane or if she runs off to another continent with a stranger might be indulging in self-fulfilling prophecies, producing the situation which he fears because of his lack of trust. The psychological problem is important in other contexts, too. A soldier who concedes that torture of prisoners could possibly be justified in some remote and undesignated circumstances may be undermining his will not to torture prisoners when the issue actually arises a few hours later. It is not surprising that Ramsey talks about the claim that there is nothing men should never do as the "most uncivilizing principle" (1968a: 135). He even refers us to Auschwitz. But Auschwitz can also be cited, with as much justice, as an outcome of an ethic of exceptionless fidelity to the state (though Ramsey does not set forth such an ethic in his article). And, more generally, an exceptionless-rule approach has often involved the perversities of moral judgment against which Joseph Fletcher and other anti-legalists have rightly spoken. Ramsey's article, however, is not designed to support such an approach. He has tried to show that *some* moral rules should be held to be significantly exceptionless. And if "significantly" means much the same as "virtually," I think he has succeeded.

He has also shown that we ought to give "first place" (1968a: 126) to many claims of justice or faithfulness which are embodied in rules of deontology or fidelity within a moral tradition. These claims have an intrinsic moral relevance and great moral weight, even though the rules are not genuinely exceptionless.

VII

In this final section I shall briefly outline and discuss three distinctively Christian considerations which Ramsey proposes in support of the possibility that some rules are exceptionless. Two of these considerations provide additional support for arguments considered earlier. The third introduces new considerations.

A. The Christian conviction that all men are *sinners* reinforces the argument that a man's private self-interest and passions may lead him into moral error if he holds such-and-such a moral rule to be revisable by his own moral judgment. Christians speak to "another law in our members" alongside our human capacity to reason as moral beings (Ramsey, 1968a: 118). The fact that sin can lead to distortions of individual moral judgment supports the need for meta-rules which are rule-strengthening.

It seems to me that even if this argument shows the need for rule-strengthening rules, it does not show that any rule should be exceptionless. And even the rule-strengthening emphasis can be challenged by another Christian conviction, concerning the work of the Holy Spirit in guiding men towards right moral judgments in difficult moral decisions, freeing them from bondage to the law. If we are talking about broad policy for Christians in general, the doctrines of sin and of the Holy Spirit cancel each other out, as it were. Christian pessimism and optimism concerning human moral insight combine—in terms of broad and general expectations concerning Christians or men generally—so as to be little different from the less dramatic reasoning of realistic secular moralists. In *particular* cases, of course, the convictions concerning sin or Holy Spirit can make a great deal of difference to the individual Christian—but not, it seems to me, in general arguments as to whether human beings generally, or Christians generally, need any rules which should be exceptionless.

B. Ramsey's stress on *fidelity*-obligations is supported by the Christian conviction that fidelity, covenants, promises, loyalty, etc., are at the heart of the theological basis for moral conduct. God has acted to establish a covenant with us and with all mankind. To this "performative" action the appropriate human response is fidelity towards God and man. This is how Ramsey puts it (1968a: 125):

> If one *begins* in Christian *normative ethics* with some such statement as "Look on all men as brothers for whom Christ died" or "Be grateful to the Lord who made us His covenant people," and if all moral reasoning is then reasoning from these "premises," then the ultimate warrant of them must be an appeal to what the Lord of heaven and earth is believed to have been doing and to be doing in enacting and establishing His covenant with us and all mankind, in all the estates and orders and relations of life to which we have been called.
>
> If it is true that in Christian ethics we are mainly concerned about the requirements of loyalty to covenants among men, about the meaning of God's ordinances and mandates, about the estates and moral relations among men acknowledged to follow from His governing and righteous will, about steadfastness and faithfulness, then it follows that in Christian ethics we can and may and must be enormously disinterested in any exception, or openness to exceptions, that would have to be justified primarily by future consequences-features, and indeed, consequences imagined in extreme, fictitious cases.

Ramsey not only sees Christian faith as a source of *emphasis* on human bonds of fidelity as the main concern of ethics, but also as a reason for *extending* the understanding of fidelity so that it covers most or all our moral obligations. Consider the following passages:

> Faithfulness-claims and canons of covenant loyalty may be the profoundest way to understand all our concepts of fairness and justice (1968a: 119).

> [Concerning rape] We may gain a fuller realization of the heinousness of unwilling sexual intercourse because we come to see more clearly the obligations created in relation to all men by a woman-being who, simply by being, claims at least this *faithfulness* of us (1968a: 127; my italics).

> In medical ethics there is a rule governing experimentation involving human subjects that this should be done only when an informed consent has been secured.... The *faithfulness*-claims which every man, simply by being a man, places upon the researcher are the morally relevant considerations (1968a: 129).

> [Concerning an argument by Jonathan Bennett in favor of abortion to save a mother's life] Bennett's other argument was concerning what *is* the relevant canon of loyalty and what *does* fidelity to two lives in conflict require in obstetrical cases. His argument did not crucially depend on consequences, other than those marked out by the faithfulness-claim upon us to save life rather than allow to die (1968a: 130, n. 63).

The idea of fidelity has here been extended so as to provide the basis for justice, for not raping a woman, for not experimenting on someone without his consent, and for not allowing a woman to die. It has become an "onlook" in terms of which *all* our fundamental obligations to human beings are understood. Why? Because "Christians look on all men as brothers for whom Christ died." It is a *fraternal* fidelity, extended from one's literal brothers to include all men.

I agree with Ramsey to some extent concerning the special Christian emphasis on human bonds of fidelity, but I would qualify this in various ways. First, there should be no *unconditional* fidelity except to God. Christian theology may say "Yes" to marriage, the state, or the religious institution called "the church," but it also says "No" where any of these purport to be a loyalty "whatever the consequences." Second, Christians can experience conflicts between different fidelity-obligations, and between a fidelity-obligation and other moral obligations. We ought not to try to resolve these problems in advance by reference to unrevisable moral rules. A Christian "onlook" which turns all moral obligations into fidelity-obligations gives a deontological color to them all, but it leaves unresolved the problems of priorities and conflicts. Third, Christians have New Testament warrant for being concerned not only about covenant-bonds between men but also about human suffering. A QB exception-clause in covenantal moral rules has Christian, and not merely utilitarian, warrant.

When I first read Ramsey's article I had a more serious worry concerning Ramsey's application of Christian covenantal theology to ethics. When I read about "all the estates and orders and relations of life to which we have been called" (1968a:125) and "the estates and moral relations among men acknowledged to follow from His governing and righteous will" (1968a: 125), I wondered whether he claimed to know, with certainty and precise definition, what these estates and orders and relations of life are. In correspondence, however, he vigorously rejects making any such claim. The interpretation of our various obligations to church, state or home in terms of covenant-fidelity involves for him a *liberal* M-approach. The approach is important, for in the past a Christian covenantal theology has been used to give a spurious divine authority to precisely defined human estates, orders and relations—often the existing social institutions and conventions of church, state and home. Ramsey, however, is content with reinforcing some traditional and *a priori* elements in morality by pointing to their distinctively Christian versions:

> Principles of faithfulness are unfolded from the elevating and directing power of divine charity. This and our intervening principles are capable of producing within Christian morality itself deeper meanings, clarifying explanations and stipulations for the "upbuilding" of the actions and the moral agency going on ordinarily (1968a: 91).

This passage, in its context, seems to presuppose a liberal M-approach —which, as we have seen, does not involve genuinely exceptionless rules.

C. Ramsey's third distinctively Christian argument as a "defender of exceptionless rules" (1968a: 133) is one which relates Christian morality to Christian *hopes:*

> The primary assumption or conviction is that the *ultimate* consequences cannot be such as to tender his (the Christian's) performance of fidelity obligations *wrong*. This is, I suppose, a sort of Kantian "postulate" which we Christians make when spelling out in thought and life the meaning of fidelity in all covenants. It is a postulate (not a mere supposition) that the grain of things cannot ultimately prove unsupportive of the doing of our fidelities under the moral constitution God makes known in His word-deeds toward us. But that is far and away different from supposing that the final worldly consequences of faithful deeds will show the success of the good (or that from taking account of that, one gets to know the meaning of the right and the good in any morally significant measure) (1968a: 133).

Ramsey has explained in correspondence that he did not mean this to imply that we should rigidly follow fidelity-rules *regardless* of consequences which are foreseeable and subject to human control, for fidelity-rules require us to consider such consequences. Rather, he was expressing Christian confidence that the unforeseeable and uncontrollable later consequences of performing a fidelity-obligation will not be such as to render the performance wrong. Such hope and trust in divine providence, however, does not warrant exceptionless moral rules. Sometime in the future I may *foresee* that the consequences of following an existing fidelity-rule would be so harmful that I ought to revise the rule.

Where a belief in genuinely exceptionless moral rules is combined with a trust in divine providence, the approach to some moral issues is often deplorable. Supposedly, we cannot be responsible for the consequences of refraining from breaking (i.e., revising) an exceptionless moral rule.

Supposedly we must never bear arms or we must never disobey a commanding officer or we must never seek a divorce or we must never use artificial contraceptives or we must never have an abortion or we must never masturbate or we must never tell a lie (except with "mental reservation"), etc., etc. If anyone gets hurt because we are preserving our moral purity, that's his tough luck (or in the jargon of theological moralists "his suffering is within the inscrutable purpose of God").

Yet a Christian hope and trust in divine providence has been a creative and renewing force. The conviction that the value and ultimate significance of our best efforts do not depend on their actual success or failure as these can be seen in history has inspired Christians to do their best and "leave the rest in the hands of God." This conviction need not involve rules which are strictly exceptionless, and it should involve a two-sided attitude towards mundane utilitarian consequences. On the one hand, these consequences matter enormously; we must do all that we can to relieve suffering and to promote happiness. On the other hand, what matters ultimately is the honest attempt, not the success. What matters ultimately is not whether we have won or lost, and certainly not whether we have "played the game" according to some allegedly exceptionless rules, but whether we have *loved.*

Yet the expression of love involves many things, including rules. And Ramsey has rightly reminded us that some of these rules are virtually exceptionless.

NOTES

[1] I am indebted to Paul Ramsey for extensive comments on an earlier draft of this essay. This does not mean that he endorses all the exegesis and criticism in this final draft. The essay first appeared in *The American Journal of Jurisprudence* 16 (1971): pp. 184-214 and is reprinted here with the permission of the author and editors of that journal.

[2] Following Ramsey, we shall be focusing attention on moral rules which are *prohibitions.*

[3] I shall not go on repeating this qualification. Henceforth we shall assume that what is called a "similar situation" involves morally relevant similarity of agents as well.

[4] Ramsey concedes this at one point (1968a:85).

[5] Her novel illustrates some of the ideas in "Vision and choice in morality," *Christian Ethics and Contemporary Philosophy*, ed. Ian Ramsey (London: S.C.M. Press, 1966), which is a reply to Ronald Hepburn—whom Ramsey quotes to support his case.

[6] Ramsey does not use the term *a priori*, but he refers explicitly to Kant. Although he is not endorsing Kant's own moral *a priori* (for Ramsey's *a priori* is part of a developing *tradition*), his main point is broadly Kantian: that we can bring moral concepts *to* experience, and not merely derive them *from* experience.

[7] Ramsey, at one point (1968a:113-114, 118), seems to forget this. He insists that it is impossible to prove the universal negative proposition that there can be no exceptionless moral rules. But this is to confuse the issue with that which arises concerning *empirical* propositions which are universal and negative. The claim that there can be no exceptionless moral rules, like the claim that "No adultery" *is* an exceptionless moral rule, is a universal negative *normative* claim.

[8] On p. 114, his second exception to the meta-rule against exceptionless moral rules may also be a form of Act-Utilitarian wedge-argument. See also p. 131.

[9] At 1968a:126 he grants that bad consequences can sometimes *override* a fidelity-obligation; but he insists that we look *first* to the fidelity-obligation, which is morally relevant in itself, apart from consequences.

[10] Ramsey seems to hold that the act could only be justified if one could somehow convey to the victim what one was really doing; see 1968a:128.

REFERENCES

D'Arcy, Eric
1963 *Human Acts.* Oxford: Clarendon Press.

Evans, Donald
1968 "Love, situations and rules." Pp. 367-414 in Gene H. Outka and Paul Ramsey (eds.), *Norm and Context in Christian Ethics.* New York: Scribners.

Fletcher, Joseph
1966 *Situation Ethics.* Philadelphia: Westminster Press.

Lyons, David
1965 *Forms and Limits of Utilitarianism.* Oxford: Clarendon Press.

McFadden, Charles J.
1967 *Medical Ethics.* 6th ed. Philadelphia: F.A. Davis.

Murdoch, Iris
1958 *The Bell.* New York: Viking Press.
1966 "Vision and choice in morality." Pp. 195-218 in Ian Ramsey (ed.), *Christian Ethics and Contemporary Philosophy.* London: SCM Press.

Narveson, Jan
1967 *Morality and Utility.* Baltimore: Johns Hopkins Press.

Ramsey, Paul
See the bibliography of Ramsey's works in this volume. Capital letters (e.g. 1950A) denote books and occasional papers; lower case letters (e.g. 1968a) denote articles.

CHAPTER III

Paul Ramsey and Traditional Roman Catholic Natural Law Theory

CHARLES E. CURRAN

The Ecumenical possibilities for Christian ethics and moral theology have come to the fore only in the last few years. Present day literature shows that Roman Catholic ethicians read and are influenced by Protestant authors and vice-versa. A Protestant or a Roman Catholic ethician today must be in constant ecumenical dialogue. Such, however, was not the case even a few years ago.

The greater openness within Roman Catholicism generally associated with the thought and the spirit of Vatican II has greatly influenced Contemporary Roman Catholic moral theology. Before that time even in the United States there was no real dialogue with the Protestant ethical tradition. The writings of such important figures in the Catholic tradition as John A. Ryan and Paul Hanly Furfey indicate little or no contact with Protestant thought. Likewise, on the part of Protestant ethicians, there was little or no dialogue with contemporary Catholic thought either in this country or abroad. Walter Rauschenbush expressed no positive appreciation of the Catholic tradition. In fact, Robert Cross (1964:xiv) has commented that Rauschenbusch's discussion of the development of asceticism, sacramentalism, hierarchy, and dogma reads today like a parody of the extreme evangelical Protestant critique of Roman Catholicism. Reinhold Niebuhr, according to Ronald Stone (1972:219-222), had some understanding and appreciation of the Catholic tradition, resisted one-sided and anti-Catholic approaches, and praised some of the changes sanctioned by Vatican Council II; but he was upset with some reactionary political alignments of the Roman Catholic Church in the 1930's and always criticized Catholic pretensions to absolute truth and authority. Niebuhr (1967) later recognized some truth in the natural law approach, but his references were usually confined to the teaching of Aquinas.

It is safe to say that no Protestant ethician in this century has shown greater interest in and appreciation of Roman Catholic ethical thought than Paul Ramsey. So strong is this concern for Catholic thought that there seems to be a feeling among some Protestants that Ramsey is a crypto-Catholic. The reasons for this lie in Ramsey's call to Protestant ethicians to pay more attention to the legitimate place of natural law in Christian ethics and his study and employment of such traditional Catholic approaches as the just war theory, the principle of the double effect, and the distinction between ordinary and extraordinary means of preserving human life. In addition, Ramsey has often sided with positions proposed by Roman Catholicism on issues such as abortion and pre-marital sexuality. He has also been a very forceful advocate of the place of universal, exceptionless norms in moral theology and has staunchly attacked the approaches of situation ethics. In the past few years when even many Roman Catholics have been disagreeing with older Catholic teaching especially as found in the addresses of Pope Pius XII and other popes, Ramsey has often gone out of his way to praise papal teaching; on one occasion (1972i: 1483) he refers to Pope Pius XII as at least a minor prophet for raising his voice against a prevalent attempt to have the personal aspect of human reproduction replaced by categories of manufacturing and product making.

A full appreciation of Paul Ramsey's Christian ethics must include a discussion of his relationship with traditional Roman Catholic theology, especially the natural law theory. There are serious problems in attempting such an evaluation, since Roman Catholic moral theology has changed greatly in the last few years. One cannot accurately describe contemporary Roman Catholic moral theology as a monolithic theory or methodology, although some traditional emphases do continue. There is now a greater appreciation of the possibility and actuality of dissent from the teaching of the hierarchical magisterium on specific moral questions. Interestingly, Ramsey (*e.g.*, 1970B: 178) has expressed his disagreement on occasion with some of these newer developments within Roman Catholic ethics. This essay will use the term "traditional Catholic moral theology" to refer to that comparatively monolithic discipline which existed before the Second Vatican Council. I dislike using the term *traditional* in this sense, but the meaning is clear if understood in this limited way.

Various difficulties for this study arise from the way in which Paul Ramsey has done Christian ethics in the course of his teaching and writing career. Ramsey has not written a definitive, systematic treatise on Christian ethics. His most systematic work is *Basic Christian Ethics* (his first book, 1950A) which shows least knowledge of and appreciation for Roman Catholic moral theology. It is a tribute to Ramsey's great intellectual capacities that his thought has developed and matured over the years, but such development also causes some difficulty in any attempt at evaluation. Furthermore, Ramsey tends to find support for his own contentions in the approaches of others, without necessarily accepting all the methodological presuppositions involved in what those others believe. Finally, his obvious delight in engaging in controversy and his rhetorical flair make the task of accurate interpretation even more difficult. In the light of the non-systematic, developmental and somewhat polemical aspects of Ramsey's writing, it is necessary to nuance carefully and accurately his attitude toward traditional Roman Catholic moral theology.

I. Ramsey's Interpretation of Natural Law in Maritain

In *Nine Modern Moralists* (1962A) Ramsey develops his own approach to Christian ethics in dialogue with and criticism of other moralists, and specifically calls on Protestant theologians to accept a concept of natural law or justice. Ramsey here (1962A: 209-256) accepts what he interprets to be a revisionist theory of natural law, proposed by Jacques Maritian, according to which there is some wisdom in man's natural decisions. Ramsey (1962A: 4-5), however, does not want to accept some of the characteristics often associated with natural law such as: natural law conceived as a realm of universal principles; an excessive rationalism which deduces universal norms from prior principles; a realm of clear light unaffected by the distortions of sin; a self-sufficient ethical stance in which Christian love does not enter to re-shape, enlarge, sensitize, and sovereignly direct our apprehensions based on the nature alone of the meaning of right and wrong action. He (1962A: 227-230) also rejects the Catholic idea of republication of the natural law by the authoritative Church teachings, an idea which in his judgment makes the natural law approach too inflexible and takes the final decision out of the court of human reason.

In *Nine Modern Moralists* Ramsey concentrates on explaining his interpretation of Maritain. In Ramsey's judgment (1962A: 209-256) Maritain affirms a natural law teaching based on the wisdom of the human judgment made by inclination (not rational deduction) in "the prism of the case." (the phrase is one Ramsey [1962A: 209-256] has taken over from Edmond Cahn). Ramsey thus interprets Maritain as rejecting the rationalistic, deductive and inflexible concept of natural law often proposed by or at least associated with Roman Catholicism in the past. He notes a development within Maritain's thought which can be seen by comparing the earlier *The Rights of Man and Natural Law* with Maritain's later exposition in *Man and the State.*

Ramsey (1962A: 217-223) interprets the later Maritain as follows. The natural law is known through "inclination" or a "vital knowledge of connaturality or congeniality" and not through a deductive reasoning process. Natural law therefore is known only *in medias res*, in social contexts, or in the prism of actual cases. Thus natural law is distinguished from *ius gentium*, which involves conceptual reason and deduction. But in Maritain the domain of natural law and that of *ius gentium* are not totally distinct. For him the natural law has been first manifested, not in inclinations, but in social patterns; that is in *ius gentium. Ius gentium* here has some characteristics similar to those of natural law and some which go beyond natural law—i.e., it is deduced by rational inference. The prohibition of murder, for instance, belongs to both natural law and to *ius gentium.*

Ramsey (1962A:219-220) finds some inconsistencies in Maritain's approach. He attributes these to a failure to break cleanly with the deductive and conceptual approach to natural law which Maritain proposed in his earlier writings. While in *Man and the State* Maritain insists that the natural law is based on knowledge through inclination and not rational deduction, he still holds that the principles of the natural law are like conclusions derived from common principles. He also maintains that the natural law follows from the first principle, do good and avoid evil, in a necessary way. Ramsey sees it as a contradiction to say that the natural law "follows from the first principle" and especially to say that it follows in a "necessary manner." Also Maritain occasionally uses the word *conceptualization* to refer to natural law even though he has theoretically restricted this word to describe only the *ius gentium* and not natural law. These inconsistencies indicate that, despite the remarkable departure that Maritain's understanding of natural law as knowledge through inclination represents from the traditional scheme of rational, deductive natural law, he occasionally lapses into the older expressions.

How accurate is Ramsey's interpretation of Maritain? In my judgment, Ramsey has somewhat distorted Maritain's position to make it buttress his own understanding of natural law as being flexible, non-rationalistic, non-deductive and contextual. At the very minimum, one cannot so totally neglect Maritain's theory of *ius gentium* and act as if it has no place in his total ethical system. Natural law is understood by Maritain in a restricted way; it is only a part of his total ethical theory.

Even more importantly, Maritain's theory is less flexible and contextual than Ramsey believes. Some of Maritain's emphasis on what follows "in a necessary way" is not merely a carry-over from an earlier position but rather remains an integral part of his mature position. He holds (1956:84-94) that natural law includes two elements—an ontological element and a second gnoseological element. Ramsey does acknowledge in a number of places in his discussion (1962A: 223-224) that Maritain's theory is based on an essentialist understanding of man and that Maritain insists on the distinction between the being of natural law and our knowledge of it, but Ramsey merely accepts the fact that there is an essence to man and does not accept the detailed ontology proposed by Maritain. In a striking contrast with Maritain, Ramsey does not develop this ontological element of the natural law as distinguished from our knowledge of it.

Maritain (1956: 86) begins his comparatively brief description of natural law by insisting that persons have a nature or ontological structure which is a locus of intelligible necessities. Further, we possess ends which necessarily correspond to our essential constitution and are the same for all. Since we are endowed with intelligence and determine our own ends, we must put ourselves in tune with the ends necessarily demanded by our nature. We can thus freely recognize and embrace the ends demanded by our nature. "This means that there is, by the very virtue of human nature, an order or a disposition which human reason can discover and according to which the human will must act in order to attune itself to the essential and necessary ends of the human being. The unwritten law, or natural law, is nothing more than that" (Maritain, 1956: 85).

The gnoseological aspect of natural law concerns our knowledge of this unwritten law of our nature which Maritain insists (1956: 89-92) is known by human reason through inclination. This is not clear knowledge through concepts and conceptual judgment, but obscure, unsystematic, vital knowledge by connaturality or congeniality.

In this light, one can properly understand the closing paragraph in Maritain's discussion of natural law (even though there might remain some verbal problem with his use of *conceptualization*—a point made by Ramsey). Maritain (1956: 94) says that the natural law is an unwritten law in the deepest sense of that expression because our knowledge of it is no work of free conceptualization, "but results from a conceptualization bound to the essential inclinations of being, of living nature, and of reason, which are at work in man, and because it develops in proportion to the degree of moral experience and self-reflection, and of social experience also, of which man is capable in the various ages of his history."

Ramsey himself does not accept such an ontological foundation for natural law; he develops his own theory in dialogue with only the second or gnoseological aspect of natural law proposed by Maritain. Maritain's exposition of the ontological aspect of natural law, as well as his insistence on the *ius gentium*, combine to make his theory less radical a revision than Ramsey claims. Ramsey's own theory of natural law, consequently, differs from Maritain more radically than he is willing to admit. Let us now explore further Ramsey's concept of natural law in the light of the traditional Catholic teaching.

II. The Theological Aspect Of The Question

To clarify and understand further the meaning of natural law in Roman Catholic moral theology it is necessary to distinguish two related but different functions of natural law. The first or theological aspect concerns the question of whether there is a source of ethical wisdom or knowledge for the Christian apart from the explicit scriptural revelation of God in Jesus Christ. Does the Christian share some ethical wisdom and knowledge with all persons because we share the same basic humanity? If one admits a non-revealed source of ethical wisdom and knowledge, how is it related to the explicitly Christian source?

The second aspect of the natural law question is the more specifically philosophical-ethical. In it one asks how the human is to be understood and how knowledge of human nature contributes to Christian ethical decision-making in terms either of virtues, goals, norms, or judgments. This aspect will be discussed in the next section.

On the theological aspect of the natural law question, Ramsey (1962A: 4-5) affirms that there is some virtue in man's ordinary moral decisions. The theological foundations for this claim are the doctrine of creation and the realization that creation and natural justice are not totally destroyed by sin, although sin is definitely present and exerting its influence. This qualification is important for Ramsey, who frequently (1968A: xiii, 479-488) condemns a natural law optimism which fails to recognize the presence of sin in the world. Specifically, he has criticized at some length (1968A: 70-90) the encyclical *Pacem In Terris* of Pope John XXIII precisely because it failed to take into consideration the existence of human sinfulness.

Moreover, Ramsey (1962A: 233-256) maintains that natural law or natural justice is not enough, nor may it be considered totally closed in itself. Christ is transforming, renewing, reshaping and redirecting natural law. Thus, for positive and negative reasons, Ramsey rejects a two-layer understanding of nature and grace (or justice and love) in which a realm of love remains above a realm of justice, which has not felt the transforming influence of love or the supernatural. For him, Christ or *agape* remains the primary distinctive and controlling aspect of Christian ethics at any level. Ramsey describes his own approach as Christ transforming natural law.

In another context, Ramsey (1961A: 22-26) describes this relationship in Barthian terminology, saying that creation is the possibility, promise and external basis of covenant, which remains the internal basis, meaning and purpose of creation. Natural justice provides the relationship of man *with* fellowman, which then must be transformed by love understood as the relationship of man *for* fellowman. Man *with* man entails at least an external system of relationships according to which each is given his due. In the order of charity, the Christian is *for* others, as Jesus Christ was the man *for* his fellowman.

Ramsey (1962A: 231-232) employs the symbols of Egypt and Exodus to explain the relationship between natural justice and Christian love. He acknowledges that there was more in Egypt than the fleshpots, for there was also a security and integration based on natural justice. But the closed world view of morality based solely on natural justice must be molded and reshaped into the form of God's saving action symbolized by the Exodus.

H. Richard Niebuhr, in his *Christ and Culture* (1956: 129-141), describes the synthesist approach of Thomas Aquinas and some other Catholic moral theologian as "Christ above culture"—a motif which affirms both Christ and culture. But there is a gulf and separation between them such that Christ stays above culture and does not truly penetrate and transform the realm of the natural or of culture.

It is important to note that Ramsey (1962A:243) recognizes that the Christ-above-culture description of Roman Catholicism is not totally accurate, especially in the light of his dialogue with Jacques Maritain. Catholic political theory does not propose that revelation or grace is simply added on to reason or nature, which in themselves remain intact and sufficiently strong and clear to furnish us with ordered structures of a just political life. Ramsey correctly points out that, in Catholic thought, grace perfects nature and revelation illumines and perfects reason. In this light, Catholic theory insists that reason can with confidence arrive at ethical truth, but also that revelation is necessary to strengthen and fulfill the suggestions of nature. Thus Ramsey sees in Maritain and in some Catholics a concept of transformism, even though he indicates elsewhere that grace does not always transform natural justice in Roman Catholic thought. Ramsey recognizes that the traditional Protestant insistence on both sin and grace puts more emphasis on the transforming aspect of love than Catholic thought does, but the difference between Protestant and Catholic thought is one of degree of emphasis on transformism and not a simple affirmation or denial of transformism.

On specific questions, Ramsey shows how his methodology operates and also how it differs from some approaches of Catholic moral theology. In his dialogue with Maritain, he (1962A: 238-244) raises the question of why the individual person should be regarded as a bearer of rights. Is this known through natural justice or through revelation which sees the person in terms of God's prior love and choice? Ramsey interprets Maritain as admitting that reason and nature alone are not sufficient for firmly establishing the rights and dignity of the individual human person in our society; these basic human rights are also founded on the religious order's appreciation of the person's relationship to a transcendent God.

Ramsey himself (1962A: 244-251) believes that the morality of covenant or Christian love is needed as the explicit theological premise actively at work in the moral life of men in every natural order in order to sustain any proper ethics, to comprehend and interpret it adequately or even to restore it in this hour of moral and political disorder. It is only the immediate presence of the claims of the righteousness of God between persons, and not any human sense of generic injustice, which asks that on occasion one should be unwilling to save his own life at the unavoidable cost of another's life. Thus does Ramsey understand the role and function of love transforming justice in this particular matter of basic human rights.

Does Ramsey consistently carry out his theory of Christ transforming natural law or love transforming justice, with its acceptance of the place of natural justice, all the while retaining *agape* or love as the controlling or primary aspect in Christian ethics? His early discussion of war published in 1961 follows such an approach. Ramsey (1961B: 3-90) appreciates the just war tradition as it developed in Roman Catholic theology, but he attempts to show that, both historically and theoretically, *agape* justifies the right to war and limits that right in the principle of discrimination. *Agape* demands that the Christian go to the aid of the neighbor whose rights are being attacked, but *agape* also demands that the attack be limited only to those who are actually bearers of force. The principle of discrimination, which proclaims the immunity of noncombatants from direct attack, is based primarily on Christian love and not on justice.

Can love transforming justice adequately describe Ramsey's more general social ethics? I do not think so. He developed and articulated this approach in the late 1950's and early 1960's. In a somewhat polemical manner, he was then attempting to indicate to his fellow Protestant ethicians that there is some value in the traditional Catholic approach to natural law and natural justice, even though he did modify the traditional Catholic approach.

One can notice a change in Ramsey's thought in his writings on social ethics in the 1960's and 1970's. There is an ever stronger emphasis on the need for order and force in the social realm because of the presence of sin, and less emphasis on love and justice. Ramsey (1968A: 5-9) laments the fact that the liberal consensus in Protestant, and to some extent in Catholic, ethics forgets the presence of sin and decries the need for power and even armed force in politics. *The Just War* (1968A: xxi) begins with a one-page fable showing that man's present life and existence are heavily influenced by sin and the fall. Ramsey's later writings in the area of political ethics emphasize the presence of sin in human existence and do not really develop at length the aspect of justice or of love transforming justice.

In the chapter considering Emil Brunner in *Nine Modern Moralists* (1962A: 207-208), Ramsey claims that the proper understanding of Christian life in society is based on the threefold divine activity of creation, preservation and redemption. Interestingly, however, on the level of the human moral activity corresponding to the threefold divine activity, Ramsey explicitly speaks only of the twofold work of love and justice, with no mention of order. *Christian Ethics and the Sit-In* (1961A: 40-65) speaks of the threefold activity of God as creating, preserving and redeeming, and relates this to the need for justice, order and love in society. But, in practice, there seems to be such a heavy stress on order that love and justice do not really exert much influence on the solution of particular questions such as voluntary and limited busing of black students out of their neighborhood into more predominantly white schools and the question of integration within the churches themselves.

The concept of the state proposed in *War and the Christian Conscience* (1961B: 15-33) downplays the role and function of justice in the state and seems to go against an isolated statement found in *Nine Modern Moralists* (1962A: 181) according to which Augustine does not pay sufficient attention to justice in his understanding of the state. Thus, in the early 60's, there was an ambivalence in Ramsey's general social ethics, but his emphasis on order in practical cases paved the way for his later insistence on order at the expense of justice.

Subsequent writings from 1967 to the present give an even greater emphasis to the negative and preserving aspect of the state in response to the sinfulness of men. In these later discussions of the state, Ramsey (1972b, 1972c, 1973j) speaks primarily of the function of preservation based on the covenant which God made with Noah never again to destroy the world. The state is seen as the means by which God will keep the world from destroying itself. There is no balancing development of a more positive aspect of the state based on creation and the needs of justice. In my judgment (as enunciated elsewhere in greater detail, 1973:11-26), the political ethics expounded by Ramsey in his writings from the middle sixties to the present cannot be described as employing the methodology of Christ transforming natural law or love transforming justice.

There is another question of consistency concerning Ramsey's theory of Christ transforming natural law proposed in *Nine Modern Moralists*. Is this position consonant with the position Ramsey took in *Basic Christian Ethics*, which was published in 1950? The author himself has indicated on a number of occasions that there is no contradiction between the two books. For instance, in the introduction to *Nine Modern Moralists* (1962A: 6-7), he maintains that *Basic Christian Ethics* develops the meaning of Christian love as the primary and distinctive aspect of Christian ethics. But, he goes on, such an approach did not deny that there could be a role and a place for natural law and natural justice in a complete system of Christian ethics. *Nine Modern Moralists* makes explicit the concept of Christ transforming natural law which could even be found somewhat in *Basic Christian Ethics*.

In *Deeds and Rules in Christian Ethics*, Ramsey (1967:122) again defends himself against the charge of any inconsistency between his exposition in *Basic Christian Ethics* and in *Nine Modern Moralists*. In the first book, he was stressing only what was primary and distinctive in Christian ethics; whereas, in the second book, he developed the proper place and function of natural law or natural justice. In fairness to Ramsey, it must be pointed out that, even in *Basic Christian Ethics* (1950A: 86), he does employ the same description of love as primary and distinctive in Christian ethics, so that his defense of his consistency is not merely a later rationalization on his part.

In my judgment, nevertheless, there is more discontinuity between *Basic Christian Ethics* and *Nine Modern Moralists* than Ramsey is willing to admit. The problem is not that *Basic Christian Ethics* emphasizes just the primary and specific aspect of Christian ethics and says nothing about natural law; rather, aspects of the theory proposed in *Basic Christian Ethics* do not allow a place for natural law and justice.

The theory of Christ transforming natural law or love transforming justice, which Ramsey proposes in *Nine Modern Moralists*, should logically affect some of the theological considerations developed in *Basic Christian Ethics*. As Ramsey points out in *Nine Modern Moralists* the acceptance of the natural law or natural justice is related to the Christian teaching on creation, but nowhere in *Basic Christian Ethics* does Ramsey give sufficient development to the role of creation in Christian theological ethics. There the central emphases on Christ and redemption seem not only primary but virtually exclusive, despite some remarks to the contrary (1950A: 337-351). Christian ethics looks only to Jesus Christ and is derived not from the human but from Jesus Christ, according to Ramsey's exposition in *Basic Christian Ethics*. This Christocentrism not only does not positively develop the place of creation, but it seems to exclude a real role for creation in Christian ethics, so that there is nothing for Christ to transform.

The theory of love transforming justice should logically also involve a theory of Christian love transforming human love, since redemption transforms creation. In *Basic Christian Ethics*, Christian love is portrayed as opposed to human love and not as transforming human love. Ramsey's Christocentric approach to love does not give an important enough place to human love so that it can be transformed. This teaching on love indicates that the Christocentric approach of *Basic Christian Ethics* truly does not supply the theoretical basis for an acceptance of creation or the natural.

III. The Philosophical-Ethical Aspect of Natural Law

The previous section of this essay has considered what was called the theological aspect of the question of natural law. Once a Christian ethicist accepts the validity of natural law or natural justice, then the question arises as to what is meant by natural law and natural justice and how ethical wisdom is derived from it. This twofold question is inherent in the term "natural" as employed in traditional Roman Catholic theology. On the one hand, nature is distinguished from super-nature and refers to what belongs to human beings as such apart from the gift of grace. But nature is also understood in a philosophical sense as the principle of operation in every living thing, so that actions should follow from nature. The natural law in traditional Roman Catholic ethics includes both meanings of nature. Ramsey's discussion also presupposes the twofold meaning of nature.

As already mentioned in the discussion of Maritain, Ramsey does not really accept the ontological and metaphysical concept of nature on which traditional Catholic natural law theory is built. Without any extensive philosophical analysis, Ramsey merely proposes the existence of an innate sense of justice or of injustice by which, in the context of the prism of the case, we can discern the right thing to do. If the reader fails to distinguish the two different aspects of natural law, he can readily claim that Ramsey's call for Protestants to accept natural law is also an invitation to accept the traditional Roman Catholic natural law theory with its ontological grounding in a universal human nature. Ramsey's insistence that he is following Maritain, and his own failure to point out explicitly that he does not accept Maritain's ontological basis of natural law, give added reason to think that his understanding of natural law is the same as, or at least very similar to, the Catholic understanding.

There is another important factor that can support the mistaken contention that Ramsey, in calling for a place for natural law in his theory, accepted the Catholic ontological understanding of nature. Catholic natural law theory, precisely because of its philosophical-ethical understanding of nature, has insisted on the existence of universal norms which are binding on all occasions. It has staunchly opposed any situation ethics. In later years, Paul Ramsey has also opposed situation ethics and stands out as the most prominent anti-situationist Protestant ethician in the United States. But the reasons for the anti-situationist approach are quite different in traditional Catholic natural law and in Ramsey.

Ramsey himself astutely points out two factors that contribute both to the emphasis on universal norms in Catholic moral teaching and to a certain type of inflexibility that he cannot accept—the republication of natural law by the authoritative teaching of the Catholic Church and the deductive logic by which conclusions are derived from first principles. Ramsey has realized that these two factors do influence the acceptance of universal norms in Catholic thought. A more fundamental factor, in my judgment, is the ontological basis of natural law—the universal nature of man, which is present in every human being. It is precisely this universal nature of man, together with a poor understanding of it in terms of a physical nature, which has been the primary reason for the insistence on universal norms in Catholic moral thought. At least, this has been the ultimate philosophical basis for such an insistence.

Although Ramsey has admitted a place for natural law in Christian ethics, his insistence on universal, exceptionless norms in moral theology does not come from his concept of natural law. He has accepted a type of natural law which affirms the validity of a sense of justice or injustice, found in the concrete judgment in prismatic cases. Thus, although Ramsey employs terminology reminiscent of the Catholic approach (for example, he [1967A: 7] speaks of general rules founded upon an apprehension of the nature of the person, his needs, and fulfillment), the nature of the person is not the foundation for Ramsey's insistence on the existence of exceptionless rules in Christian ethics.

Ramsey's own position on the place of norms in Christian ethics and his justification of general rules has evolved in the course of his writings. There is one chapter in *Basic Christian Ethics* (1950A: 46-91) which can readily be interpreted (Sellers, 1970: 196) as opposed to any universal norms and principles in Christian ethics. Yet, later, Ramsey defends the existence of such norms. In my judgment, there is some discontinuity in Ramsey's developing teaching on universal, exceptionless norms, but not as much as might appear on the surface. Many of the statements appearing in *Basic Christian Ethics* (1950A: 46-91) should be interpreted in the light of a Protestant rhetoric against the law and its use in Christian ethics.

The first basis for Ramsey's later insistence on exceptionless norms in Christian ethics is the concept of *agape* or Christian love, which is the same concept first expounded at great length in *Basic Christian Ethics* (1950A: 92-152). Christian love is obedient love of the neighbor and his needs in the same way that God has loved us. As God is faithful to his covenant, so must man keep his; as God shows mercy and forgiveness, so must man; as God's love gives all according to man's need and not merit, so should the Christian. Christian *agape* is disinterested and unclaiming regard for the needs of the neighbor. Later, in *Nine Modern Moralists*, Ramsey (1962A: 290) describes our love for our neighbor under the one univocal term of faithfulness. On the basis of this understanding of love, Ramsey later develops his insistence on exceptionless norms.

Deeds and Rules in Christian Ethics (1967A: 44-45) tries to show that the very meaning of *agape*, understood as faithful love, will at times result in universal judgments about ways of acting. There are bonds of fidelity existing among persons, and the individual is not free at any given moment to break these bonds. Rules, properly understood, are in no sense opposed to *agape*, but rather agape itself leads to the existence of universal, exceptionless rules. The Christian in no way opposes rules to agape. Thus the concept of love which Ramsey first proposed at great length in *Basic Christian Ethics* is the primary reason, or at least the reason Ramsey propounded first and in greatest detail, proving that there are exceptionless moral norms in Christian ethics. Ramsey (1968a: 120-135) later developed this concept of exceptionless rules based on *agape* in terms of canons of loyalty.

Second, the notion of *agape* which Ramsey accepts logically involves an emphasis on exceptionless rules. He (1967A: 108-109) admits that if agapism is not a distinctive type of ethical theory which is neither teleology nor deontology, then it is more truly called a type of deontology. This approach is consonant with Ramsey's theory of eschatology, for right action cannot be derived from any consequences or goods to be obtained in an age which is being fast liquidated. Such a deontological understanding of *agape* in Christian ethics is opposed to a situationist's view that would see good consequences and benefits as a justification for breaking norms in certain circumstances.

In his insistence on the existence of rules of practice, Ramsey (1967A: 123-144) develops an additional reason for the existence of exceptionless norms in Christian ethics. Relying on the two concepts of rules distinguished by John Rawls, Ramsey now emphasizes the need for rules of practice in Christian ethics. He goes so far as to contend that the very existence of Christian social ethics depends upon whether this second possible justification of general rules has a legitimate place in systematic reflection on the Christian life. Thus, the third reason for Ramsey's insistence on the existence of exceptionless rules comes from his use of Anglo-American philosophy. It is this type of philosophical ethics, rather than Catholic natural law theory, that the later Ramsey uses to bolster his contention about the existence of exceptionless rules. He often appeals to the principle of universalizability which is frequently mentioned in contemporary philosophical literature. The influence of analytic thought is readily seen in his long essay, "The Case of the Curious Exception" (1968a). Ramsey, in a recent article (1973a: 210) explicitly acknowledges his dependence on such philosophical insights rather than on traditional Catholic natural law theory as the best theoretical explanation of and warrant for general moral norms.

Ramsey's insistence on exceptionless moral norms has bases other than the traditional Catholic natural law theory. His use of these theoretical justifications of moral norms furnishes additional proof of the thesis that Ramsey himself does not accept the philosophical and ontological understanding of nature which is the ultimate philosophical basis for the traditional Catholic acceptance of universal norms.

IV. The Principle of Double Effect

In order to show the implications of my argument, I should like to conclude with an illustration. There has been no particular aspect of Catholic natural law theory which Ramsey has emphasized more than the principle of double effect. A study of his use and understanding of this traditional Catholic concept will be quite revealing and will support the contention that Ramsey really does not much depend upon Catholic natural law theory. In his first extended discussion of abortion, Ramsey (1968g: 78) argues that Protestants should adopt as a rule of practice a distinction between direct and indirect abortion which Roman Catholicism unfolds for the charitable protection of human life in cases of irreconcilable conflict of equals.

Again, in his latest article on abortion, Ramsey (1973a: 212) claims there are only three possible solutions to conflict situations involving human lives: (1) One can remain an equalitarian and stand aside from cases of lives in conflict. (2) One can abandon equalitarianism and justify taking one life on the basis of comparable value and worth. (3) One can, while not standing aside, remain an equalitarian and be driven to moral reasoning in conformity with the famous principle of the double effect. Ramsey puts himself in the third category, but, in the process, so revises the principle of double effect that it is no longer recognizable as such.

Ramsey (1961B: 45-59; 135-153) first utilizes the principle of the double effect in his discussion of just war. The same Christian love which justifies war to protect the neighbor in need also gives rise to the principle of discrimination affirming the immunity of non-combatants from direct attack because they are not bearers of force or harm. The concept of direct attack is then explained in great historical and theoretical detail in the light of the Catholic teaching on the principle of the double effect; Ramsey also points out his differences with the Catholic position.

Ramsey's understanding (1961B: 54-59) of the evolution of the principle of double effect is as follows: Thomas Aquinas did not express the fully developed principle found in contemporary moral theology. Thomas does not talk about the question of the physical structure of the act itself but only about the intention. In his famous article on killing an unjust aggressor (in the *Summa Theologiae* [II-II, q. 64, a. 7]), Thomas maintains that one can never intend to kill the aggressor; rather the killing always has to be indirect. Catholic theologians after Aquinas insisted that the good effect not only be the immediate object of the intention but also the immediate material object of the physical act. In the light of this more developed understanding of the principle of double effect, many Catholic theologians found it difficult to describe the killing of the unjust aggressor in self-defense as only indirect; the aggressor is killed directly as a means of saving one's own life. The act of directly killing the unjust aggressor is an inherently right means because of the injustice of the aggressor. The principle of the double effect was then limited (and in Ramsey's opinion rightly so) to cases of killing innocent persons on one's own authority, and did not apply to the case of unjust aggression.

Ramsey (1961B: 39-59) criticizes this development, not on the basis of its internal logic, but rather as indicating a full shift to the category of natural justice rather than love. According to natural justice the aggressor loses his right to life and can be directly killed. Augustine did not allow any killing in self-defense because Christian love would never allow one to kill another in order to save one's own life. In the light of Christian love, a person does not lose his right to life because of his injustice. Christian love protects the weak, the helpless and even the unjust, and surrounds them all with immunity. Ramsey sees a love motif still somewhat present in Thomas because the latter would never allow one to *intend* to kill an unjust aggressor. But, in the final development of the principle of the double effect, justice has become the controlling category so that one can directly intend and directly do the killing of the unjust aggressor who has lost his right to life.

Ramsey's explanation of the principle of discrimination, not only in his earliest works but consistently throughout his writing on war, has been based on the understanding of direct attack which has been developed in Catholic natural law theory. It is not merely a question of intention but also involves the doing of the deed itself. *In War and the Christian Conscience* (1961B: 172-183) and in *Nine Modern Moralists* (1962A: 251-256), Ramsey states just one area in which he disagrees with the Catholic understanding of direct and indirect and its application to conflict situations involving life. In the comparatively rare situation of the birth-room conflict between the life of the mother and the life of the fetus, traditional Catholic moral theology would not allow either life to be directly taken, even if the result is that both will die. In Ramsey's judgment, this is truly a case where morality must exit from the closed system of natural law and be transformed by love which would allow the direct killing of the fetus to save the life of the mother.

Through the work of Bouscaren, Ramsey (1961B: 172-183) is aware of late nineteenth century Roman Catholic controversies about permitting the direct killing of the fetus to save the life of the mother. However, Church authority intervened through decrees of the Holy Office and declared that the fetus could never be directly aborted. Ramsey points to this authoritative intervention to indicate again that the problem of inflexibility in Roman Catholic natural law ethics might not come from the concept of natural law itself but rather its republication or authoritative interpretation by the Church.

In his first article devoted exclusively to abortion, originally delivered as a paper in 1966, Ramsey (1968g: 80-82) continues his criticism of what he understands as the Catholic teaching which allows the unjust aggressor to be directly killed because by his guilt he has lost his right to life. In Ramsey's perspective of Christian love and righteousness, the determination of right conduct cannot be determined by the innocence or guilt of the aggressor. It is not formal aggression (guilt or innocence) but material aggression which justifies the taking of life to prevent the aggressive action, just as in the case of warfare one can directly kill combatants, not because of their subjective guilt or innocence, but because they are bearers of hostile force. In the conflict situation involving the life of the fetus and the life of the mother, Ramsey no longer appeals to *agape* to justify the killing, rather he redescribes the act. In this conflict situation, the act is directed toward the incapacitation of the fetus from doing what it is doing to the life of the mother and is not directed toward the death of the fetus as such. Ramsey suggests that such an approach is truly in keeping with the teaching of Aquinas himself. "The stopping of materially aggressive action is the highest possible warrant for the killing of men by men (if life cannot otherwise be saved), not the aggressor-innocent distinction" (1968g: 86). In a later version of this article, Ramsey (1971e: 22-23) recognizes, in the light of comments made by Richard McCormick, that in accord with the teaching of Aquinas such an action should be called indirect; but he still prefers the term justifiable direct abortion, because such terminology requires all to accept the fact that there are two personal termini of a single action and that truly the life of the fetus is taken.

Ramsey has made some comparatively minor clarifications in his ensuing discussions; but, for our purposes, it is sufficient to consider his most recent extended discussion of abortion—a long review article of the books by Daniel Callahan and Germain Grisez. Here again, Ramsey (1973a: 220-221) retains his position that the crucial question is whether the target of the "deadly deed" is the life of the fetus or, alternatively, what it is doing to the mother. The act is done with physical or observable directness but is justifiable if the target is the death-dealing function of the fetus. From what Ramsey has written, it is fair to describe the act as physically or observably direct because the fetus is directly killed, but morally indirect because the act is targeted against the death-dealing function of the fetus.

In the light of Ramsey's discussion of double effect, three comments are in order. First, his earlier disagreement with Catholic teaching in the conflict situation of the life of the fetus and the life of the mother appealed to the concept of love transforming justice, but later he employed purely rational arguments to redescribe the human act as preventing the fetus from doing its deadly function. This definitely indicates a change in his thinking and may also show that the concept of love transforming justice is no longer as central in his thinking as it was in an earlier period.

Secondly, I think Ramsey has consistently misinterpreted, at least to a degree, the Catholic teaching on directly killing an unjust aggressor. Ramsey interprets the majority contemporary Catholic position as holding that the aggressor by his guilty action has lost his right to life and therefore can be directly killed both in the order of intention and in the order of the material act itself. He indicates that Thomas was still influenced by Christian love in maintaining that one could kill the aggressor but not directly intend his death. However, the Catholic position was not based on the subjective guilt or innocence of the person. A simply materially unjust aggressor could be directly killed; neither guilt nor innocence is the determining factor, but the very fact of being a bearer of force or an aggressor.

In fairness to Ramsey, there are, in my judgment, some ambiguities and even inconsistencies in the majority Catholic opinion that could bring about confusion. Those (e.g., Zalba, 1953: 275-286) who allowed the direct killing of the aggressor to save one's own life, then restricted the principle of the double effect to the killing of the *innocent* on one's own authority. Their use of the term *innocent* certainly favors Ramsey's interpretation. Nevertheless, one must recall that this same theory did allow direct killing of a materially (not formally) unjust aggressor. The decisive factor was never subjective guilt or innocence but the material fact of aggression or attack.

It is also true that after the decisions of the Holy Office in the late nineteenth and early twentieth century, Catholic theology did not allow the application of the teaching on directly killing an unjust aggressor to be applied to the fetus in the womb. One could readily assume that the justification rested on the fact that the fetus could not be subjectively guilty. But the reason proposed for not applying such a teaching (at least by all the twentieth century manuals I have read and supported by Bouscaren, 1944: 3-64) is not that the fetus cannot be guilty but that the fetus in the womb is not truly involved in aggression and is only trying to live and survive. These authors deny that the action of the fetus constitutes aggression. (In my judgment even a knowledge of the Catholic tradition argues for a change in this teaching so that the fetus can be killed to save the life of the mother.)

In response to remarks of Germain Grisez that he is really talking about materially unjust aggression, Ramsey (1973a: 219-220) says that he was in no way thinking of the category of *materially unjust* aggression, but only of actual aggression of one innocent human upon another. Despite the inaccurate terminology, I believe that by materially unjust aggression the Catholic tradition meant actual aggression. One could directly kill a person who was a bearer of aggression and thus threatening one's life. Thus it seems that Ramsey and the traditional Catholic teaching were closer than he recognized on this point.

In this context, I also disagree with Ramsey's theory that Thomas Aquinas did not allow one to intend killing the unjust aggressor because he was still operating on the basis of Christian *agape* in the tradition of Augustine, whereas later Catholic teaching on the basis of the guilt of the aggressor allowed one to directly intend the death of the aggressor. The later Catholic teaching was not founded on such a non-agapistic understanding of justice. In addition, there is no evidence that Thomas employed *agape* in his reasoning. The later Ramsey acknowledges that by redescribing the human act as targeted on the death-dealing function of the fetus one can conclude on purely rational grounds without necessarily invoking *agape* that the defender should not intend to kill the aggressor.

The third and most important observation about Ramsey's continuing application of the principle of double effect is that, in his latest statement of it and even earlier, he has really not *revised* the traditional Catholic theory but has *rejected* it. However, he himself never admits that he has rejected it. The most significant and important condition of the double effect, according to Catholic discussions, is the condition which holds that the good effect must be equally as immediate as the evil effect in the order of physical causality. The evil effect cannot be the means by which the good effect is produced. Ramsey

(1961B: 55) properly understood this, because he described the principle of the double effect as requiring that the good must not only be the formal object of the intention but also the immediate material object of the physical act. Likewise, Ramsey employed this understanding of the concept of direct in describing the principle of discrimination.

In conflict situations, Ramsey is now denying that the act is necessarily wrong if the abortion is the immediate material object of the physical act. In fact, the physical structure of the act is no longer determinative for Ramsey, at least in some cases. Life can be taken with observable and physical directness, but the crucial moral problem is whether the intention of the act is the incapacitation of the fetus from doing what it is doing, the prevention of the aggressive function, or the stopping of the deadly deed perpetrated on the mother. Ramsey limits his consideration to the conflict situation involving the life of the fetus and the life of the mother; but, even in other conflict situations involving abortion and other values, he would have to settle the morality, not on the basis of the immediate material object of the act, but merely on the basis of proportionality. In these conflict situations, the physical structure of the act has no moral significance for Ramsey. He could readily maintain that the only proportionate reason justifying an abortion is the life of the mother; but, as I have pointed out elsewhere (1973: 128-130), there is some ambivalence in Ramsey on this point. It is clear, however, that Ramsey (as well as many a Catholic author writing today) does not apply the contemporary understanding of the principle of the double effect to abortion cases. (On this see David Smith's essay in this volume.)

Conclusion

Paul Ramsey both agrees and disagrees with traditional Catholic natural law theory, but the area of disagreement is much greater than might appear at first sight. From the perspective of the theological aspect of natural law, he accepts a place for natural law or natural justice, but rightly insists on its being integrated into the Christian vision, including sin and transformation by love. From the philosophical perspective, he does not accept the ontological basis for natural law proposed in the manuals of moral theology. Ramsey's own insistence on exceptionless rules does not follow from his acceptance of natural law. Although Ramsey frequently says that he is following the principle of the double effect, his own teaching on the solution to conflict situations in abortions does not follow that principle. He does, however, follow the concept of direct killing in his exposition of the meaning of the principle of discrimination which protects noncombatants from deliberate direct attack.

REFERENCES

Bouscaren, T. Lincoln, S.J.

1944 *Ethics of Ectopic Operations.* 2nd ed. Milwaukee: Bruce Publishing Co.

Cross, Robert D.

1964 "Introduction to the Torchbook edition." Pp. viii-xx in Walter Rauschenbusch, *Christianity and the Social Crisis.* New York: Harper and Row Torchbook.

Curran, Charles E.

1973 *Politics, Medicine, and Christian Ethics: A Dialogue with Paul Ramsey.* Philadelphia: Fortress Press.

Maritain, Jacques

1956 *Man and the State.* Chicago: Chicago University Press, Phoenix Book.

Niebuhr, H. Richard

1956 *Christ and Culture.* New York: Harper and Row Torchbook.

Niebuhr, Reinhold

1967 *Love and Justice: Selections from the Shorter Writings of Reinhold Niebuhr.* Ed. D.B. Robertson. Cleveland and New York: Meridian Books.

Ramsey, Paul

See the bibliography of Ramsey's works in this volume. Capital letters (e. g. 1950A) denote books and occasional papers; lower case letters (e.g. 1968a) denote articles.

Sellers, James

1970 *Public Ethics: American Morals and Manners.* New York: Harper and Row.

Stone, Ronald H.

1972 *Reinhold Niebuhr: Prophet to Politicians.* Nashville and New York: Abingdon Press.

Zalba, Marcellinus, S.J.

1953 *Theologiae Moralis Summa*, Vol. II: *Theologia Moralis Specialis; Tractatus de Mandatis Dei et Ecclesiae.* Madrid: Biblioteca de Autores Christianos.

CHAPTER IV

Paul Ramsey's Task: Some Methodological Clarifications and Questions

PAUL F. CAMENISCH

I. The Task of Christian Ethics

Just as Paul Ramsey asserts that prudence must be in the service of some prior principle (1961B: 4), so method must be in the service of some prior task. Consequently the only proper starting point for considering any ethicist's methodology is to ascertain what task that method is designed to effect. I see this as a significant question since I am presently convinced that there are several different valid and historically authenticated tasks of Christian ethics and that different tasks set in motion different methods of ethical reflection and different modes of moral action.

Ramsey's position is that a major task of Christian ethics is serving the neighbor. And that mode of serving the neighbor which according to Ramsey is crucial for Christian ethics is the shaping and maintaining of the ethos of modern society in order to protect the rights and integrity of individuals from encroachment and violation by the society and/or its ethos. This statement will no doubt strike many readers as at best a generous and at worst an incorrect assessment of Ramsey's purpose. It therefore requires documentation.[1] Ramsey has explicitly stated this concern more than once. For example, in his introduction to *Who Speaks for the Church* he refers to ". . . our proper task of nourishing, judging, and repairing the moral and political *ethos* of our time" (1967B: 15; see also 1967A: 9).

To the extent that "repairing and maintaining the *ethos*" can be taken as one way of saying "preserving social order," this element in my statement of Ramsey's purpose will raise few problems. In fact some of Ramsey's critics have attacked him on precisely this point of emphasizing order at the expense of justice (Curran, 1973: 37) or, in his concern for order, of being overly solicitous for the interests of the state (Deats, 1968: 34).

It is the second element of my statement of Ramsey's purpose which will raise the difficulty for most readers, the suggestion that his concern for a society's ethos, its moral order, is a form of or a means to his concern for protecting the rights, prerogatives and integrity of the individual. Ramsey makes this connection when he states in a recent article that ". . . law and ethics have primarily to do with individuals and proscribing the violation of individual human beings. . . ." (1973d: 15). And in a more extended and, for our purposes, more pointed statement in "The Case of the Curious Exception," he says:

> It should be noted . . . that it is incorrect to say that the defender of exceptionless rules is the one who places collective or societal values first, and is insufficiently compassionate or open to exceptional action that may take the individual's good more into account. The reverse is the case. It is the defender of exceptionless rules who would build a floor under the individual fellow man by minimum faithfulness-rules or canons of loyalty to him that are unexceptionable, while it is the proponent of future possible exceptions who may be placing societal and gross consequence-values uppermost (1968a: 133).

The fact that Ramsey's concern with the social ethos is a concern for protecting the individual is also evident in his relative indifference toward judging the moral performance of individuals. For example, it is the reshaping of the "abortifacient society" rather than "the praise or blame of individual actions or agents" which motivates his analysis of abortion (1971e: 23). And the "excessive individualism" he criticizes in Protestant ethics is not a doctrine which exalts the good of the individual at the expense of the societal good; it is, rather, a concern to judge the individual's acts instead of systems and institutions which affect individuals.

Further support for this thesis comes from Ramsey's characterization of contemporary society. Some dangers in it which concern him are: the possibility of behavior control (1972e: 174); moral-bond-destroying atomistic individualism (1967A: 44); trends in this scientific and secular age destructive of substantive morality (1971e: 27); atmospheric humanism and liberal progressivism (1970A: 17); "the vast technological alienation of man" (1970A: 89); dualism and mentalism which will end by seeing "everyone [as] a useful precadaver" (1970B: 209); and the loss of passion from modern technical life (1962A: 108). It is clear that for the most part these trends and characteristics are distinguished, *not* by the threat they pose to social order, but by the threat they pose *to the individual* in the name of social order, domination and progress. It is also clear that as Ramsey looks at contemporary society his concern focuses, not in some abstract sense on that society for its own sake, but rather on

> . . . the groundlings—creatures of this world come of age—who do not have the moral courage or the ethical concepts, the religious daring or the theological concepts, with which to radically challenge the basic assumptions of a technological civilization (1970A: 130).

The alert reader will note that virtually all the evidence cited so far is drawn from Ramsey's more recent writings about various bio-medical problems. Such an observation suggests, of course, that I have taken a relatively recent concern of Ramsey's, which has arisen in the context of bio-medical ethics, and tried to see it as a crucial theme in all of his work. Charles Curran, for instance, would seem committed to such an interpretation when he writes: "I have criticized Ramsey's political ethics for not giving enough importance to the value of individual human life, and I have criticized his medical ethics at times for giving too much importance to the individual" (1973: 221).

It is true that this concern for the individual does emerge in the later Ramsey with increasing frequency and passion. But that is not to say that this is a new concern in his thought. Ramsey's earlier writings on sexuality repeatedly return to the various ways in which individuals are, in that area of life, suffering at the hands of the society and the regnant ethos. The battle there takes on rather different shape, however, because society's most significant incursions in that area are not of the overt and documentable sort which occur in the bio-medical field. Rather, they occur there in the shaping of the mores, the moral atmosphere, and the formation of the individual's own values and conscience—by which he himself then "chooses" to surrender much of the deeper significance of human sexuality and human beginnings, and thus renders himself and his fellows less "sanctified" and more vulnerable before the society.[2]

My suggestion is that Ramsey's major concern in his writings on sexuality and human beginnings was not to whip experimenting teenagers into line but rather parallels his defense of the individual so prominent in his bio-medical writings. In the case of sexuality, that defense takes the form of assisting the teenager, and all of us, in retaining some sense of the deeper levels and significance of human sexuality and human beginnings in the face of increasing societal indifference or even animosity toward them.

Admittedly Ramsey's writings on war are the most difficult to fit under my present hypothesis. Explicit statements on behalf of the individual and the worth of his life are disappointingly rare in Ramsey when he is engaged in the complexities of the just war theory. But a number of points must be made before a fair judgment can be rendered on whether Ramsey has abandoned his commitment to the individual and the value of his life in that context.

In relation to war there are a number of possible ways of affirming and protecting the value of the individual, his life and his rights. One such way is that of a pacifist who, by taking a stand against all war, opposes any harm which comes to persons through war. Ramsey, as is well known, rejects the pacifists' way, not because he takes concern for individuals less seriously than pacifists do but because he disagrees with their conclusions as to the best method for effectively implementing that concern. His rejection of those conclusions derives largely from his noting, whether correctly or not, a frequent and disquieting coincidence between doctrines of total peace (which would include at least some forms of pacifism) and doctrines of total war. This latter, of course, is a much more serious threat to life and other values than is Ramsey's just or limited war position. (See, for example, 1968A: xi, 42-69.)

Having rejected as unsatisfactory the pacifists' attempt to exclude all wars, the only way to protect persons is to distinguish between those causes of or motivations for war which can and those which cannot make morally tolerable the human losses involved in any war. *Ius ad bellum* here stands as a protector of individuals by letting pass only those causes which, being pressed by arms, hold some promise of preventing more evil to individuals than they cause. Under the proper circumstances the concern for individuals becomes a reason for war rather than against it. Ramsey finds grounds for this assertion in the experience of the early Christians:

> The change-over to just-war doctrine and practice was not a "fall" from the original purity of Christian ethics; but however striking a turning-full-circle, this was a change of tactics only. The basic strategy remained the same: responsible love and service of one's neighbors in the texture of the common life (1961B: xvii).

But even this requirement that only those wars which can be seen as serving the neighbor shall be permitted is not enough; so Ramsey goes further, insisting in his treatment of *ius in bello* that even in such conflicts as these, certain limitations on the means used must be observed. Thus Ramsey arrives at the just war position and struggles to formulate the *ius in bello*, not because some lessening in his concern for individuals has permitted this, but because his concern for individuals, for providing them with workable and realistic protection, has driven him to it. Among the requirements of the *ius in bello*, Ramsey's unwavering defense of the principle of discrimination serves as testimony to his continuing concern for the life of the individual—here, of course, most especially that of the noncombatant.

Of course some readers will look at these limits set by Ramsey's *ius in bello* and see, not the evils they exclude, but the harm they permit or perhaps even legitimate. They do of course serve both functions; but one must ask which function, the excluding or the including, is the one which drives Ramsey to struggle with the whole set of issues. It borders on the grotesque to suggest that it is the desire to legitimate some forms of violence that motivates just war theorists, a suggestion which James W. Douglass tends toward when he writes: ". . . the just war's moral logic is basically in the service of violence as an opponent of injustice. . . ." (1968: 176). Ramsey, and any right-minded just war theorist, would rightly insist that just war theory is basically in the service of justice (even love) even to and beyond the point at which violence is required to defend it.

I have not here undertaken to defend Ramsey's just war theory as the most appropriate Christian response to war. My claim is that all of Ramsey's work, including that on war, should be assessed in relation to the task he has set himself and the concerns which move him to it. I do not interpret Ramsey as everywhere and always exalting the individual, his rights, needs, convictions and even whimsies, above the society and its rights, needs, etc. Since any serious reader of Ramsey's works will know such an interpretation to be false, I will not document the other side of the tension in which Ramsey and all of us are here caught. (See, for example, Ramsey's discussion of selective conscientious objection, 1968A: 92-93.)

I have suggested that Ramsey's concern for the individual, his integrity and his rights is a crucial driving force in his ethics; that this concern extensively shapes the task Ramsey sets for himself—that of protecting the individual, largely through the shaping and maintaining of a livable ethos; and that this concern and this task are the absolutely necessary starting points for understanding Ramsey's methodology. I will now attempt to support this interpretation by looking at various areas of Ramsey's thought where these concerns exert significant influence on his methodology.

II. From "love" to "covenant"

It is well known that from very early in Ramsey's career "love" has dominated his exposition of Christian ethics: "The central notion or 'category' in Christian ethics is 'obedient love'. . . ." (1950A: xi). This love is not a teleological orientation to some good (1950A: 148), but is rather a matter of a deontologically right relation to the neighbor (1950A: 148) whereby one exists for the other person (1947c: 189). Part of the right relation is, of course, the unselfish seeking of the neighbor's good, but it is the relation, not the good, which is the fundamental concern of Christian ethics.

More recently, however, there has been in Ramsey's articulation of the Christian's ultimate norm a rather evident shift toward a much more extensive use of the ideas of covenant, and what I take to be the derivative notions of canons of loyalty and fidelty claims. Of course Ramsey in no sense sees the "love" and the "covenant" terminologies as mutually exclusive alternatives. They have from the beginning been closely interrelated, even interdependent, in Ramsey's thought:

> The covenant means unconditional obedience; it means unclaiming love. In this book, the basic norm for Christian ethics has been called "obedient love" because of its intimate association with the idea of "covenant" and with the "reign" of God (1950A: 388).

And in 1962 he refers to "the single covenant-meaning of love" (1962A: 185). Furthermore, as late as 1968, he exhibits a broad tolerance, in some sense even an indifference, toward the question of which terminology is to be used, when he refers to "the ultimate norm in Christian ethics (*agape*, or whatever is a more adequate name for our basic Christian perspective upon the moral life). . . ." (1968a: 73).

The as yet unresolved problems which enter Ramsey's thought with the idea of covenant are those of the origin, the authority and the content of the covenants under which we live. With regard to the ethical significance of men's covenants there are two sorts of possible answers to be given to the question of their origin. One can say either that covenants originate at the will of the agent(s) bound by them or that they originate outside of and independent of the will of the agent(s) so bound. The first account gives us a relatively simple and persuasive answer to our second question—covenants so understood have authority and are obligatory, because the agent has freely and knowingly bound himself by them. But this answer raises another problem by portraying moral obligation as so voluntaristic that some might suspect that it ceases to be moral obligation. Ramsey shows this concern in a rather different context (1967A: 163), but I feel certain that he would also raise it here were all our covenants to be viewed in this way.

The other account of the origin of our covenants solves the problem of voluntariness, for covenants originating outside the agent's will or assent can in some respects be more easily viewed as fully obligatory in themselves. But this raises the question of how they can then bind the agents coming under them for whom most moderns want to retain a considerable amount of autonomy if their actions and obligations are to be viewed as truly moral. (For such a concern in Ramsey with regard to the question of infused virtues, see 1947c: 187.)

Ramsey seems to vacillate on this point, indicating a preference first for one and then for the other of these two answers and consequently moving back and forth between the attendant problems he must, or at least should, deal with. One of his most explicit statements on this question comes down emphatically on the side of at least some covenantal obligations originating independently of the bound agent.

> . . . Christian ethics makes ultimate appeal to a divine performance, making proto-typical use of something that is also said in the analysis of human performatives, namely, that it is not only one's own committing action that creates an obligation; one can also be put under obligation to someone by *their* conduct rather than one's own. . . . (1968a: 123).

And Ramsey proceeds in his medical ethics to operate to a considerable degree on the basis of this answer when he writes of the claims which women

(1968a: 127), men (1968a: 129; 1970B: 68) and children (1968a: 131; 1970B: 12) rightfully make upon us simply by being, or by being who they are—women, men and children—, or by being what they are—sick or dying (1968a: 131).

But at other points Ramsey softens and possibly even reverses this position on our being bound by obligations which we have no part in originating. Concerning the obligations of Christians, a softening comes when on the very next page after the above quotation concerning performatives, he writes: "In any case, we mean and should mean in Christian ethics to say that there are correlative performative understandings of moral acts, relations and situations that arise from our faith-commitment or acknowledgment of God's performatives and his mandates" (1968a: 124, see also 133). Now this is not to say that we will our obligations into being, but neither is it to say that we are obligated by the simple act of another. The agent's own being through his "faith-commitment or acknowledgment" has entered into the coming-into-being of this obligation in a significant way. And concerning men in general, although admittedly written from the point of view of his "moral and religious premises," Ramsey says, ". . . the *conscious acceptance* of covenant responsibilities is the inner meaning of even the 'natural' or systemic relations into which we are born and of the institutional relations or roles we enter by choice" (1970B: xii. Italics added). But most problematic in the light of Ramsey's above strict assertions concerning covenants and their contingent obligations and claims which are simply "there" is his statement that:

> While our bodily existence and the integrities of twinship or of familial society are the conditions of the possiblity of covenants of utmost faithfulness among men on earthly pilgrimage, these elements of dust from which we are created do not by nature bind us to such covenants. The latter are *free actions* as one goes with grace among the equally needy (1970B: 185. Italics added.).

Now this appears to be a virtual reversal. It may not be. It may be merely the invoking of a different sort of covenant—those freely entered into. But reversal or not, this is a telling confirmation of my thesis that Ramsey is exceedingly concerned about protecting the individual from society, for Ramsey's asserting the existence of covenants and claims independently of any human willing of them almost always occurs in those bio-medical contexts where such covenants and claims serve to assure the individual adequate care and to protect him from societal encroachments. On the other hand, the revision just cited occurs in a context where covenants might be appealed to by the society to legitimate inappropriate claims upon the individual on behalf of one with whom he is presumed to have covenanted, that is, to bring to bear upon him the "obligation," whether he is willing or not, to surrender his organs for transplantation. At that point Ramsey protects the individual (the donor-to-be) not by invoking independently existing covenants but by making the "covenants" invoked contingent on the individual's freely entering into them.

Now Ramsey, like the rest of us, cannot have it both ways—unless he means to suggest that there is more than one kind of covenant, some of which in some sense pre-exist the individuals who come under them, and others of which come into being only at the will of the covenanting ones. This would be a plausible suggestion and one which Ramsey possibly puts forward when he writes: "By nature, choice, or need we live with our fellowmen in roles or relations" (1970B: xii). Since roles and relations here arise in a discussion of covenants and canons of loyalty and seem in Ramsey's mind to be derivative from them, I take this to be a comment also about covenants. But are "nature, choice or need" meant to be alternative grounds for all the covenants we live in, or is each of the three suggested as the basis of some of our covenants? At least one previous statement, referring to "their elected and their nonelected covenants of life with life" (1967A: 123), seems to assume that there are various sorts of covenants we all live under. But then Ramsey needs to say this more clearly and then to get on with the job of indicating the character and the location of the various types in human experience. For there are fundamental questions concerning ethical method and content which can be clarified only after these questions are addressed. (For the present author's own struggling with some of these issues, see Camenisch, 1970.)

Concerning Ramsey's shift in emphasis from "love" to "covenant" terminology, it only remains for me to suggest some possible reasons for this shift. The first suggestion hinges on a point yet to be made concerning Ramsey's interest in affirming and/or establishing continuity of various sorts in the moral life and experience. If that concern is playing an increasingly significant role in Ramsey's thought (as I think it is), then the increasing use of covenant ideas such as canons of loyalty and claims of fidelity, in preference to love or *agape* ideas, is partly understandable on the basis of the larger and more explicit role they give to continuity within the moral life of the idividual agent, in the agent's dealings with various other individuals and within the overall structure of the society itself shaped by covenants. For example, Ramsey writes concerning marriage:

> The biblical covenant view of marriage, which lies behind our marriage law, affirms the will's competence to bind itself from one moment to another throughout all change, and therefore its competence to bind itself to another person and thus to exhibit a fuller freedom (1967A: 45).

This affinity between ideas and Ramsey's concern for continuity is all the more significant when one realizes that in his earlier writings Ramsey had fairly sharply dissociated love from some of the most common embodiments of continuity in the ethical life, rules and laws: "Christian ethics is emancipated from all preconceived rules and laws by Christian love for neighbor *permitting* everything to be done which the neighbor needs, absolutely everything, without a single exception" (1947c: 194; see also 1950A: 79-80).

Given his past treatment of love from this perspective, which (whatever he himself has done with it since) remains persuasive to many persons, it is not surprising that Ramsey has found a new set of expressions for the ultimate Christian norm more consonant with and conducive toward continuity and stability in the moral life of individuals and societies and in the moral bonds by which they are related to one another. This increasing use of the continuity-sustaining covenant terminology is of course more understandable also in the light of Ramsey's conviction, reflected both above in the characteristics of contemporary society which concern him and below in his statement about our time of "lapsed links," that the creation or defense of such continuity is perhaps the form of service currently most needed by all our neighbors.

A second possible reason for, or fortunate benefit of, the shift to covenant concepts is the fact that these ideas (as ethical ideas) seem to have more parallels in general human experience than does love *as an ethical concept.* In fact, as most Christian ethicists by now know, the first thing to be done by anyone setting out to use "love" as an ethical concept is to dissociate the idea as he uses it from the myriad uses it has in the culture at large. This seems not to be the case with "covenant," the meaning of which seems to be relatively stable across the religious/non-religious line. The increasing use of covenant terminology seems quite plausibly related to the fact that in his recent writings Ramsey has seemed increasingly content to extract and extend the moral wisdom which he finds already operative in the human community or among the conscientious professionals in a given problem area, and less concerned therefore to supplement, correct or "transform" it on the basis of Christian insights. For example he writes in "Shall We 'Reproduce'?": ". . . a negative moral verdict against in vitro fertilization need invoke no other standards of judgment than *the received principles of medical ethics.* I have appealed to no religious and to no other ethical criteria" (1972h: 1350; see also 1972i, 1970A, 1973j and 1973k). The emergence of a set of central concepts, and therefore of a logic by which they move and a method by which they are applied, all of which are shared by Christian and non-Christian makes the transition to this style of ethical reflection much easier and perhaps more easily justifiable.

One caveat should be entered here. Covenant might be understood as a *form* of relation compatible with various possible contents. If that is the understanding many non-Christians have of it, then the fact that the Judeo-Christian understanding of covenant has always been specifically a covenant of love, as we know love from God's dealings with us, should warn us away from making too much out of or presuming too much from the occurrence of covenant ideas outside the Christian community. We must, in other words, look carefully also at the content of such covenants. This is a caution which I at present have no reason to believe Ramsey has any more need of than do the rest of us, but it is worth stating for any who want to employ covenant ideas in the doing of Christian ethics.

III. Consequences

For many readers my suggestion above that Ramsey's ethics is extensively shaped by his concern for the neighbor, that he be served through Christian action, will seem to fly directly in the face of Ramsey's deontology and his critical stance toward the use of consequences in moral reflection. Consequences are often viewed as things which happen to persons, and deontological rules are often suspected of being largely impersonal regulations originating from sources remote from individuals and the sorts of problems they face. We can show that such assumptions are often operative by citing Charles Curran's interpretation of Ramsey's ethics, which gives rise to the following comments in his recent book on Ramsey: ". . . Ramsey too easily justifies war in the name of *agape*" (1973: 76); "In general, I think Ramsey does not give enough importance to the role of teleological considerations" (1973: 85); "I have criticized Ramsey's political ethics for not giving enough importance to the value of individual human life. . . ." (1973: 221). Admittedly these three statements occur in Curran's book at considerable distance from one another. Nevertheless, seen in the context of Curran's critical comments throughout the book, they seem to coalesce in Curran's mind to become the interrelated elements of a single trend in Ramsey's thinking—a trend which, by de-emphasizing consequences, moves further and further from concern for concrete individuals.

The first thing to be said on Ramsey's behalf is that he by no means eliminates consequences as irrelevant to ethical reflection and moral decision-making. Rather, he is simply concerned that they be restricted to their appropriate place in moral reasoning, where they are exceedingly important:

> In ensuring that man shall remain man when and after he does any of these projected procedures for the increase of knowledge and for his own improvement, consequences are an important consideration. In fact there is nothing more important in the whole of ethics than the consequences for good or ill of man's actions and abstentions—*except* right relations among men, justice, and fidelity one with another. The moral quality of our actions and abstentions are determined both by the consequences for all men and by keeping convenant man with man (1970A: 122).

This is to grant consequences, and hence the interests of the persons to whom they happen, considerable importance in ethical decisions, but it is also to locate them as coming after other, deontological considerations. This subordination is stated even more clearly and emphatically elsewhere, most often concerning the relation between the two principles of just conduct in war, the principle of proportion (a teleological or consequence-weighing guide) and the principle of discrimination (the deontological principle of noncombatant immunity):

> . . . an assessment of any proposed action should first be made in terms of discrimination, in order to determine the actions that are ever permissible. Then one has to choose, from among actions that are morally tolerable because they are not indiscriminate, those

actions that should be done because of an apt proportion between their good and evil consequences (1968A: 431; See also 1968A: 116 and 1961B: 4, 159).

This proper locating of consequences is as far as Ramsey's interest in restricting their influence goes. To exclude them totally would be immoral as Ramsey indicates when, speaking of "genetic imprudence" in a context which makes the calculating of consequences a large part of prudence, he asserts that "imprudence is gravely immoral" (1970A: 57). All Ramsey would have us remember is that we cannot invert that statement and say that prudence (in and of itself) is moral: "Morality may be prudent without being moral *because* it is prident" (1968A: 406, note 5).

Moreover, and more importantly, Ramsey rightly insists that to assume that a choice must be made between persons and rules is to misunderstand rules or to underestimate their variety. The Christian, says Ramsey, lives in a world populated by persons, not by rules. But Christian love in its experience with persons can discern "the human" and "the good for man" (1967A: 126ff.) and from these can formulate rules: "General-rule agapism . . . in Christian ethics . . . begins with persons and then devolves or discerns the rules" (1967A: 131). Ramsey may, of course, be wrong about this capacity of love to discern rules on the basis of its knowledge of persons and their good; and/or he may be wrong concerning the specific rules love devolves or discerns. But both of those would be mistakes rather different from and less serious than the mistake of putting rules before persons. For these rules, if love discerns them, are put forward not to displace persons but precisely on persons' behalf: "[T]he question at issue is whether there are principles that embody love for persons. . . ." (1967A: 24).

Such rules can serve persons by insistently putting forward the constancies of their essential humanity and their true good. These person-centered rules should therefore have priority over immediate consequences, the occurrence and moral significance of which are less constant and which, therefore, constitute less reliable moral guides. Furthermore, according to Ramsey, persons are quite likely to suffer more rather than less if the calculation of immediate and direct consequences is given the primary role in moral reflection and decision-making: "The likelihood of making a mistake by applying *agape* directly on one's own in particular cases of a given sort is greater than the likelihood of making a mistake by following the rule" (1967A: 126). Thus an act which might in its direct and immediate effects be loving, might nevertheless "because of its side-effects, its *indirect* results, tend to break down the social practice of a rule of behavior which 'generally' embodies love" (1967A: 126).

IV. The Morality of Means

The major source of Ramsey's opposition to the awarding of first place in ethical reflection to consequences is found, however, in his observation that a goal-dominated ethic often loses either its capacity or its will to subject to careful moral scrutiny the means employed to attain that goal. An ethic totally, or even primarily, committed to certain ends often becomes morally careless about the means employed and inquires only about their efficiency in producing that end. Such prudent, that is, goal-seeking, consequence-calculating ethics are "well calculated to reduce every present reality—people and principles no less than facts—altogether to what they may do to bring in the future" (1961g: 48).

This concern about the "menializing" of too much of life and of persons themselves, and therefore the concern to nurture a morality of means to prevent this, is a theme of some long standing in Ramsey (See 1961A: 86, note 28); but it appears to be invoked with ever increasing frequency in light of a number of goals which Ramsey fears many men currently see as absolutely imperative, and which therefore distract them from moral criticism of the means by which those goals are to be attained. Some goals Ramsey has challenged are: avoidance of nuclear holocaust in the "politics of fear" (1961B: 192ff.); procreation of a child at any cost/risk (1970A: 59); infinite extension of bio-medical knowledge and techniques; and the survival of the race in the face of gene-pool deterioration (1970A: 29-30). When any of these goals become absolutely imperative, persons will suffer either because morally uncriticized means to these goals will be employed or because persons themselves will be reduced to means. In both cases persons will suffer not because consequences or goals have been ignored but rather because consequences and goals *only* have been attended to. (See for example, 1970A: 61.)

Against such encroachments upon persons and the essential forms of their lived-out humanity in the name of absolutely imperative ends, Ramsey wants most emphatically to assert the irreducibility of persons to means only. In terms of the issues of just war and the relations of persons to political goals, for instance, the point is stated this way: "Not nations but first persons are elevated to citizenship in another city and to a destiny kept between themselves and God which prohibits any man from reducing them wholly to the status of means useful in attaining some historical goal in the life of the kingdoms of this world" (1968A: 163).

This same concern shapes much of Ramsey's reflection on contemporary bio-medical issues. For example, in his discussions of medical treatment of and experimentation on children, Ramsey struggles to keep ever present in the minds of all practitioners and parents the fact that "fidelity to a human child also includes never treating him as a means only, but also as an end" (1970B: 35). And it is this same concern in relation to adult patients and subjects that would seem to give the requirements of a reasonably free and adequately informed consent its significance in Ramsey's mind, for the consenting patient/subject has, in the recognition of his right and capacity to give or withhold consent, been treated as an end, and to the extent that he does now become a means, he has himself consented to that (1970B: 2-6 and throughout).

According to Ramsey, Christians are armed to oppose any such reduction of persons to means only, not only by their specifically moral insights and commitments concerning the nature of persons as ends, but by their eschatological view of life in this world which should prevent any worldly end from appearing to be absolutely imperative: "Eschatology has at least this significance for Christian ethics in all ages: that reliance on producing *teloi* or on doing good consequences, or on goal-seeking, has been decisively set aside" (1967A: 108). For example, living in the light of the Christian eschaton gives one more room for an ethics of means than facing the "eschaton" a genetic cul-de-sac alone would permit (1970A: 29-31).

Richard McCormick has made one partly valid response to Ramsey's critical stance toward the role of consequences in moral reflection by suggesting that Ramsey's opposition to consequences turns out to be a family fight among different sorts of consequentialists. This suggestion is based on the fact that Ramsey has on occasion invoked consequences in order to reject them (McCormick, 1972:538, 542). The consequences Ramsey wants to limit are in fact only those of a certain sort. The picture of these consequences which I extract from Ramsey's various writings includes three major characteristics. First, they tend to be the *exclusive* claims upon us subordinating, if not eliminating, other considerations such as persons, justice, etc. Second, these consequences tend to become embodied in or epitomized by some goal so distant and so compelling that it removes moral value from presently existing persons and moral pressure and criticism from the intervening distance and so threatens to leave the means of traversing that distance subject only to the criterion of efficiency.[3] Third, the consequences Ramsey limits are seen by him as hard "empirical" realities, either events, states of affairs or "goods" which follow from but are not themselves a part of the act performed.

Ramsey sometimes opposes the use made of such "hard" consequences in ethical reasoning on the basis of a better grasp of that very kind of consequence. This is his approach when he sees the consequentialist as having engaged in too foreshortened a calculation of consequences. But Ramsey's basic move here is to appeal to a different *kind* of consequences, consequences which contrast sharply with those characterized above. His preferred consequences would be: valuable precisely because of their relation to persons, their humanity and their "good"; important in the present as well as the future and so stimulating sensitivity to the (im-)morality of present means;[4] often not empirical nor separable from the act itself but rather a dimension of the act—for example, the violation of the child's claims upon us is the same thing as experimenting non-beneficially upon him, it does not "follow from" it. It is this last characteristic of Ramsey's "consequences" that permits him to see the "thin edge of the wedge" argument as unimportant in rejecting non-beneficial experimentation on children: "The argument is rather that to begin to experiment on children in ways that are not related to *them* as subjects is already a sanitized form of barbarism; it already removes them from view and pays no attention to the faithfulness-claims which a child, simply by being a sick or dying child, places upon us and upon medical care" (1968a: 131). The "consequences" Ramsey has in mind here, then, are such things as the observation/violation of: canons of loyalty, right relations among persons, covenants, essential forms of humanity such as parenthood, etc.

It should be clear that we are rapidly approaching or have already passed the point at which it becomes unhelpful and uninformative, if not incorrect, to call these elements "consequences," since that term, as Ramsey rightly sees, has generally pointed toward a rather different sort of consideration. Whatever more might be said on this point, it should be clear that Ramsey is a person-alist, that his critical stance toward consequences in moral reasoning represents not a lessening of his concern for persons and their good but is in fact a manifestation of that very concern. The rejection of non-beneficial experimentation on a child is based on Ramsey's concern that that person not be "menialized," that his claims on us not be violated. His concern for sexuality's "present, immediate meaning in itself" (1967A:177) is a concern that that relation and the persons thereby related to one another not be seen only as means to some future good or to someone else's well-being and thus that it and they not be denied present human significance. His concern that parenthood as a "basic form of humanity" not be manipulated and altered beyond recognition in and by the bio-genetic revolution is a concern for what will be lost to persons when and if this happens: "Human parenthood is, in the language of Karl Barth, a basic form of humanity. To violate this is already dehumanizing, even if spiritualistic or personalistic or mentalistic categories are invoked to justify it" (1970A:131, see also 109, 123, 130). These may well not be "goods" or consequences which an empirically oriented consequentialist would recognize as such. But there can be little doubt that they express a deep and abiding concern for persons and not for rules-instead-of-persons.

V. Continuity in the Moral Life

Exceptionless rules in and of themselves should not be seen as a major focus in Ramsey's thought; they are more helpfully and more accurately viewed as one possible and rather limited manifestation or embodiment of a larger concern. That larger concern I will here call simply continuity in the moral life. I shall attempt to show in a later critical section that Ramsey has not significantly furthered this larger concern in his defense of exceptionless rules. But first it is necessary to identify the cause of Ramsey's concern for continuity.

In his essay on "Responsible Parenthood" Ramsey wrote:

> This is an era of "lapsed links." Essential moral bonds have eroded, not only in the actuality of modern life but from many of our theological conceptions. The continuity of one moment or action with another moment or action in the integrity of an individual's life, the bond of life with life in the covenant of marriage, a vital inner relation between the life of the soul or mind and one's bodily life, the union between procreation and conjugal love in the purposes and meaning of marriage and in human sexuality, the congeneric connection between conscious life and nascent life, a sense of heritage or "piety" between the generations of men—all these ingredients of the fabric of human existence have weakened where they are not altogether lacking (1967h:343).

This rather varied set of trends is here brought together in part because of the source or sources they share. Two such common sources that Ramsey would cite are the "blinkers of momentalism" (1967A:112) and the "atomistic individualism of secular thought." This latter he sees as the source of act-agapism in contemporary Christian ethics and as the "acid that eats away at moral relations, and at the very idea that there are moral bonds between man and man, or between one moment and another" (1967A:44).

In Ramsey's view, these various trends tend not only to isolate each moral agent from all others and from morally significant larger entities such as society, but even to isolate each of his moral decisions[1] acts from all his other moral doings. Thus they threaten the individual with significant harm both by severing him from the sustaining and protecting web of moral relations, obligations, duties and rights which have traditionally surrounded the lives of civilized persons and by severing him from his own moral past and future. They therefore leave him marooned and directionless in the present moment of decision.

Ramsey opposes these various trends for a variety of reasons which range from act-agapism's seeming incompatibility with scripture (1967A:118, 158), to an understanding of the logic of moral language and reasoning which appears to render some of the more "momentalist" positions untenable (1968a:67; 1967A:165). But high among Ramsey's movitations here is his concern for protecting the individual, and for giving the individual the tools and resources to protect himself, against the various harms he so evidently could suffer from such trends. If this is correct, then Ramsey's concern about these trends and his defense of solutions to them are best understood if they are viewed in the light of Ramsey's task.

Just as Ramsey realizes that he is here addressing a variety of related trends in modern social and ethical thought which have a variety of impacts on society, so he has seen that there is an equally varied group of antidotes for them. In *Deeds and Rules* he refers to several of these: "The question is simply whether there *are* any general rules or principles or virtues or styles of life that embody love, and if so what these may be" (1967A:112). And in "The Case of the Curious Exception" where Ramsey seeks to make his terminology more precise than it had been in the past, he notes that:

> Heretofore, when treating the methods and the options for adducing or elaborating the full contents of a normative ethics upon the basis of the ultimate norms in Christian ethics . . . I have used the word "rule" as shorthand for "principles," "orders," "ordinances," "ideal," "direction," "directives," "guidance," the "structures" of *agape* or of *koinonia* life, the "style" of the Christian life, the "anatomy" or "pattern" of Christian responsibility—as well as for "rules" strictly so-called (1968a:73).

It is perhaps understandable that "rule" has been used to refer to this considerable variety of elements since they are all means by which Ramsey, in opposition to the anti-rule theory of situation ethics, can, as he puts it, draw attention to the similarities among situations, persons, marriages, etc. (1970b:423). Nevertheless, one must welcome a "tightening up" of Ramsey's terminology whereby the reference of such terms as "rules" will be focused more sharply. Unfortunately one must ask whether, in narrowing the reference of the term "rule" to rules properly so-called, Ramsey has not permitted these other entities to recede to the background so that now rules properly so-called must carry the entire load of continuity once shared by these other elements. Some such misstep as this seems the only explanation for the emphasis Ramsey now puts on the idea of unexceptionable rules and principles.

Generally valid rules are certainly one way of providing the continuity—stability, security, reliability, constancy, consistency—which Ramsey would like to see restored to modern moral life. But these other means listed by Ramsey are also valuable tools in any such enterprise and in some cases they do not raise the difficult methodological and normative problems which attach to the idea of exceptionless rules. However, the most telling response to Ramsey's recent focus on general rules in order to restore continuity to the moral life is that it does not further the cause nearly so much as Ramsey's emphasis would seem to indicate. This judgment can be supported by a variety of points.

Ramsey's certainty about the exceptionless character of the moral wisdom or direction to be found on any of the levels of moral discourse seems to decrease as he moves from ultimate norms through the intermediate stages of principles and rules to the level of prudence, or particular decision/action. At the highest level, an exceptionable ultimate norm would be a strange creature indeed since any thing which is exceptionable may be presumed to be so in the light of some higher norm. At the other end of the spectrum, the realm of prudence, we shall see that the entire question is disqualified for quite different reasons. Thus the question of exceptionless moral wisdom is most crucial on the levels of principles and rules. Of these two, it is the level of principles which Ramsey has for a longer time and with greater conviction seen as offering exceptionless guidance. Although I find Ramsey's distinction between rules and principles not to be maintained with sufficient clarity and rigor, it does seem reasonably clear that he is less insistent on there being exceptionless rules. And certainly his commitment to such is of more recent origin, for he wrote in 1968: "I judge I have [hitherto] not altogether committed myself to the conclusion that there are *rules* to which there are no exceptions" (1968a:74). The crucial observation to be made here, given Ramsey's lesser conviction about exceptionless rules, is that any uncertainty on this issue at the level of rules is virtually impossible to prevent from carrying over to principles since Ramsey repeatedly asserts that the distinction between rules and principles is a relative one (1968a:74, 75, 76, 94).

But the uncertainty attaching to the exceptionlessness of principles also arises from the fact that future possible counter instances might show them not to be generally valid: "If it could be shown that to act in accord with one of these love-formed principles of conduct is in a particular situation not what love itself directly requires, then that was not a general principle of conduct but a summary rule only" (1968a:112; cf. 132). This is a rather surprising statement for a man who has so many times argued against holding all principles open to future possible consequence-based exceptions. But Ramsey seems here finally to have granted the point to those who, according to him, would prejudice the whole discussion of rule-agapism from the beginning by defining it "in such fashion that this means that a Christian should obey a rule 'even though the action called for is seen not to be what love itself would directly require' " (1968a:111).

In making the occurrence of such a case a way of distinguishing between general principles or rules and summary rules, Ramsey has greatly weakened general rules and their reliability in guiding conduct by making them general only on condition of the non-occurrence of such cases in the future. To the extent that Ramsey sticks to this position (and perhaps he must to avoid an unloving application of a love-embodying rule), his general rules do not permit us to stop testing each decision by what love directly requires here and now anymore than do others' summary rules. Furthermore, he writes:

> There are also always situations in which we are to tell what we should do by getting clear about the facts of that situation and then asking what is the loving or the most loving thing to do in it. The latter may even be at work in every case of the creative casuistry of in-principled love going into action (1967A:5).

Moreover, even if and where exceptionless guides are established, they are apparently only negative ones: "The case of the curious exception concerns only the matter of *prohibitiva*." And this, Ramsey readily admits "is only a small part of morality" (1968a:135). And even here the rigor of the rules is further lessened when Ramsey concedes that while the condemnation in such *prohibitiva* is clear, equal clarity does not attach to the matter of which acts they refer to. Love must continue to struggle to define those "prohibited breaches of promise which can never express love" (1967A:30), or to identify the *prohibited* suicide (1961B:185. Evans, 1971 [and Chapter II of this volume] on Ramsey's "liberal M" approach to exceptionless rules is helpful here.)

Finally, Ramsey grants a large role in Christian ethics to summary rules (for example, 1967A:162), to exceptionable moral principles (1968a:68), and to act agapism, or at least to what looks very much like it (1967A:5; see also 1967A:121, 107 and 143). But when it comes to general or unexceptionable principles and rules, Ramsey's conclusions are almost always stated in terms of the *possibility* of exceptionless guidance: "I conclude, therefore, that there is no rational moral argument that can exclude the possibility that there are exceptionless moral rules, in some moral matters" (1968a:112); "it cannot be shown that Christians or just men should never say Never" (1968a:134); "doing everything that love requires . . . may include more than single acts" (1967A:23, note 6). Thus the element which Ramsey most insistently champions in order to provide the continuity-stability mentioned above is precisely the one whose status as a viable alternative Ramsey himself seems to admit is most subject to question. I would hope, therefore, that Ramsey's legitimate concern about such continuity will lead him to further efforts to extract and extend the forms of continuity which can be contributed by those other elements in moral reasoning, summary rule agapism and even act agapism, which are assured a place in ethical theory.

One must ask also how much continuity in terms of specific obligations incumbent upon individuals has been gained—even where exceptionless rules and principles have been offered with considerable confidence—when, as we shall see below, all such guidance draws up short at that final and crucial stage of decision/action, the realm of prudence: "However definitely a rule discriminates right from wrong, it cannot tell us '*This* is right or wrong'" (1968a:94).

Thus, if I can summarize without caricaturing, all of Ramsey's impressive argumentation on behalf of exceptionless principles and rules has resulted in giving us the *possibility* of *negative* rules and principles which require a *continuing interpretation* to discern what they forbid, are to be held to as exceptionless only in the *absence* of love-violating counter-instances, and are prohibited by the inviolable rights of prudence from making pronouncements in individual cases. *That* is not much in the way of positive rule making as a means to continuity. And if, as I suggested, continuity was what Ramsey was primarily after in his pursuit of exceptionless rules, one must ask at this point if the game has been worth the candle.

But whatever conclusion we reach on Ramsey's success in his defense of exceptionless principles/rules, or the wisdom of his relying so heavily for continuity on exceptionless principles/rules, it is clear that his involvement with this whole set of issues is largely accounted for once again by his concern for the individual and his conviction that the pursuit of continuity or stability through exceptionless rules is one important way of meeting that concern. (See, for example, 1968a:133.)

VI. Prudence

Although Ramsey occasionally uses "prudence" to refer to the calculation of consequences, his dominant usage of the term, and ours in the following comments, is to mean by it those various capacities and functions of and demands upon the moral agent which come into play as he struggles to travel the distance between the ultimate norms, principles and rules he draws upon and the particular decision/action he alone can and must arrive at in a given instance.

Ramsey's most frequent and emphatic caveats about encroachments upon the prerogatives of the individual at this point in his moral life are issued on behalf of professional personnel such as politicians, military men, medical doctors and researchers, all of whom work in fields of specialized knowledge and/or responsibility concerning the subject matter of whose decision-making the moralist, the theologian or the church itself has, as such, no competence. Here Ramsey as a church ethicist realizes that he labors under the same limitations which he asked the churches to observe in their moral deliberations and pronouncements in his critique of the 1966 Geneva Conference on Church and Society:

> . . . a Christian ethicist is only a church ethicist; his "competence" ideally and that of the church ideally is the same; neither is that of statecraft or particular political judgments. . . . I deny myself, professionally as a Christian ethicist, everything that I ask churches and churchmen, speaking as such, to deny themselves in the claims they assert" (undated "Apologia. . .": 35-36).

Ramsey seems to have several supporting reasons to offer for these limitations on ethical reflection and moral guidance vis-a-vis the agent. First there is the issue of the relevant facts of the case which may be accessible only to the specialist because of his "location" in relation to the problem and only comprehensible to him because of his special training which enables him to assess and interpret them (for example, 1968A:336, 484; undated "Apologia.. .":33). Second, there is the fact that the decision should be made by the party or parties who have been given and who will have to bear responsibility for it, a role which moralist or church bears only when it is the agent (1961B:162).

And, third, there is the nature of moral judgment and experience itself which seems to preclude ethical theorists as such from pre-empting the agent's prudential responsibilities by making particular pronouncements. This third factor refers first of all to the fact that ethics deals with *sorts* of acts (undated "Apologia. . .":33), and that rules therefore, as already noted above, "cannot tell us '*This* is right or wrong'" (1968a:94). Or, as Ramsey elsewhere says, the ethicist "has no special competence in subsuming cases" (undated "Apologia. . .":40). Second, the moral life is such that "there may be on the outskirts of the moral life, in regard to every sphere or sort of behavior, situations that cannot be penetrated by moral reasoning, situations where ambiguity reigns, where more or less arbitrary decison alone can limit wrong doing. "(1973d:27). And finally, with specific reference to Christian ethics, Ramsey says:

> It is high time for it to be acknowledged on all sides that not every decision is a moral decison, and not every moral decision is a Christian decision. The bearing of God's will and governance in relation to every aspect of human life cannot possibly be construed in such fashion that supposes that there is a Christian shape or style to every decision. Concerning a great many choices it has to be said that only a deliberately or inflexibly imprudent decision would be wrong, or an uncharitable exercise of prudence. The principle of prudence (among a Christian's teachings) definitely refers the matter in question to the magistrate or to the political process for decision; and Christians as such can say no more than that this is the case (1967A:135-136).

Now some of the above mentioned reasons for hedging prudence around to protect its area of operation from intrusion have special reference to, or perhaps better, have special meaning with reference to, specialists. One such example would be the element of access to and understanding of the facts involved in the decision. But it is also true that all of these elements in some significant sense apply to every moral decision/act. In other words, Ramsey's case for respecting the integrity and role of the specialists' prudential judgments is at the same time a case for respecting the integrity and role of every moral agent's prudential judgment. No one can quite duplicate his access to and understanding of the facts as they now affect him. No one else can arrogate to himself the responsibility he bears for the values at stake and the decisions made. Hence it would seem to be both a moral and a logical mistake (1968a:95ff.) to think that ethical reflection can replace any agent's own prudential judgments and decisions, that it can close the gap logically between rule and decision/act. Ramsey is not saying, of course, that ethics must not intrude on prudence because the prudential judgment is not a moral judgment and/or does not involve moral values. Here Charles Curran (1973:51-52) misconstrues Ramsey's position.

One could, of course, raise the question of whether Ramsey himself has always observed these barriers which should separate the ethicist *qua* ethicist from particular judgments. For example, his complete rejection of *in vitro* fertilization (1972h:1346) and of self-immolation (1968A:471-472), while still being about *sorts* of actions and hence in that sense rules, refer to acts which seem to be so easily and certainly identifiable (unlike, for example, marital infidelity), that the relevant rule appears indistinguishable from a judgment against all particular acts falling under it. More troublesome yet is the overstepping of these limits in Ramsey's judgments about the Viet Nam war: his 1967 statement that "In any correct use of moral language, this has been a limited war whose conduct has been held within the test of discrimination . . ."

(1967a:43); his statement at the same time that the March 10, 1967 bombing of the Thainguygan iron and steel complex was not discriminate because it constituted an attack on the society and the future of North Viet Nam; and his assertion that our involvement in Viet Nam was a case of "counter-intervention" (1968A:34).

But whatever the number and nature of the violations we might find of Ramsey's own restrictions on ethical discourse and on the ethicist's competence, the validity of his position on those restrictions is not to be tested by his own observance of them. In fact, he has recently stated explicitly that if such violations have occurred on his part, it is the violations and not the restrictions which he rejects:

> . . . if I were chiefly concerned to approve or disapprove a particular war, or have given the appearance of doing so, that was a serious departure from my task as an ethicist whose chief concern and sole competence is the moral discourse governing such decisions (undated "Apologia . . .":35).

Here again, then, in his discussion of the issue of prudence, a surety and support is offered to any embattled individuals who feel that their integrity, their responsibility and their consciences as moral agents are being usurped by a society, an ethos, a church, or an ethicist which would seek to eliminate the need for their own prudential judgments and decision making in their moral life:

> What is at stake in keeping statements of ethico-political principle separate and distinct from their specific application is the integrity of the office of political prudence, and the right of persons in their official capacities of magistrate or citizen not to have their consciences faulted, their freedom in the slightest degree overborne, if they disagree . . . . [and] not to have their final weighty responsibility in the exercise of political prudence in the slightest degree eased when it happens that they agree with one of these particular judgments . . . . (1967B:108-9).

If there is casuistry in Ramsey, or in Christian ethics as Ramsey understands it, then it is not the casuistry which with equal certainty traverses all stages between ultimate norms and concrete decision/action. Rather, the reflective task of ethics extends from ultimate norms, through two sorts of principles and possibly several sorts of rules, to its halting place at the boundary of the realm of prudence, that inviolate place where occurs the mystery of the subsumption of cases. This is the point at which the ethicist's task *qua* ethicist ceases and the matter is left in the hands of the agent who presumably has the necessary access to and understanding of the facts involved and who bears the responsibility for the decisions made and the actions taken.

VII. Conclusion

Paul Ramsey's writings constitute not only a large but a very rich and very complex authorship. There are, no doubt, several threads or themes which could be used as illuminating guides through it. What I have done here is to take one such theme which is supported by and helps to illuminate significant elements in Ramsey's thought. The theme chosen is a simple one: Ramsey's conviction that concern for the neighbor must, in our time, focus on aiding the neighbor in defending himself against those various forms of societal encroachment and violation which tend to dehumanize, menialize and isolate him. This theme is not only unifying thread throughout Ramsey's work, but at particular points—the move from "love" to "covenant," the treatment of consequences, the morality of means, the concerns for continuity and prudence in the moral life—it is so crucial to Ramsey's task that the interpreter who fails to give it a central role will run the risk of misconstruing Ramsey's thought.

NOTES

[1] Here and throughout I will draw on both Ramsey's distinctively methodological works (especially 1967A and 1968a) which concentrate in his more recent writings, and his normatively ethical ones, which span his career. The most significant reason for not confining myself to Ramsey's later methodological writings is the fact that those writings have been far too much shaped by, and by that I mean in part narrowed down to, issues arising from the situation ethics or the principles *vs.* context debate. I say "*too* much shaped by" because the debate centering on this set of issues has, it seems to me, gotten in the way of the central task of Christian ethical reflection, that of offering Christianly-informed moral guidance to the members of the Christian community. That task requires engagement with a much broader spectrum of issues, which is not to deny that it also required some engagement with "situation ethics" issues once they had been raised and spread abroad. But given the extent to which contemporary American religious ethics has suffered from this same narrowing down, I would not want to contribute to continuing this focus by locating Ramsey's importance for questions of method only in relation to this set of issues.

[2] A good example of such a surrender (in Ramsey's view) which has corrupted not only individuals, but one branch of the church is the United Methodist Church's acceptance of the "tissue" theory of fetal life whereby that church now addresses "the world—the culture generally—with a conclusion it has already reached" (1970e:186).

[3] This characteristic of the consequences that he opposes contrasts sharply with the love on behalf of which he opposes them: ". . . *agape* does not first and always face toward the future alone. Rather does *agape* face in the present also toward a man's existing neighbors and companions in God, seeking to determine what love permits and requires to be now done or not done toward them" (1961B:4).

[4] If we view this concern of Ramsey's in conjunction with his concern about the short-sightedness of some consequentialists as seen in his response to summary-rule ethicists, it would seem that Ramsey is working both sides of the street. That is, when consequentialists are near-sighted, Ramsey criticizes them for losing sight of the long term implications of their actions. And when they look too far into the future he chides them for ignoring the persons and the moral issues, especially the morality of means, close at hand. Of course either tendency in an extreme form is a serious fault and should be corrected. Ramsey should recognize that this tension is inherent in the very structure of human ethical reflection and action and so must not be charged against the consequentialist as such.

REFERENCES

Camenisch, Paul F.

1970 "Good Reasons for Judgments of Moral Obligation and their Use in the Theological Ethics of Emil Brunner." Unpublished doctoral dissertation, Princeton University.

Curran, Charles E.

1973 *Politics, Medicine, and Christian Ethics: A Dialogue with Paul Ramsey.* Philadelphia: Fortress Press.

Deats, Paul

1968 Untitled interview. Pp. 17-35 in James Finn (ed.), *Protest: Pacifism and Politics.* New York: Random House.

Douglass, James W.

1968 *The Non-Violent Cross.* New York: The Macmillan Company.

Evans, Donald

1971 "Paul Ramsey on exceptionless moral rules." *American Journal of Jurisprudence* 16:184-214. Also this volume, Chapter II.

McCormick, Richard A., S.J.

1972 "Genetic medicine: notes on the moral literature." *Theological Studies* 33 (September): 531-552.

Ramsey, Paul

Undated "Apologia Pro Vita Sua—one decade, that is." Pp. 33-48 of an unpublished typescript.

For other references, see the bibliography of Ramsey's works in this volume. Capital letters (e.g. 1950A) denote books and occasional papers; lower case letters (e.g. 1968a) denote articles.

Part Two

WAR AND POLITICAL ETHICS

CHAPTER V

Morality and Force In Statecraft: Paul Ramsey And the Just War Tradition

JAMES TURNER JOHNSON

The purpose of this essay is to consider the relation of Paul Ramsey's thought on war to classic just war doctrine. I will argue that his position is importantly different from the classic doctrine both in the sources on which it relies and in the main use to which it is put. If some—perhaps at times Ramsey himself—have thought of his just war theory as a continuation of the just war tradition of thought, then I want to try to specify how this both is and is not the case. In pursuit of these aims it will be necessary first to examine the definition and requirements of classic just war doctrine, then to explore certain aspects of Ramsey's thought in connection with related aspects of the classic doctrine, and finally to define the different senses in which both Ramsey's and the classic doctrine attempt to provide a bridge from the moral to the political (though the very large question of what constitutes a valid politico-moral doctrine must be left unanswered here).

The key to all that will be argued in what follows is found in two words: *charity* and *strategy*. *Charity* is above all Ramsey's norm for developing a just war doctrine. For him the thought on war of both Augustine and Thomas Aquinas expresses this norm, and that is why they are of interest to him. So far as the just war tradition as a whole is Christian, Ramsey regards it to be an expression of charity. His use of the tradition is such as to focus upon and bring to prominence the presence of charity in it, because this is necessary to relate the tradition to his own thinking, in which charity occupies the place of primacy. But it is important to note that just war doctrine in its classic form is not solely a product of *Christian* moral thought but derives also from two distinct *secular* traditions: the chivalric code and the legal idea of *jus gentium*.

In the second place, Ramsey's writings on war have been heavily weighted by consideration of questions of moral military *strategy*. Preoccupation with strategy pervades *War and the Christian Conscience*, the book in which Ramsey first developed his position, and though he later drew out the implications of this position for questions of tactics, strategy still has an edge in *The Just War*. Classic just war doctrine, however, placed its emphasis elsewhere. So far as the classic doctrine was Christian, it was far more developed on the question of the rightness of going to war (*jus ad bellum*) than on that of what it is right to do in war (*jus in bello*). Further, the rudiments of a *jus in bello* which the Church did develop (and which became part of the classic just war doctrine) had nothing whatsoever to do with strategic questions. The same is true of the secular contribution, which (though having a well-developed *jus in bello*) concentrated entirely upon tactical matters. Ramsey, in sharp contrast to the Christian contribution to classic just war doctrine, has hardly touched the *jus ad bellum*. His well-known twin criteria of proportion and discrimination, which are the central features of his thought on war, belong to the *jus in bello*. Ramsey assumes, for the purposes of his analysis, the *rightness* of going to war so as to work out the best (in various senses) *way* of waging war. This changed emphasis is determined neither by the norm of charity nor by his role as a Christian ethicist, I suggest, but rather by his concern with questions of strategy.

On this matter of Ramsey's preoccupation with strategic questions there are a great many problems which cannot be addressed here. Why, for example, does Ramsey direct his attention in this direction, in contradistinction to those who have gone before him in the tradition? I think (without here being able to prove) that the answer lies clearly in the advent of thermonuclear weaponry, which raised strategic questions far above tactical ones in the minds of military planners. But there may be a more general reason also. The whole history of just war thought in the modern period has seen a gradual erosion of the *jus ad bellum* taking place simultaneously with increased attention to developing the *jus in bello* (the reasons for this development are beyond the scope of the present essay, but see Johnson, 1973a: 219-224; 1973b; 1975: Chapters III, IV). Ramsey's concern with the *jus in bello* appears as a recent stage in this long-term trend.

Ramsey's just war doctrine needs to be reconsidered both in its relation to the classic doctrine and in its contemporaneity, as well as in terms of its contribution to the historical development of thought on justice in war generally. Placing him correctly with regard both to classic just war doctrine and our contemporary world is necessary to understanding whatever is unique and creative in his thought on war. It will also suggest the place Ramsey's position occupies in the continuing development of thought on the limitation of war. We need first to consider the nature of the classic doctrine.

I.
Classic Just War Doctrine, Its Development and Its Purpose

Among those who have written on just war doctrine during the past two decades there is general agreement as to the contents of that doctrine in its classic form. It has two main components, usually identified by the Latin terms *jus ad bellum* and *jus in bello*, which cover the right to make war and what it is right to do in war, respectively. The *jus ad bellum* includes four main requirements: a just war must be fought on proper authority, for a just cause, with right intent, and for the end of peace. The requirements of the *jus in bello* are two: provision for noncombatant immunity and weapons restrictions (these correspond broadly to Ramsey's two *jus in bello* principles, discrimination and proportionality, though there is some overlapping of categories).

Though it is essentially correct, historically speaking, to conceive the classic just war doctrine in this way, it is *not* correct to find just war doctrine in this relatively well-specified and complete form in the theologies of Augustine or Thomas Aquinas. These two theologians occupy singular places in the development of just war theory (with a special debt being owed by the tradition to Augustine), but historically just war doctrine in its classic form emerged only at the end of the Middle Ages and into the beginning of the modern era. A central figure in the final stages of this development was the sixteenth-century Spanish Dominican Francis de Vitoria, who is claimed as one of their own both by churchmen (as a neo-scholastic theologian) and by international lawyers (because he provided the groundwork on which Grotius, Gentili and others built). Around the year 1540 Vitoria prepared two works treating the subject of war: *On the Indians (De Indis)* and *On the Law of War (De Jure Belli)*. Here a just war doctrine with all the elements outlined above can clearly be identified; Vitoria's work on war represents the first clear and complete statement of what has come to be conceived as the classic requirements of the doctrine of just war. Vitoria was consciously attempting to spell out the implications, for the conditions of his own time, of scholastic thought on war; he thus provides a direct link with the theory of war of the high Middle Ages. But unconsciously he prepared the groundwork for what was to become in succeeding centuries the secular science of international law, and thus he represents also the future development of just war thought outside and away from the walls of the Church's moral system.

A convenient benchmark for locating classic just war doctrine historically, then, is provided by Vitoria's two works on war from the middle of the sixteenth century. Actually (see Johnson, 1975: Chapter I), the elements of classic doctrine were already present by the close of the fifteenth century, but it is only in Vitoria (and others from the "Spanish school" who wrote at about the same time or later, such as Molina and Suárez) that these elements are assembled consciously into a complete doctrine. But whether we date classic just war doctrine to the 1490's, to 1540 (Vitoria) or to the 1580's and later (Suárez), my point is the same: the Catholic tendency to regard Aquinas as *the* definitive just war theorist (exemplified in Albert Vanderpol's *La Doctrine scholastique du droit de guerre*, 1919) and the parallel Protestant tendency to look to Augustine for definitive precedent on just war matters (as in Roland Bainton's *Christian Attitudes toward War and Peace*, 1960) are misleading if not simply wrong. There was no just war doctrine, in the classic form as outlined above, before the end of the Middle Ages.[1]

Thus when Ramsey in *War and the Christian Conscience* explicitly derives his theory through consideration of both Augustine and Thomas Aquinas, he appears to be doubly in error. That this is not in fact the case follows from the nature of his use of these seminal figures. Unlike, for example, Vitoria, who was consciously trying to carry forward the scholastic tradition into his own age, Ramsey uses Augustine and Aquinas because of the insights on the requirements of charity which he perceives in them. They are not interesting to him because they state the essence of a historical tradition that must be revered and maintained; it is rather as if they were contemporaries with him in thinking out the implications of charity for Christians confronted with war. Ramsey uses not the *tradition* but the *theology underlying the tradition* as his norm; he is a systematic thinker rather than historical or traditionalist. I shall return to this point below.

To address another common misconception, if it is incorrect to look to theorists living before the end of the Middle Ages for just war doctrine in its classic form, it is equally wrong to conceive the classic doctrine as narrowly *Christian*. I do not here mean to point to the antecedents of Augustine's thought on war in the teachings of the OT or in Roman theory and practice; it is not necessary to go that far back into the past. Rather I mean to point to the multiple forces which together produced classic just war doctrine in the late Middle Ages: scholastic theology and canon law, to be sure, but also the waning chivalric code and the secular study of law. It is impossible here to do more than paint the picture of this multiple parentage with a broad brush, though I have developed the evidence in detail elsewhere (Johnson, 1975: Chapter I).

Augustine's influence on the developing just war tradition needs to be carefully stated, as it was not nearly so pervasive as seems generally to be thought today. His systematic thought on war, contained almost entirely in *The City of God, Against Faustus*, and *Questions on Joshua* (for a complete list see Curran, 1973: 72, n. 52), was all but forgotten for several centuries after his death. When it began to come to the surface as a focus of the Church's position on Christian participation in war, what emerged was not the whole of Augustine's teaching but only a few easily-stated guidelines drawn from it. These guidelines formed the core of medieval Christian just war doctrine, and there is good reason to begin with them when tracing the ancestry of classic just war doctrine.

Gratian's *Decretals* (published about 1148) contained the definitive abstraction of Augustine's thought on war for the high Middle Ages. The *Decretals* held a place of great significance in the developing code of canon law, and their influence can be found not only in later canon law but also in the writings of scholastic theologians. Gratian drew from Augustine three main points on war: a definition of just war (*Decretals*, Part II, Case XXIII, Question II, Canon II),[2] a statement on just cause for war (Question I, Canon IV),[3] and a brief passage limiting legitimate participation in war (Question VIII, Canons IV, XIX).[4] A definition from Cicero, through Isidore of Seville, even precedes Augustine's in the text (Question II, Canon I).[5]

Thomas Aquinas did not proceed far beyond Gratian's canons in his own theory of just war, though he treated the matter at more length and, instead of simply *copying* Augustine's words (Gratian's method), attempted to *reason* within the framework provided by them (*Summa Theologica*, II/II, Question 40 "On War"). Further, Thomas systematized Gratian's relatively unsystematic excerpts so as to produce a unified theory of just war, whereas Gratian's concern had been merely to provide *ad hoc* canons bearing on war. But this systematization is Thomas' chief contribution; for content he leans on Gratian and, through him, on Augustine. Thomas' requirements for just war (right authority, just cause, right intent, to secure peace) (Art. 1), which provided the core of the classic doctrine's *jus ad bellum*, came from Augustine through Gratian. Like the canonist before him Thomas did little on the matter of limiting the prosecution of war, only prohibiting participation in war to certain churchmen (Art. 2). But Thomas quoted at more length than Gratian the passage from Augustine on right intent (Art. 1), and he took it out of the specific context given by Gratian: whether Christians may ever without sin participate in war. This opened a small crack in the door to reading the requirement of right intention in two ways: not merely as pertaining to the motives of the prince as he contemplates whether to make war, but also as requiring that war be conducted so as to manifest no signs of wrong intent.[6] This provided a theoretical base from which to build a doctrine on *jus in bello* not simply limited to lists of categories of persons who ought not to take part in war. But Thomas Aquinas, it must be stressed, does not pass through the door which he begins to open, and his position on war remains almost entirely a doctrine on *jus ad bellum*.

Besides Gratian and Thomas Aquinas, the third major source for the specifically Christian element in late medieval just war theory was the treatise *De Treuga et Pace (Of Truces and Peace)* entered into the canon law by Pope Gregory IX in the thirteenth century. The significance of this treatise lay in its restricting further than Thomas and Gratian the classes of persons to be spared the ravages of war. Monks, friars, other religious, pilgrims, travelers, merchants, and peasants cultivating the soil are added to the priests and bishops named by both earlier writers. Since those who did not participate in war ought also not to have war made upon them, the expanded listing in *De Treuga et Pace* represents a serious move in the direction of defining noncombatant immunity. Moreover, this treatise also includes an opening to further development of such restriction on war, since it requires that the goods, animals, and (in the case of peasants) land of those named be exempt, along with the persons themselves, from the ravages of war. But this treatise still halted a long way from a complete *jus in bello*. Nothing is said about weaponry, and it remained for later contributors to the just war tradition to fill out the idea of noncombatancy by adding women, children, the aged, the infirm, and certain other civilians to the Church's listing (*De Treuga et Pace*, Title XXXIV; see also Johnson, 1971: 154-169).

What, then, did the church have to say about war in the high Middle Ages? On the side of the *jus ad bellum* was to be found a doctrine which has remained substantially unchanged down to our own time, based in Augustine's definition of just war. This doctrine focused mainly upon the question of lawful participation in war by Christians and sought to define the terms for such participation, without addressing the further question of *how* the Christian ought to fight once he has been given leave to do so. On the side of the *jus in bello* was to be found explicitly only lists of persons who had no part in war because of their functions in society. Some of these could never be soldiers (priests, bishops, religious), while others might leave off their regular occupations for that of fighting (merchants, peasants, pilgrims, other travelers). But so long as these latter kept to their own business (buying and selling, farming, *etc.*), they had the same rights to immunity from war as the churchmen had. The church's rudimentary and incomplete lists of noncombatants comprised the whole of its *jus in bello*, though openings were left for a fuller doctrine to develop later on. But this later process was mainly the result of secular forces, not specifically Christian ones. The *Christian* component of classic just war doctrine, then, is essentially the *jus ad bellum* of that doctrine (see further Johnson, 1975: Chapter I).

In contrast, an overriding concern for the *jus in bello* (along with little on the *jus ad bellum*) can be found in the two *secular* sources which helped to shape the just war tradition in the late Middle Ages. The complementarity of approach made possible a synthesis between churchly and secular attempts to limit war. The result was a doctrine incorporating the strengths of both sets of parents. It is *this* doctrine which Vitoria promulgates and which has come to be regarded as "the" just war doctrine.

One of the two secular sources helping to shape late medieval just war thought was the chivalric code of conduct, whose life history parallels that of knighthood itself. The Hundred Years' War (1339-1453) provides a convenient historical reference by which to date the demise of the chivalric code on warfare and its incorporation into a growing European consensus on just warfare. It is difficult for us today to comprehend the idea of wars fought by the rules of chivalric conduct, according to which battles were sometimes regarded as large-scale games designed to test the valor of the opposing players. At Agincourt, for example, the sense of knightly propriety was such that the French and English heralds could stand together on a hill overlooking the battle below them so as to mark the conduct of the two sides; it was the heralds, at last, who declared the day won by the English, and the French King-at-Arms (master herald) who conveyed this to his sovereign. But whatever our inability to conceive of stylized, game-like warfare as enforced by the heralds (who, as a special class, were steeped in the requirements of chivalry and were accorded certain prerogatives to enable them to perform their various functions as umpires over the "games" of war, judges over the morals of ordinary knights, and arbiters of suits between members of the knightly class), it is from the code of chivalry which defined such warfare that much of the just war doctrine's *jus in bello* has derived.

While chivalry was supreme at the beginning of the Hundred Years' War, by its end in the mid-fifteenth century the characteristic form of chivalric warfare (one-on-one encounters by mounted, heavily-armored knights) had disappeared and the code of conduct which had informed chivalry was no longer observed. Only two residues remained of this code: its high ideals, increasingly held up to ridicule (as in the story of *Don Quixote*) and the law of arms, that part of the code which governed the actual employment of the knight and his armament in battle. But the chivalric law of arms did not persist intact.

On the one hand it was expanded, simplified and regularized to be made to apply to the new type of common soldier who had appeared with the coming of gunpowder. This tendency produced a succession of military manuals of conduct prepared by generals and sovereigns to serve as regulations for their subordinates under arms. Gustavus Adolphus' *Swedish Discipline* (from the early seventeenth century) is a widely-known example of this type of manual, and it was very influential in its own time. Others of less broad impact were written earlier, and still other manuals came later. The current United States field manual *Law of Land Warfare* is a contemporary example of the same type of book.

On the other hand the law of arms was abstracted from the chivalric ideals and joined to even higher ideals as part of the developing just war tradition.

This was accomplished largely through the writings of such influential bridge-builders as Honore Bonet (1343-ca. 1400) and Christine de Pisan (1368-after 1429), who equated (one is tempted to say confounded) the rudimentary provisions of the churchly *jus in bello* with the more extensive chivalric limits on what might rightly be done in war. The result was a much fuller *jus in bello* than was known by Thomas or Gratian or even the author of *De Treuga et Pace*. Two brief comparisons using Bonet's *L'Arbre des battailes* (*Tree of Battles*, written between 1382 and 1387) must suffice here to indicate the lines of this gradual process of amalgamation. First, Bonet makes explicit the reason why the peasant's land, the merchant's goods, and the animals of both must be as immune from war as the peasant and merchant themselves. Why, Bonet asks, does an ox have the privilege of noncombatant immunity? Because, he responds, the ox plows the soil and does not make war. But by extension anyone or anything whose business is other than warmaking ought to have the same immunity (Coopland, 1949: 188). Thus Bonet states what is only implied in *De Treuga et Pace*. Second, Bonet adds to the listing of noncombatants in the canon law those classes of persons who were by the chivalric code to be protected by knights. Thus women, children, the poor, and others who are too weak to protect themselves came to be set alongside those the church had exempted because their social function was other than warmaking (Coopland, 1949: 189). Bonet's book set a pattern for later bridgebuilders, and gradually the chivalric law of arms and the churchly *jus in bello* were woven together into a single doctrine (see further Johnson, 1971: 154-156).

Another secular set of ideas, this one emergent rather than waning, also conditioned the development of just war doctrine in the late Middle Ages: the legal concept of *jus gentium*. Though the term *jus gentium* comes from Roman law, late medieval lawyers used it in a somewhat different sense from their Roman predecessors. Among the latter the term had referred to two distinct and partially contradictory ideas: a positive law deducible by reason from the general principles of the natural law, and the general law which governed members of the Empire not Roman citizens. In either case the *jus gentium* was conceived as a law common to all men, though a particular civil law (*jus civile*) might further govern a man who lived in the territory controlled by a particular ruler. In the Middle Ages the Roman concept of *jus gentium* as positive law which expresses in rational form the natural law was connected and identified with the concept that Mosaic law expresses God's will for man in the state of nature. Thus the *jus gentium* became much more specific than it had been under the (fundamentally Stoic) Roman conception. Again, the late medieval lawyers converted the idea of *jus gentium* as the law of peoples not Roman citizens into a concept of a kind of "common law" of Christendom, contained and expressed in a growing body of customs and agreements among sovereigns and their agents.[7] By the higher normative conception of *jus gentium* God's dealings with Israel became a legitimate basis for purely secular law (as opposed to the ecclesiastical canon law, which had of course made use of the OT right along); by the "common law" conception secular law is increasingly taken out of the hands of higher authorities (such as the Holy Roman Emperor or the Pope) and put in those of regional sovereigns, who in turn tended more and more to be conceived as drawing their authority from their subjects (Hamilton, 1963: Chapter II).

Several results of this development interest us. In the long run, the loss of secular power by churchly authorities and, correspondingly, a widening split between the spheres of authority of ecclesiastics and of secular sovereigns led to the conviction that holy war could ultimately be ruled out: no pope had the right to call up an army (a secular power), while no prince had the right to make war in a holy cause (a matter pertaining to the church's authority) (Johnson, 1975: Chapters II, III). In the short run the results were also significant: a gradual growth of a set of agreements among sovereigns ratifying old customs (among them those pertaining to war) and establishing new ones by mutual consent. Just war doctrine, by this time belonging to the sphere of old customs, thus came to be taken over into secular law and modified there in accord with princely agreements.

In short, four sources pour into the making of just war doctrine in its classic form. From the side of the church there are inputs from both canon law and scholastic theology (here I have treated only the very first contributions in these lines); from the secular side there is the influence of the waning chivalric law of arms and that of the emergent legal concept of *jus gentium*. In the truest sense, then, classic just war doctrine is not a specifically *Christian* doctrine (even though all the contributors to it were Christians by religion); it is better to call this doctrine a product of *Christendom*, because of the combination of secular and religious forces which together produced it. Of particular importance in the forging of this combination was the complementarity of the two sets of sources: the *jus ad bellum* from churchmen, the *jus in bello* from secular theory and practice. It is especially relevant for understanding later just war doctrine, including that of Paul Ramsey, to emphasize that the classic *jus in bello* was provided mainly from secular sources. Though the beginnings of a position on limiting the conduct of war can be discerned in scholastic theology and canon law, they remain but beginnings.

What are the elements of a fuller *jus in bello* provided by the secular sources? From the chivalric code came regulations governing the conduct of soldiers under arms, specification of noncombatants so as to include all classes of persons who for one reason or another could not or did not bear arms, and the idea of war fought according to certain rules higher than those of military necessity. From the *jus gentium* came agreements specifying conditions of noncombatancy, rules for sieges, safe-conducts, truces and other day-to-day problems of war, along with the general tendency to forge into positive law the customs of war which had persisted for generations. Indeed, so unequal are the churchly and the secular contributions to the *jus in bello* that it is only in retrospect, after the church's tentative restrictions on who might be a soldier have been joined with the much more wide-ranging secular contributions, that the church can be seen as itself having a *jus in bello* of its own. Any argument that limits on conduct of war are grounded in theological norms must be made very carefully, then; systematically they may be so, but historically they come from purely secular sources.

Finally, it should be noted that the secular sources, particularly the *jus gentium* idea, involved a tendency to undercut the *jus ad bellum* of the church and produce a concept of justified war by mutual consent of the belligerents. This concept, often identified by the French term *compétence de guerre* (which reduces the *jus ad bellum* to one requirement, authority or *compétence*), does not become a serious problem for theory on the limitation of war until the eighteenth and nineteenth centuries. In the classic just war doctrine, as exemplified in Vitoria's two works from the middle of the sixteenth century, the *jus ad bellum* and the *jus in bello* are present in complementary strengths—as they never were before and have not been since.

II.
PAUL RAMSEY'S JUST WAR DOCTRINE AND THE TRADITION

There are two places, both in *War and the Christian Conscience*, which are definitive for Ramsey's use of the just war tradition and his own particular methodology. These are Chapter Two, "The Just War According to St. Augustine," and Chapter Three, "The Genesis of Noncombatant Immunity," where Ramsey probes the thought of Augustine and Thomas Aquinas in search of the rationale behind their positions on just war. In neither place does the treatment of either of these key figures in just war tradition become, however, a simple matter of tracing the movement of the tradition so as to discern where it seems to be pointing—though this is what a historian of ideas would do, as would a theologian who regards the line of development of a traditional doctrine as itself providing the norm for what he must do as the heir of that tradition. Ramsey instead turns to Augustine and Aquinas because of what he believes they discern about the requirements of charity in cases like those encountered in connection with war.[8]

The chapter entitled "The Just War According to St. Augustine" is Ramsey's only direct consideration of the right to go to war (though a *jus ad bellum* can be inferred from elsewhere, notably the essays titled "Selective Conscientious Objection" and "Robert W. Tucker's *Bellum Contra Bellum Justum*"; 1968A: Chapters 5, 17). I wish to note only one point about that treatment: Ramsey uses Augustine's doctrine of the state, borrowed from Roman theory and modified in accord with charity, to argue that the later just war tradition was wrong in declaring there to be one just and one unjust side in just wars. For Augustine, Ramsey argues, the ambiguities of life in this age of mixture between heavenly and earthly cities produce conflicts in which "the existing justice . . . may tragically be on both sides" (1961B: 29). But as Charles Curran notes, there is some disagreement whether this interpretation of Augustine on justice in war is correct: "Roland Bainton interprets Augustine as saying that only one side could be just; whereas Frederick Russell admits that for Augustine both sides could have a just cause, but one is more just" (1973: 73).[9] The correct reading of Augustine on this point is too complicated a matter to be decided here. But one thing is certain: for over a thousand years after Augustine the just war tradition assumed that wars might be fought between one just and one unjust party, and that men could tell the difference. Christian participation in war was limited to fighting on the just side against the unjust. With Vitoria, however, there clearly emerges a concept of simultaneous ostensible justice—the idea that both sides in a war may justifiably think themselves in the right because of the evidence available to them (Johnson, 1973a: 220; 1975: Chapters III, IV).[10]

Vitoria was concerned with cases in which the claims of justice are so confused men cannot sort them out so as to determine the *truly* just side; Ramsey, though, goes further in his interpretation of Augustine, arguing that the heavenly and earthly cities are so intermingled that real justice and injustice must inevitably be mixed together in all human claims. The result is the same, whether the simultaneous justice is conceived as only ostensible or as real. Vitoria and his successors in the field of international law used the idea of simultaneous ostensible justice to argue for a stricter adherence to the limits of the *jus in bello*, and this is also Ramsey's line of argument: "The 'just' war which seeks peace . . . has its own intrinsic limits" (Ramsey, 1961B: 30).

What is at stake in this argument? For Ramsey, to find grounds for the concept of simultaneous ostensible justice already in Augustine's thought, whatever the just war tradition later said, means that a charity-based just war theory can never clearly discriminate in favor of one side or social system and against another (1961B: 32). It can never be used to justify wars of the "righteous" against the "unrighteous," of one ideology against another. That the just war tradition up until the sixteenth century allowed such wars under the rubric of "war for religion" opened the way to the argument sometimes made by proponents of holy war, that the justness of one's own cause was so great and the injustice of one's opponents so gross that war should be made against them with no quarter.[11] Where such a *jus ad bellum* existed, it is not surprising that a serious attempt to frame a *jus in bello* was so long coming. Vitoria appears to have understood this connection, for his argument for simultaneous ostensible justice is tied, on the one hand, to a rejection of war for religion as just cause, and on the other, to an argument stressing the need for adherence to strict limits in fighting wars (Nys, ed., 1917: *De Jure Belli*, sections 18-19, 27-30; *De Indis*, section III, 7). So too, Ramsey's interest in grounding the idea of simultaneous ostensible justice in Augustine's charity-inspired doctrine of the state is to reject, on the one hand, the cold-war mentality which made of the East-West confrontation an absolute ideological impasse which could only be settled by an all-out thermonuclear war, while on the other hand he attempts to build up a *jus in bello* which determines the limits for use of thermonuclear weapons. Understood in this way, "The Just War According to St. Augustine" becomes a necessary theoretical step justifying the *jus in bello* preoccupations of the remainder of *War and the Christian Conscience*.

In the following chapter, "The Genesis of Noncombatant Immunity," we come to a discussion critical for establishing Ramsey's own perspective upon just war doctrine. No other single portion of his work on war better illustrates his constructive and theological, rather than historical, use of Augustine and Aquinas. In the case of Augustine, rather than looking to *The City of God, Against Faustus*, or *Questions on Joshua*, the Augustinian sources that figured most prominently in the development of the historical just war tradition, Ramsey instead treats *De Libero Arbitrio* and *The Duties of the Clergy* (1961B: 35-37).[12] In the case of Aquinas, instead of referring to the question on war (*Summa Theologica* II/II, Question 40), Ramsey draws on an entirely different question, that on self-defense (Question 64). In both cases his concern is with the justification of defense against attack by force, a matter which he finds extremely instructive for questions of morality in war and in statecraft generally.

Augustine, Ramsey notes, distinguishes between defending oneself against an assailant and defending one's neighbor. "The striking thing about the views of Augustine," he writes, "is that, while he was quite realistic . . . about the necessity and justifiability of public defense and the Christian's responsibility for it, nevertheless he saw no cause for private self-defense" (1961B: 34).[13] As Ramsey interprets Augustine, it is impossible to imagine that self-love does not play some part in self-defense, and so this is unjustified. But defense of one's neighbor can be an act of charity free of self-love. In the case of soldiers it is thus not only the law which allows them to kill the enemy; it is that their acts protect from harm their neighbors in the state. Augustine in this manner justifies the killing of combatants by other combatants. But, Ramsey notes in passing, Augustine refuses to allow the Christian to avail himself of the right to self-defense, though it is allowed in the law of the state. This opens up the question whether any person who acts in defense, whether of self or of another, ought morally always to do all that the law allows (Ramsey, 1961B: 35-39).

For an answer to this question Ramsey turns to Thomas Aquinas. "[T]he striking thing about the views of Thomas Aquinas is that . . . he was . . . reluctant to justify the direct killing even of the enemy, or of an unjust aggressor, as in itself intrinsically right" (Ramsey, 1961B: 34-35). In support of this judgment he quotes Aquinas: "Wherefore if a man, in self-defense, uses more than necessary violence, it will be unlawful: whereas if he repel force with moderation his defense will be lawful, because according to the jurists, *it is lawful to repel force by force, provided one does not exceed the limits of a blameless defense*" (*Summa Theologica*, II/II, Question 64, Article 7; Ramsey, 1961B: 40, emphasis in text). Commenting on the passage in which this sentence appears, Ramsey argues, "The only case in which it is right to intend to kill even an unjust assailant would seem to be when, in acting for the public defense, one refers this intentional killing as a means to the public good" (1961B: 40). Here his concerns are to develop the rule of double effect, by which it is necessary to intend to do harm for the public good to justify killing in war, and by which also it is only allowable to harm noncombatants if their hurt is not directly intended but a secondary effect of justifiable defense directed against combatants or other forces of war. This is a central theme throughout not only the rest of this chapter but also the remainder of the book.[14] But elsewhere Ramsey develops the very same passage from Aquinas in a different, if equally interesting, way. In a chapter of *The Just War* entitled "Incapacitating Gases" (1968A: Chapter 19) he points out that *killing* an enemy is only one means of *incapacitating* him. If less final means of incapacitation are available, they are morally preferable (1968A: 471). This argument too should be understood as in response to the question posed earlier, whether someone acting defensively ought to do all that the law allows. Whichever derivation of Aquinas he uses, Ramsey's answer is No. And, as in the case of his interpretation of Augustine, his argument is that charity informs the conclusions reached: "Profoundly at work in [Aquinas'] line of reasoning is what *justice transformed by love* requires to be extended even to him who wrongfully attacks" (Ramsey, 1961B: 43-44, emphasis added).

Ramsey's concern to draw out the implications of charity, rather than to bring up to date the just war tradition, gives him a marked independence from the developing tradition. This independence characterizes his theory on war throughout and sets him off from most contemporary Catholic just war thought as well. It further removes any necessity for him to become an apologist for elements retained in the tradition with which he might be uncomfortable. These he can simply leave out of his own developing doctrine.

III.
Ramsey and Strategy

It is his almost exclusive concern with the *jus in bello* which leads Ramsey in the direction of criticizing strategic models—as already noted, a possibility completely overlooked in the development of classic just war doctrine.

"Strategy," as Clausewitz defined it, is "the theory of the use of combats for the object of the war." This is a definition not only commonly accepted today but also applicable to the period in which classic just war thought took shape, the late Middle Ages. Two broad types of strategy may be defined within the bounds set by Clausewitz, as military historian Russell Weigley notes following German commentator Hans Delbrück. They are "the strategy of annihilation, which seeks the overthrow of the enemy's military power; and the strategy of attrition, exhaustion, or erosion, which is usually employed by a strategist whose means are not great enough to permit pursuit of the direct overthrow of the enemy and who therefore resorts to an indirect approach" (Weigley, 1973: xxii). The fundamental difference between these two kinds of strategy is their dissimilar objects: the complete overthrow of the enemy's power to make war *vs.* the blunting or turning aside of that power so as to frustrate the enemy's objectives and to avoid harm, so far as possible, to one's own side. These different objects determine the employment of available means of warmaking, whether those means consist of nuclear missiles, World War I tanks, a regiment of light dragoons, or fully-armored knights on horseback. Nevertheless, there is a certain historical, if not a logical, connection between possession of overwhelming force and pursuit of a strategy of annihilation. Superior military strength plus the element of surprise enabled Germany to overrun Poland, the Netherlands, Belgium, and finally France at the start of World War II; thereafter the war became defined by strategies of exhaustion or attrition, as each side tried to wear the other down. The nuclear superiority of the United States during the decade after World War II helped to produce the idea of a pre-emptive strike against the Soviet Union as a means of overwhelming Communism once and for all. But also a factor in the growth of this idea was the historical American preference for strategies of annihilation, a preference which Weigley documents throughout *The American Way of War*.

Delbrück linked the strategy of attrition with military weakness, implying that where there are the necessary resources a strategy of annihilation will *always* be followed. This is questionable even as a historical observation, and it surely does not follow from the types of strategy themselves. It is the role of the head of state and his advisers to define the objects of policy and to tailor military strategy accordingly. This, in turn, determines which of the weapons and weapons systems will be utilized. To understand whether and how a particular strategy is justified, then, requires first of all understanding what are the policy objectives of the government in power in a given state, and whether these are justified or not. This is substantially how Ramsey employs his just war theory: first discounting unlimited policy aims with his introduction of the concept of simultaneous ostensible justice, then building a framework of moral considerations within which only strategies of limited war will fit. We must inquire how he does this, but first we ought also to inquire into medieval use of the two types of strategy and the relation of just war doctrine to them.

While most medieval wars exemplify strategies of attrition, there were some which clearly were waged with annihilation as their aim. The first crusade was one such, and when a later crusade turned its wrath upon the heretic Albigensians to utterly destroy them, it became another. These wars were not essentially different in their strategic goals from the French Wars of Religion and the subsequent Thirty Years' War—two examples from the century of conflict which followed on the Reformation. The common characteristic of these wars, post-Reformation and medieval alike, is that they were holy wars, that is, wars fought for the cause of religion. But "religion" in these cases meant little if anything more than we now mean by "ideology"—a way of defining one's friends and one's enemies by their beliefs. This suggests that the message can be extrapolated into our own time: wars fought for ideological reasons tend to be wars of annihilation (see also Johnson, 1973a: 219-224).

So long as just war theory remained within the realm of Christian theology and canon law exclusively or even mainly, such religious/ideological causes for war were regarded as just, and strategies of annihilation were tacitly accepted.[15] But with the post-Reformation split in Christendom, and more importantly with the amalgamation of secular and religious ideas to form the classic just war doctrine of the fifteenth and sixteenth centuries, such causes were disallowed in the mainstream of just war thinking. Vitoria again is a convenient example: he devotes a considerable part of *De Jure Belli* to ruling out war for cause of religion and grounding just war in purely natural law causes (see further Walters, 1971: 346-351; Johnson, 1975: Chapters III, IV).[16] The result was that just war doctrine in its classic form accepted only wars which, in one way or another, belonged to the realm of politics. These were, moreover, wars *limited* by the new *jus in bello* produced by the late medieval developments in just war theory.

Two patterns in the relation of just war theory to strategy thus emerge from the period of development of classic just war doctrine. First, the churchly doctrine of the late Middle Ages justified wars for religious causes as well as wars for reasons strictly political: defense of property, retribution for some harm done, and so forth. The former (which I have identified with ideological war) tended toward strategies of annihilation. The influx of secular ideas ultimately led to repudiation of this kind of cause and with it the unlimited mode of warfare which sometimes accompanied it. This left only wars for causes political in nature, and these were, in the Middle Ages as well as in the time of Vitoria, limited (though to different degrees) by the *jus in bello*. But in neither case was there any concern for strategy as such or for criticizing strategic models. Strategy, indeed, as a concept had not yet been invented.

For Ramsey, conversely, the existence of alternative strategies and competing strategic models was, when he began to write on war, an inescapable reality. Preoccupation with strategy in some sense reached a zenith in the early years of the age of nuclear weaponry, for suddenly such weapons made it possible to think of wars which would never be fought (the realm of tactics) because of strategic advantage clearly communicated to the enemy. The development of game theory and its use by military and civilian strategists furthered the tendency to make of war a gigantic game—though a very serious game indeed. *War and the Christian Conscience* entered the arena of American debate over strategy, and the *jus in bello* Ramsey developed there had primary reference to problems of strategic nuclear deployment. Though the appearance of the problem of defining moral limits to counterinsurgency war allowed Ramsey (1968A: 427-536) to apply this thought to tactics as well, the balance in *The Just War* is also toward matters related to strategic considerations: nuclear war, deterrence, and the like.

For Ramsey the only acceptable strategies are those of limited war—of "attrition," using Delbruck's term, though it is an odd term in this context. For in nuclear war the wearing down of the enemy's forces could be achieved almost instantaneously by an interchange of missiles, and, moreover, the morally-acceptable counter-forces strategy Ramsey proposes in *War and the Christian Conscience* might well have the effect of *annihilating* the enemy's military power (see Ramsey, 1961B: 229-230, 260-261, 275-282, 294-296, 320-323). The sense in which Ramsey's counterforces strategy is a limited-war strategy can be understood best by considering what was his real adversary in the 1961 book: the idea of counter-society or counter-people warfare, well expressed in the doctrine of massive retaliation (though given other shapes as well). Massive retaliation is aimed at deterrence through the threat of a massive nuclear strike upon the population centers of an enemy should he, in a way no matter how small, make a warlike move. Such a strategy of deterrence Ramsey criticizes (see the references immediately above) as both disproportionate and indiscriminate, hence morally wrong. Indeed, Ramsey is not even happy with a counter-force strategy such as that proposed by Herman Kahn (Ramsey, 1961B: 260-261). Such a strategy would require targeting one's own missiles so as to destroy those of the enemy—with the implication, of course, being that a preemptive strike would be necessary to destroy the enemy's missiles before they left their launch pads. Ramsey's preference, counter-forces warfare, is an explicit attempt to incorporate Aquinas' position on the allowable limits to defensive action into strategic theory. Specifically, Ramsey would have nuclear weapons (and other types of weapons as well) constructed and targeted so that they could destroy or turn aside an enemy's attacking forces (see 1961B: 275-276). Assuming the effectiveness of such a strategy, it might well in practice produce the annihilation of the enemy's forces; yet it is a limited-war strategy in the twin senses that it *proportionately* responds to the enemy's attack and *discriminately* seeks out the attacking *forces* (and not the population centers of the enemy nation) to prevent their doing harm to one's neighbors in his own state. The counter-forces strategy expresses Ramsey's willingness to think about actually *fighting* a thermonuclear war, not just about deterring it with a force so massively destructive it could never morally be used (see also 1961B: 314-316). This sets him off from both some civilian strategists (notably those who, like John Foster Dulles, advocated a nuclear deterrent so massive and so awesome it would never have to be used) and also fellow theological ethicists like John C. Bennett (see Bennett, 1962: 100-112), for whom the possibility of fighting a nuclear war was, in Herman Kahn's word, "unthinkable."

Much more could be said about the implications Ramsey's concern with strategy have for his just war theory. Among other things, for example, it leads him away from considering *who* noncombatants are, since definition of moral strategy requires only the recognition that there *are* noncombatants in the vicinity of a missile's target (see, for example, 1968A: 59). In my opinion (1971) the just war tradition offers some quite explicit guidelines for defining combatants and noncombatants, and anyone wishing to work in just war theory in our own time would do well to attempt to formulate such guidelines also. That Ramsey does not do so follows, I suggest, implicitly from his strategic concerns. In any case, he needs more explicit definition of noncombatants for his principle of discrimination to be applied intelligently by decision-makers all the way down to soldiers in the field. But such application has to do with *tactics*, not strategy.

One might also construct a detailed, point-by-point comparison with a classic just war theorist like Vitoria to show how Ramsey's strategic concerns produce different emphases in the *jus in bello* generally. Given their differing concerns, the strength of Ramsey's doctrine is the weakness of the classic just war doctrine as expressed by Vitoria, and *vice versa*. That is, Ramsey's preoccupation with strategic considerations allows him a more universal usefulness (through his general principles of discrimination and proportion), but at the same time his lack of a more specific *jus in bello*, a strength of classic doctrine, makes his work less useful in practical law-of-war application.

Space considerations do not allow expanding the two former points here; I want only to bring them to view as indications of the wider implications Ramsey's strategic concerns have for his just war theory. One final matter I would like to deal with at more length, if still only in a programmatic way. This is the matter of the appeal Ramsey wishes to make to secular strategists, practical politicians and military men.

The roots of Ramsey's just war theory are in an Augustinian appeal to charity in a world where until the end of time there exists an ambiguous mixture of the City of God and the City of Earth (1961B: Chapters Two, Three, Afterword; compare 1973j: 111, where he compares his teacher H. Richard Niebuhr with "the great Augustine"). Ramsey understands charity to be at the bottom of just war theory as he derives it, a conception which can be identified with the phrase (originally from Reinhold Niebuhr but modified slightly by Ramsey), "love transforming natural justice." Perhaps better is the terminology used near the end of *War and the Christian Conscience*: "[t]he definite fashioning of justice by divine charity" (1961B: 305). As Ramsey first understood his role in this gradual transformation or fashioning, it was to lay out as clearly as possible the requirements of the ethical claims confronting man; these requirements he attempts to draw directly from charity. At this stage in his thinking he makes the distinction, "ethics is a practical *scientia*, while political practice, like an art, requires *doing*" (1961B: 309, emphasis in text), by which he implicitly sets himself, as ethicist, over against the political decision-maker. The implicit distinction is underlined by his terming the political realm one of "deferrable repentance"—Ramsey's way of indicating that the requirements of politics and those of ethics (specifically just war theory) might often conflict (1961B: 309). There is at this stage in his thinking some recognition that the Christian ethicist and the political practicioner have something in common (the area in which natural justice is being transformed by charity), but Ramsey does not dwell on this.

It must be admitted, however, that in the realm of secular policy-making and strategic analysis, direct appeals to charity are likely to amount to very little. Accordingly, in his latest paper, instructively entitled "A Political Ethics Context for Strategic Thinking" (1973j), Ramsey turns to the ground shared by himself and the secular strategists with whom he would communicate. "Our quest should be," he writes, ". . . for the ethical ingredient in foreign policy formation, for the wisdom peculiar to taking counsel amid a world of encountering powers, for—as a sub-set—the laws *of* war and *of* deterrence so long as these are human activities properly related and subordinated to the purposes of political communities in the international system" (1973j: 125, emphasis in text). The language he uses is reminiscent of his earlier position (1961B: Afterword), where he also spoke of providing "a moral context" for political decisions (1961B: 311), but now he takes the further step of presenting just war doctrine as an *inherent* requirement of politics itself (1973j: 132-136). Charity as the ultimate source of just war principles is not treated here at all.

It is one thing to note this change; it is another to understand it properly. It is, I think (and have tried to suggest), a change in *emphasis*, not in substance. Ramsey represents his 1973 treatment of just war principles as a restatement of his earlier position (1973j: 132, 133, 135), and as I have noted the language is also similar to that of 1961B. But now he wants to stress that just war requirements are "internal" to politics, not "external" (1973j: 125). What has happened here?

As only the suggestion of an answer, I see an important likeness between this metamorphosis in Ramsey's thought and that in Christian just war doctrine as it became transformed into the classic doctrine as expressed by Vitoria and others. From Thomas Aquinas to Vitoria there was a gradual submergence of divinely-based norms so as to enable a more direct claim of relevance to be made to the political sphere. Ramsey's latest entry into the arena of ethics and strategy bears a strong resemblance, I suggest, to Vitoria's attempt to fashion a just war doctrine wholly on a base in natural law. There is no space here to conduct the inquiry that would prove or disprove this interpretation. But, if it is correct, it would help also to explain Ramsey's method in his writings on medical ethics, where again the principal appeal is to what we might call "common moral sensitivity" in the community at large (see, for example, 1970B: xi-xii). If my association of Ramsey's recent method with Vitoria's appeal to natural law is correct, further, an investigation of my hypothesis would tend to reveal something about the idea of natural law in Ramsey's thought—a problem usually approached through his use of Thomas Aquinas. But these are problems beyond the scope of this essay.[17]

Conclusion

I have aimed, in this paper, at the general goal of examining Ramsey's relation to classic just war theory. This has necessitated a capsule description of the development of the classic theory out of religious and secular sources during the late medieval period. To show Ramsey's position with regard to the just war tradition and the classic doctrine I have treated two central concerns in his writings on war and politics: appeal to the norm of divine charity, and definition of a *jus in bello* in the context of strategic thinking. Finally, I have suggested that his concern for strategy has led him to submerge the appeal to charity beneath a kind of "natural-law" claim that just war theory is an inherent requirement of politics understood rightly. Overall, Ramsey's relation to the just war tradition has been described in terms of his use of key figures from the tradition for their particular insights into the requirements of charity, while Ramsey's dual concern with charity and strategy has been offered as a principal reason for differences between his position and that in classic just war doctrine. I have *not* tried, in this paper, to hold up to view all the likenesses between Ramsey and the Christian just war tradition or the classic doctrine, though there are many. Because of these likenesses Ramsey belongs squarely in the tradition of just war thought. But more important, he is a constructive and creative thinker, as evinced by the differences I have dealt with here. The significance of his just war thought lies in both observations.

NOTES

[1] I leave aside here the whole matter of attempts to ground theories of just war in figures outside the mainstream of development, such as Helmut Thielicke's attempt to set Luther up as the primary figure for guidance in his own theory of the moral limits to warfare: *Theological* Ethics, II: *Politics*, 1969: 460-472.

[2] "Those wars are customarily called just which have for their end the revenging of injuries, when it is necessary by war to constrain a city or a nation which has not wished to punish an evil action committed by its citizens, or to restore that which has been taken unjustly."

[3] Though this passage is too long to quote here, the contents are the familiar requirements of right authority, right intent, just cause, and the end of peace. The context in the *Decretals* is the question whether Christians may without sin participate in war.

[4] Participation in war is specifically denied to clerics and religious. No other classes are mentioned.

[5] "A war is just when, by a formal declaration, it is waged in order to regain what has been stolen or to repel the attack of enemies."

[6] In Augustine's words, repeated by Gratian and Thomas, wrong intention includes "the desire for harming, the cruelty of avenging, an unruly and implacable animosity, the rage of rebellion, the lust of domination and the like."

[7] I set off the term "common law" to indicate that I am not identifying it with the common law of Anglo-Saxon legal tradition; yet I use this term to suggest that there is a similarity of tone between the medieval *jus gentium* and the English common law: both, for example, rested heavily on established custom and developed following common practice among men.

[8] Because of this particular interest of Ramsey's it is not important whether he knows the full history of the development behind classic just war doctrine. His concern is to go to the normative roots of that doctrine and all other formulations in the Christian just war tradition, that is, to probe to the requirements of divine charity, which is for him the ultimate moral norm on which all Christian just war thought is based. Of course, it is quite relevant that the classic formulation of just war theory is in Ramsey's past, for without it one can only wonder whether Ramsey, any more than Augustine or Aquinas, would have been led by charity to produce a doctrine so single-mindedly weighted toward the *jus in bello*.

[9] Ramsey himself recognized the controversial nature of his argument: "*If Augustine believed* that there is always only one side that can be regarded as fighting justly in the wars in which a Christian will find himself responsibly engaged, he should not have believed this" (1961B: 28); again, "The just war theory *cannot* have meant for him the presence of justice on one side, its absence on the other" (1961B: 31, emphasis added).

[10] Vitoria held, however, that God could always tell which side was truly in the right. After Vitoria a concept of simultaneous ostensible justice (without, to be sure, any assumption of divine omniscience) flourishes in secular international law, eventually giving birth to the doctrine of *competence de guerre* — the idea that a sovereign alone has the right and authority to decide when a war will be just for his state, and so to initiate war.

[11] Witness, for example, the bloodthirstiness of this passage from Henry Bullinger's *Decades*: in some cases, he writes, "the magistrate of duty is compelled to make war upon men which are incurable, whom the very judgment of the Lord condemneth and biddeth to kill without mercy" (Harding, 1849: 376). Bullinger was, of course, a Protestant and a contemporary of Vitoria; only slightly later English Catholic Archbishop William Allen raised the same flag of unsparing prosecution of war for religion by calling for the slaying of unfaithful Christians (*i.e.*, Protestants) "from the highest to the lowest without exception" (1583: 103).

[12] Curran's statement that "[t]he only texts Ramsey cites are from Book XIX of the *City of God*" (1973: 73) is inaccurate; it applies only to Ramsey's discussion of Augustine in Chapter Two.

[13] Ramsey made the same distinction for himself earlier, in a discussion of what the Good Samaritan *might have done* on the Damascus Road (1950A: 169-170).

[14] For discussion of Ramsey's use of the principle of double effect and the meaning of this principle in traditional Catholic natural law theory, see Charles Curran's essay in Part I of this volume.

[15] For more on the use of religious cause to justify war see Walters, 1971: 119-127; 1973: 585-590; Johnson, 1975: Chapter I. On the relation between religious cause for war and unsparing prosecution see Bainton, 1960: 148; Walters, 1973: 591-592; Johnson, 1975: Chapter II, Appendix.

[16] Walters, however, argues that Vitoria retains some religious causes for just war. I can accept this interpretation only if it is understood that for Vitoria these traditionally religious causes have lost their divine sanction and are allowed only for reasons based in natural law. For example, Vitoria admits that it is just for soldiers to protect Christian missionaries from attack by the Indians they are endeavoring to convert. But notably the reason they may do this is the natural-law right of free passage to be accorded peaceful men in foreign lands, and not the religious purpose of the missionaries. The same reason allows protection of traders, explorers, and others, so long as their purpose is peaceful. For Walters on this from Vitoria see his essay in this volume.

[17] I do not here intend to equate Ramsey's use of natural-law concepts with Vitoria's or with traditional Catholic natural-law theory generally, but merely to point to a similarity of method

between Ramsey and the sixteenth-century theorist of just war. For criticism of Ramsey's use of natural law, see Charles Curran's essay in Part I of this volume. Curran, however, argues by comparing Ramsey with the traditional Catholic concept of natural law, and the burden of his argument is that Ramsey is no Catholic on this matter. The suggestion I offer above is methodologically quite different: to focus upon the *similarities* between Vitoria's and Ramsey's respective moves away from overt appeals to theological norms toward other bases in men's common moral wisdom. If such a positive comparison proves valid, it should tell us more about both the content and the intent of Ramsey's idea of natural law than does the negative comparison done by Curran.

REFERENCES

Allen, William, Archbishop
1583 *A True, Sincere, and Modest Defence of English Catholiques that suffer for Their Faith both at home and abrode.* London: William Cecil.

Bainton, Roland
1960 *Christian Attitudes toward War and Peace.* Nashville and New York: Abingdon Press.

Bennett, John C. (ed.)
1962 *Nuclear Weapons and the Conflict of Conscience.* New York: Charles Scribner's Sons.

Bonet, Honore see Coopland, G. W. (ed.)

Bullinger, Henry see Harding, Thomas (ed.)

Coopland, G. W. (ed.)
1949 *The Tree of Battles of Honore Bonet.* Translated from the French *L'Arbre des battailes.* Cambridge, Massachusetts: Harvard University Press.

Curran, Charles E.
1973 *Politics, Medicine, and Christian Ethics: A Dialogue with Paul Ramsey.* Philadelphia: Fortress Press.

Hamilton, Bernice
1963 *Political Thought in Sixteenth Century Spain.* Oxford: Oxford University Press.

Harding, Thomas (ed.)
1849 Henry Bullinger, *The Decades. The First and Second Decades.* Cambridge: Cambridge University Press.

Johnson, James T.
1971 "The meaning of non-combatant immunity in the just war/limited war tradition." *Journal of the American Academy of Religion* 39/2 (June): 151-170.
1973a "Ideology and the *Jus ad Bellum*: justice in the initiation of war." *Journal of the American Academy of Religion* 41/2 (June): 212-228.
1973b "Toward reconstructing the *Jus ad Bellum.*" *Monist* 57/4 (October): 461-488.
1975 *Ideology, Reason and the Limitation of War.* Princeton: Princeton University Press.

Nys, Ernest (ed.)
1917 Franciscus de Victoria, *De Indis et De Jure Belli Relectiones.* (Classics of International Law series, ed. by James Brown Scott.) Washington: Carnegie Institute.

Ramsey, Paul
See the bibliography of Ramsey's works in this volume. Capital letters (e.g. 1950A) denote books and occasional papers; lower case letters (e.g. 1968a) denote articles.

Thielicke, Helmut
1969 *Theological Ethics, II: Politics.* Philadelphia: Fortress Press.

Vanderpol, Albert
1919 *La Doctrine scholastique du droit de guerre.* Paris: A. Pedone.

Vitoria, Francis de see Nys, Ernest (ed.)

Walters, LeRoy B.
1971 "Five Classic Just-War Theories: A Study in the Thought of Thomas Aquinas, Vitoria, Suarez, Gentili, and Grotius." New Haven: unpublished Yale University Ph.D. dissertation.

1973 "The just war and the crusade: antitheses or analogies?" *The Monist* (October): 584-594.

Weigley, Russell F.

1973 *The American Way of War: A History of United States Military Strategy and Policy*. New York: Macmillan Publishing Co., Inc.; London: Collier Macmillan Publishers.

CHAPTER VI

Historical Applications of The Just War Theory: Four Case Studies In Normative Ethics

LeRoy Walters

Paul Ramsey, especially in his book *War and the Christian Conscience* (1961B), has provided us with an insightful historical survey of the just war tradition. However, Ramsey's overview concentrates almost exclusively on intellectual history, on the just war *thought* of Augustine, Thomas Aquinas, Luther, Calvin, and others. Except for references to the destructive possibility of contemporary nuclear warfare, *War and the Christian Conscience* devotes relatively little attention to the socio-political context in which the just war theory has been formulated or applied.

The aim of the present essay is to complement the work of Ramsey by attempting to reconstruct the social-historical situation in which several of the just war theorists thought and wrote. The method of the essay will be to analyze the four pre-modern cases in which just war theorists most explicitly and in greatest detail applied just war categories to particular wars or military campaigns. At the conclusion of these case studies, then, we shall consider what generalizations, if any, can be formulated on the basis of this brief foray into history.

The search for appropriate case studies leads first, and most obviously, to Francisco de Vitoria (d. 1546), who applied just war categories to the Spanish conquests in Latin America, 1519-1539. A second author, Hugo Grotius (d. 1645), is well-known as a major systematic just war theoretician. Less well known is that in his early writings he employed just war theory in analyzing two concrete cases, the Dutch-Portuguese disputes (1595-1609) over the East Indian trade, and the first phase of the war (1567-1609) between Spain and the Netherlands. In the case of the latter war, we are fortunate in being able to compare Grotius' views with the opinions of two other just war theorists, Balthasar Ayala (d. 1584) and Alberico Gentili (d. 1608). Finally, thanks to an excellent recent monograph (Belch, 1965), we are able to add a fourth case study: the relatively unknown Polish canon lawyer Paulus Vladimiri (d. 1435) and his opponents evaluated the fifteenth century struggle between the Teutonic Knights and Poland-Lithuania by appealing to major emphases in the just war tradition.

Three of our theorists, Vitoria, Gentili, and Grotius, wrote major systematic treatises on just war in addition to commenting on particular cases. In these systematic works, four issues received primary attention:

1. *Whether* warfare is ever morally justifiable.
2. *Who* may wage war (authority).
3. *For what reasons* war may be waged (cause or *jus ad bellum*).
4. *How* war should be waged (intention and means or *jus in bello*).[1]

Generally speaking, the post-medieval theorists accorded greater emphasis to the issues of cause and means than to the first two questions. In our concluding section, we shall investigate the extent to which the theorists-as-commentators discussed the four issues outlined above.

There are, as well, several general questions on which the present study may shed additional light:

1. Was there diversity of viewpoint at the theoretical level within the just war tradition?
2. Did the just war theorists discuss the problem of religious war?
3. When two or more theorists analyzed the same war, did they agree or disagree in their assessments?
4. Were the theorists generally supportive of, or critical of, the wars waged by their own nations?

At the conclusion of each case study and in the final section of the essay, we shall return to the consideration of these questions.

We turn, then, to the case studies. Within each study we shall begin by sketching the macro-historical background of the theorist or theorists. These sketches will be based upon modern historical works and will be framed as accurately and objectively as possible. Next, biographical data concerning the theorist(s) involved in each case study will be adduced. Against this macro- and micro-historical background each just war theorist's ethical analysis of a contemporary conflict will be presented. At the conclusion of each case study we shall briefly examine the significance of our findings. The four case studies will be discussed in chronological order.

I

The Teutonic Knights, a military religious order, had originated in the Holy Land during the final decade of the twelfth century. In 1226 the Holy Roman Emperor, Frederick II, granted to the Order a vast expanse of pagan territory along the coast of the Baltic Sea. Included in the grant were the lands of Pomerania and Prussia. According to the text of Frederick's grant, its purpose was to enable the Teutonic Knights to "invade and obtain the land of Prussia for the honour and glory of the true God" (Belch, 1965: 102).

By a combination of conquest and federation the Teutonic Knights gradually acquired most of the territories bordering on the Baltic Sea—including some territories traditionally claimed by the neighboring nations to the south, Poland and Lithuania. For their part, Poland and Lithuania formed a union in 1386. The reasons for the union seem to have been partly military, partly religious. Militarily, Poland and Lithuania stopped waging war against one another and formed a united front against the Teutonic Knights. On the religious front, the pagan leader of the Prussians, Jagiełło, was converted to Christianity, was crowned king of Poland-Lithuania, and led his countrymen to accept Christian baptism.

Eventual military confrontation between the Knights and Poland-Lithuania was predictable. Constant, minor skirmishes escalated in 1409 into full-scale warfare. The Order was allied with Sigismund of Hungary and assisted by Christian crusaders from many parts of Europe. Poland-Lithuania was aided by Tartars and Schismatic Russian Orthodox believers. Despite a decisive battle (Tannenberg) and a peace agreement in 1410, hostilities continued. Finally, the papal legate arranged an armistice. The belligerent parties agreed to submit their dispute to the Council of Constance for resolution.[2]

These Polish-Prussian conflicts formed the backdrop for the life of Paulus Vladimiri. Born about 1370 in a northern province of Poland, the young Vladimiri was well aware of the activities of the Teutonic Knights. Indeed, his native district of Dobrzyń was the target of frequent raids by the Order. Between the late 1380's and 1410 Vladimiri studied the arts and law at the University of Prague and canon law at the University of Padua. His main professor in Padua was the learned canonist, Francis Cardinal Zabarella. In 1410 Vladimiri returned to his native Poland, where he began to teach canon law at the University of Cracow. During the succeeding decade Vladimiri devoted major attention to problems of international diplomacy and particularly to a series of territorial disputes between Poland and Lithuania. He served as the legal adviser to the Polish delegation at an arbitration proceeding in Buda in 1412 and, as a member of the Polish delegation at the Council of Constance, gradually emerged as the leading proponent of the Polish point of view (Belch, 1965: 115-139).

The two works in which Vladimiri most clearly worked out the theoretical foundations of his just war views were both written in 1415, while he was attending the Council of Constance. The longer treatise was entitled "On the Power of the Pope and the Emperor with respect to Infidels" (hereinafter cited as *De potestate*). The shorter work, a memorandum entitled "The Opinion of Hostiensis" (*Opinio Hostiensis*) summarized the context of the *De potestate* in terms of 52 "conclusions" (Belch, 1965: 164-165). In the following paragraphs we shall briefly note the major emphases of the longer treatise.

Vladimiri's *De potestate* employed two distinct modes of argumentation, the one historical or descriptive, the other more theoretical and normative. In the introductory section of the work, Vladimiri provided a historical review of the relationships among the Poles, infidels, and Teutonic Knights. According to him, the Knights had originally been admitted to Poland by the Polish princes for a definite and limited end, namely, to help the Poles resist the attacks of the savage Pruthenians (Prussians) and other infidels. However, when the Pruthenians had been successfully subjugated, the Knights remained, took possession of Prussia, and created there a powerful state.

In Vladimiri's view, this unnecessary consolidation of power by the Order led to a series of further abuses. The Order regularly attacked the neighboring, peaceful tribes of infidels, particularly on the twice-yearly feasts of the Blessed Virgin. Despite the conversion of the Lithuanians to Christianity in 1386, the Knights did not cease their acts of aggression. Indeed, the Friars attacked the neophytes with greater ferocity than before. Finally, the Order turned against its original benefactor, Poland, and by force of arms seized large tracts of Polish territory (Belch, 1965: 781).

Vladimiri devoted the second section of the *De potestate* to a more theoretical analysis of three pivotal issues: the authority of the Pope, the authority of the Emperor, and Hostiensis' views on the relations between infidels and Christians. On the first point, Vladimiri argued that the Pope "has jurisdiction over all men, but his authority is that of a loving father whose function is to maintain justice and order and not to injure his children" (Belch, 1965: 782). In Vladimiri's view, the Pope had power to punish infidels for committing crimes against the natural law, but *only* for such crimes. Consequently, he maintained that the Supreme Pontiff could deprive infidels of their kingdoms only if the infidels had gained possession of those territories through violating the law of nations. According to Vladimiri, the Saracens had unjustly seized Christian territory in the Holy Land; thus the Middle-Eastern Crusades were justifiable military actions. In contrast, the pagan Prussians had been lawful possessors of their own lands.

On the second issue, the power of the Emperor, Vladimiri flatly denied that the Emperor had any special jurisdiction over infidels, unless such authority had been explicitly given to him for a legitimate reason by the Pope. The clear implication of Vladimiri's argument was that Emperor Frederick II's grant to the Teutonic Knights lacked the slightest vestige of legal validity.

Finally, Vladimiri directly confronted the opinion of Hostiensis, an influential thirteenth century canon lawyer and a contemporary of Thomas Aquinas. According to Hostiensis, since Christ had transferred all power and authority to Peter and his successors, pagan possession of any territory or property, unless the possessors were subject to Christians, was *ipso facto* unjust. It thus followed that, for Hostiensis, the mere unbelief of infidels was a sufficient cause for war, and a Christian military campaign against pagans was by definition a just war. Against this opinion, Vladimiri posed the authority of Innocent IV and Thomas Aquinas, who had conceded to infidels a natural law realm of legitimate dominion over both property and fellow infidels (Belch, 1965: 783-786).

Within a year, four known polemical replies to Vladimiri's views had been penned. In turn, Vladimiri launched literary counterattacks on the most influential critiques of his own writings. We shall not here attempt to pursue in detail this complex chain of thesis and antithesis. Rather, we shall briefly examine the most cogently argued response to Vladimiri's position, namely, the "Treatise concerning the Status of the Teutonic Order of the Blessed Virgin Mary and Their Battles against the Infidels" (hereinafter cited as *Tractatus*), written in 1416 by Ioannis Vrebach de Bamberga (Belch, 1965: 886-887).[3]

Descriptively, Vrebach's *Tractatus* assumed that Lithuania was still pagan and that the pagan Lithuanians continued to commit crimes which deserved the punishment of war. For his normative position, Vrebach relied upon Hostiensis' view that infidels have no right to political independence. Explicitly contradicting Vladimiri, he argued that the infidels were not the sheep of Christ but were, instead, beast-like. The twentieth century historian Stanislaus Belch summarizes Vrebach's thesis in the following words: "Their mere non-recognition of imperial power makes them rebels and persecutors of the Church, of the empire and of Christians. Hence war against infidels is always just, particularly in the case of the Teutonic Order where war is authorized by papal and imperial privileges and universally recognized as just. To oppose the fulfillment of the Order's mission is, therefore, to oppose the Church. On this same ground Christian princes cannot enter into any alliance with such rebels" (Belch, 1965: 1113).

Several aspects of the dispute between Vladimiri and his opponents deserve comment. In the first place, it is clear that divergent descriptions of historical events underlay the theorists' differing normative judgments concerning the Polish-Prussian conflict. To cite one example, Vladimiri and Vrebach disagreed markedly in their answers to the factual question: Are the

Lithuanians pagans or converts to Christianity? A second factor compounded this disagreement: Vladimiri and his opponent Vrebach subscribed to competing versions of the just war theory. A war which seemed, according to Hostiensis' just war thought, to be morally justifiable was condemned by Vladimiri on the basis of arguments developed by two other authoritative just war theorists, Innocent IV and Thomas Aquinas.

This first case study also provides initial data concerning several other questions raised in the introductory section of the essay. In this case political and religious factors seem to have been closely intertwined. Vrebach, at least, was not hesitant to call a religious war a just war. Second, while the question of means in warfare was present in the theorists' writings—particularly in Vladimiri's complaint about the ferocity of the Teutonic Knights—the primary emphasis fell on the questions of just cause and legitimate authority for war. Finally, both Vladimiri and his opponents employed the just war theory to justify the actions of the sides which they supported; the only restraints proposed were directed toward the actions of the opposing side.

II

The first half of the sixteenth century constituted Spain's "Golden Age." A significant aspect of Spanish supremacy was the activity of its explorers in the New World. Shortly after Columbus' well-known voyages to North America, the *conquistadores* undertook journeys to Central and South America. Between 1519 and 1521 Hernán Cortés gained ascendancy over the Aztecs in Mexico. Later, other *conquistadores* led numerous expeditions to the interior of present day South America.

The Spanish conquest of Peru seems to have provided the immediate context for Vitoria's thought on justice in warfare against the Indians. In the early 1530's Pizarro—accompanied by one of Vitoria's former pupils, Vincente Valverde—led a group of adventurers into the mountain kingdom of the Incas. The most decisive incident of the campaign involved Pizarro's band and the Inca monarch, Atahualpa. Initially, Atahualpa extended, and the Spaniards accepted, generous hospitality. However, Pizarro and his followers soon changed tactics. Under the guise of holding a formal conference with Atahualpa, the Spaniards seized him by force and launched a surprise attack on his followers. William H. Prescott, in his epic nineteenth century history of the Peruvian conquest, described the ensuing massacre as follows:

> Pizarro saw that the hour had come. He waved a white scarf in the air, the appointed signal. The fatal gun was fired from the fortress. Then springing into the square, the Spanish captain and his followers shouted the old war-cry of "St. Jago [Santiago] and at them!" It was answered by the battle-cry of every Spaniard in the city, as, rushing from the avenues of the great halls in which they were concealed, they poured into the *plaza*, horse and foot, each in his own dark column, and threw themselves into the midst of the Indian

> crowd. The latter, taken by surprise, stunned by the report of artillery and muskets, the echoes of which reverberated like thunder from the surrounding buildings, and blinded by the smoke which rolled in sulphurous volumes along the squares, were seized with a panic. They knew not whither to fly for refuge from the coming ruin. Nobles and commoners—all were trampled down under the fierce charge of the cavalry, who dealt their blows right and left, without sparing; while their swords, flashing through the thick gloom, carried dismay into the wretched natives, who now, for the first time, saw the horse and his rider in all their terrors. They made no resistance—as indeed they had no weapons with which to make it. Every avenue to escape was closed, for the entrance to the square was choked up with the bodies of men who had perished in vain efforts to fly; and such was the agony of the survivors under the terrible pressure of their assailants, that a large body of Indians, by their convulsive struggles, burst through the wall of stone and dried clay which formed part of the boundary of the plaza! It fell, leaving an opening of more than a hundred paces, through which multitudes now found their way into the country, still hotly pursued by the cavalry, who, leaping the fallen rubbish, hung on the rear of the fugitives, striking them down in all directions (Prescott, 1847: I, 381-382).

Having taken Atahualpa prisoner, the Spaniards demanded a huge ransom in gold for his release. The required ransom was duly collected by Atahualpa's agents. The Spaniards, however, fearing the king's influence on the Incas, accepted the ransom but defaulted on their promise: they sentenced Atahualpa to death for his alleged crimes. At the insistent urging of Valverde, the chaplain of Pizarro's group, Atahualpa was converted to Christianity moments before he was scheduled to be burned alive. In response, the Spaniards graciously changed the mode of his execution from burning to strangulation (Prescott, 1847: I, 437-447).

Vitoria, born in Burgos about 1492, was educated at the Dominican convent San Pablo de Burgos and later in Paris at the Dominican College of St. James and the University of Paris. In 1523 he returned to his native Spain, where he began teaching theology at the College of St. Gregory in Valladolid. Three years later, he accepted a prima professorship at the University of Salamanca. There he was to remain from 1526 until the end of his distinguished career in 1546.

It was only rather late in life that Vitoria turned his scholarly attention to the question of Spanish conquests in the New World. Although his first teaching position had been in Valladolid, seat of the Council of the Indies, Vitoria seems not to have discussed the Indian's plight in his early lectures. During the mid-1530's, however, one finds scattered traces of his interest in the Indians. In a letter dated November 8, 1534, he noted that mention of recent events in the Indies, particularly in Peru, "makes my blood run cold" (Scott, 1934: 78-82). The following year Vitoria presented a lecture entitled "On the Obligation to Be Converted When One First Attains the Use of Reason." Basing his address on Thomas Aquinas' discussion of unbelief in the *Summa Theologiae*, II-II, question 10, Vitoria sought to determine what, if anything, pagan barbarians were bound to believe in order to be saved. Later in 1535 Vitoria's lectures on the secunda secundae of the *Summa* occasionally touched on the Indians, sometimes even mentioning them by name.

The year 1536 seems to have marked a decisive watershed in Vitoria's thinking and writing about the Indians. One modern scholar attributes this change to a first-hand report delivered to Vitoria by his former pupil, Valverde. As we have noted, Valverde had earlier accompanied Pizarro to Peru and had participated with some enthusiasm in the campaign against the Incas. Back in Spain for a short period, he seems to have provided his former teacher with a detailed account of the Peruvian conquest (Hoffner, 1947: 190-191). Whatever the reason, during the years 1537-1539 Vitoria's comments on the Spanish conquest became much more direct and pointed. In 1537 or 1538 he announced a lecture inoffensively entitled "On Temperance." When the lecture was actually given, it included a stinging attack on many of the theoretical foundations for Spanish colonialism. Frightened by the uproar occasioned by his lecture, Vitoria carefully sought to gather and destroy all manuscript copies of his lecture (Beltran de Heredia, 1967: XXVI). A year or two later, however, Vitoria publicly presented his major work on the Indian question, the lecture entitled "On the Indies" (hereinafter cited as *De Indis*).

In this tripartite work Vitoria concentrated primary attention upon the question of just causes for war against the aborigines. The first part of *De Indis* sought to establish that the Latin American aborigines were true owners of their own lands and possessions before the arrival of the Spaniards. According to Vitoria, there were only three grounds on which such Indian ownership could have been denied, namely, that the Indians "were sinners or were unbelievers or were witless or irrational" (*De Indis*: I, 4).[4] After having denied that mortal sin effaces the image of God in man, Vitoria also attacked the thesis that unbelief invalidates ownership. Like Vladimiri, Vitoria based his refutation squarely on Thomas Aquinas' view that unbelief alone does not destroy the natural law basis of legitimate ownership. As for the third argument, Vitoria noted that, far from being witless or irrational, the Indians had "polities which are orderly arranged and they have definite marriage and magistrates, overlords, laws, and workshops, and a system of exchange, all of which call for the use of reason; they also have a kind of religion" (*De Indis*: I, 23).

In Part II of *De Indis* Vitoria turned to an analysis of illegitimate titles, or unjust causes, for Spanish military action against the Indians. Like Vladimiri, he denied that the Emperor or the Pope possessed sufficient temporal power to grant Indian territories to the Spaniards. In a bold departure from tradition, Vitoria also sought to refute an opinion of Innocent IV, namely, that the Pope could punish unbelievers for sins against the natural law. Vitoria seemed to acknowledge that sins against nature occurred among the aborigines, e.g., "cannibalism, and promiscuous intercourse with mothers or sisters and with males" (*De Indis*: II, 15). However, he argued that the Pope lacked jurisdiction to punish infidels for such offenses.

The concluding section of Vitoria's *De Indis* listed eight potentially legitimate grounds, or just causes, for war against the aborigines. Among these, four were of primary significance: (1) the denial to the Spaniards of the right of innocent passage through Indian territory, (2) the harassment of Christian missionaries, (3) the persecution of Indian converts to Christianity, and (4) the killing of innocent persons in religious rites or for cannibalistic purposes. Throughout this section of his lecture, Vitoria repeatedly emphasized that even if a just cause for war existed, the war should be waged moderately, with a proper regard for proportionality, and "with an intent directed more to the welfare of the aborigines than to [the Spanish wariors'] own gain" (*De Indis*: III, 12).

A summary of Vitoria's treatise inevitably fails to capture the liveliness of his style and the acuity of his perception. For example, he ventured the psychological observation that the Latin American Indians, far from being malevolent, might be genuinely terrified by the Spaniards. As he put it, "It is . . . to be noted that the natives being timid by nature and in other respects dull and stupid, however much the Spaniards may desire to remove their fears and reassure them with regard to peaceful dealings with each other, they may very excusably continue afraid at the sight of men strange in garb and armed and much more powerful than themselves" (*De Indis*: III, 6). Vitoria was also rather forthright in criticizing alleged Spanish excesses in the New World conquests. Without denying that the wars had been "carried on by men who are alike well-informed and upright," he nonetheless noted that "we hear of so many massacres, so many plunderings of otherwise innocent men, so many princes evicted from their possessions and stripped of their rule" (*De Indis*: I, 3).

Several general comments can be appended concerning this second case study. Vitoria's extended discussion of the just-cause question suggests that, on this issue at least, there existed even in the sixteenth century a plurality of just war *theories*. The rival theories against which Vladimiri had protested so vigorously a century earlier seem to have continued as live options in Vitoria's day. Thus Vitoria, too, found it necessary to deny that papal or imperial grants or mere unbelief constituted sufficient grounds for just war. In addition, Vitoria's apologia for the rationality of the Indians seems to have been directed against a neo-Aristotelian variation of just war thought which saw in the New World aborigines a modern example of "natural slaves."[5]

We have noted that the writings of both Vladimiri and his opponents tended to justify the wars waged by their own sides. It seems clear that Vitoria's treatise was composed with two purposes in mind, the one *restrictive*, the other *apologetic*. When he denied certain grounds for war and criticized the conduct of his Spanish countrymen, Vitoria sought to restrain the violence of warfare. On the other hand, Vitoria accepted the legitimacy of eight grounds for warfare against the Indians, thus seeming to justify, at least in general terms, Spanish foreign policy in Latin America.

There are other parallels between the works of Vladimiri and Vitoria which should be mentioned in passing. Both writers confronted military conflicts in which religious and political motives were curiously mixed. Generally speaking, Vladimiri sought to downplay the religious factor in the Polish-Prussian war; Vitoria, on the other hand, expressly accepted several carefully circumscribed religious grounds for just war. A further parallel is that one sees mirrored in the writings of each author a clash at the frontiers of Christendom, in one case at the borders of northeastern Europe, in the other, across the seas in Latin America. In both instances the just war theorists sought to protect real or alleged unbelievers from the military excesses of Christian imperialism.

III

The first phase (1566-1609) of the struggle between Spain and the Low Countries forms the backdrop for our third case study. The major events in this prolonged and highly complicated conflict can be summarized as follows. Through dynastic succession the seventeen provinces of the Low Countries (present-day Belgium, Luxemburg, and the Netherlands) had come under the rule of Emperor Philip II of Spain. Philip, a zealous defender of the Catholic faith, sought to assert his political authority over the provinces as well as to counter the growing influence of Protestantism there. To accomplish the latter end, he demanded that the local magistrates and nobles introduce the Inquisition into the Low Countries.

Some of the more militant nobles in the Low Countries—particularly in the northern provinces—resisted Philip's order and appealed to his regent for religious toleration. Simultaneously, a grass roots iconoclastic movement broke out. Spurred on by Calvinist and radical Reformation preachers, the movement gradually spread to numerous areas of the Netherlands. Images, church windows, and pictures were smashed, and books and manuscripts were destroyed. Philip responded in 1567 by sending his best general, the Duke of Alva, and 10,000 troops to the Low Countries. Alva sought to suppress the rebellion by force; during several years of occupation 8,000 suspected heretics were executed. Despite these stern measures and an impressive series of military victories, Alva was unable to pacify the Low Countries.

A second wave of military action began in 1576 with the so-called "Spanish Fury." A group of Spanish occupation forces in Antwerp, bitter because they had not been paid, mutinied. During a period of several days they seized local property, set fire to public buildings, raped women, and killed between six and seven thousand citizens. Outraged by this incident, the Low Country provinces united, at least temporarily, against the authority of Spain. Philip II responded by sending Alessandro Farnese of Parma to the Low Countries with 20,000 troops. In 1578 Parma was appointed governor-general of the Low Countries.

The Dutch-Spanish conflict was to drag on for almost three decades.

Through a combination of diplomacy and military force Parma was able to recover the southern, predominantly Catholic, provinces (present-day Belgium and Luxemburg) for the Spanish Crown. The Protestant northern provinces, however, declared their independence from Spain in 1581 and resisted Parma's armies. They received assistance in the mid-1580's from Queen Elizabeth I of England, who, eager to weaken her Spanish archenemy in any way possible, sent Robert Dudley, Earl of Leicester, and a contingent of 6,000 troops to their aid. By the mid-1590's the eventual independence of the northern provinces (the present-day Netherlands) seemed assured (Koenigsberger, 1968: 264-281, 297-301).

The struggle between Spain and the Low Countries was explicitly commented on by no fewer than three major sixteenth and seventeenth century just war theorists. The three theorists—Ayala, Gentili, and Grotius—expressed their viewpoints on the war in works written in 1581, 1598, and 1604-1606, respectively. After reviewing the careers of these three theorists, we shall examine how each of the three applied just war categories to the Dutch-Spanish conflict.

Balthasar Ayala (1548-1584) was born in Antwerp to noble parents. His father, a native of Burgos in Spain, had obtained citizenship rights in Antwerp in 1531-1532. Ayala, after having received his licentiate in law from the University of Louvain, was appointed in 1580 to the prestigious post of auditor-general to the Spanish army of the Netherlands. In this position Ayala served as military judge and judicial adviser to Philip II's governor-general, Alessandro Farnese of Parma, and accompanied him on his military campaigns in the Low Countries. Ayala's major work on the just war, *On the Law and the Duties Connected with War and on Military Discipline*, written in 1581 while he was auditor-general, was dedicated to the governor-general (Westlake, 1912: I, ii-vii).

Alberico Gentili (1552-1608) was born in San Ginesio, Italy. After completing studies for a doctorate in law at the University of Perugia in 1572, he served as praetor and municipal lawyer in Ascoli and San Ginesio for several years. In 1579, however, Gentili and his father, both Reformed Protestants, found it necessary to flee Italy in order to escape the Inquisition. Gentili made his new home in England, where he taught civil law at Oxford, first as a tutor, and later, beginning in 1587, as Regius Professor. Gentili's work on war, *On the Law of War*, was initiated in 1588, shortly after Queen Elizabeth had sent military aid to the Low Countries and immediately prior to the anticipated attack on England by the Spanish Armada. Gentili dedicated the completed work to his countryman Robert Devereux, second Earl of Essex, who had accompanied English forces to the Netherlands in 1585-1586 and had served as general of the cavalry during the attack of the Spanish Armada (Holland, 1898: 1-19; Van der Molen, 1968: 35-60).

The third theorist, Hugo Grotius, was born at Delft in the province of Holland in 1583. A precocious child, Grotius pursued studies in philology, history, law, and theology at the University of Leyden from 1594 to 1597. One year later, at the age of fifteen, he completed his doctorate in law at the University of Orleans in France.

The years 1599 to 1613 mark the first phase of Grotius' long and varied career. After spending several years in a private law practice in the Hague, Grotius assumed public office in 1607 as Attorney General (*Advokaet Fiscael*) to the provinces of Holland, Zeeland, and West Friesland. He was to hold this post until 1613. During the same period Grotius produced two works of importance to our study. Appointed official historiographer of Holland in 1601, he worked between 1601 and 1612 on a major chronicle entitled *The History of the Netherlands, 1560-1609.*[6] In this work Grotius described in detail the prolonged struggle between the Spaniards and the Low Countries. Between 1604 and 1606 Grotius penned his first major work on international law, *On the Law of Prize* (hereinafter cited as *De jure praedae*). In this treatise Grotius formulated a systematic restatement of the just war theory and sought to show its relevance to recent historical events.[7] Although the primary focus of *De jure praedae* was the Dutch-Portuguese conflict in the East Indies (see Part IV below), Grotius also drew upon his research on the history of the Netherlands to comment on the Dutch-Spanish war (Vreeland, 1917: *passim*; Van Eysinga, 1952: *passim*).

Given the divergent political contexts of our three theorists, it is perhaps not surprising that they viewed the struggle between Spain and the Low Countries from distinctive angles of vision. To Ayala, the upheaval in the Netherlands was an affront both to the authority of God and to the legitimate rule of the Spanish Emperor. In the dedicatory letter of *De jure et officiis bellicis* he wrote to the governor-general, the Prince of Parma:

> It is our hope, Most Serene Prince, that . . . your surpassing valor and wonderful skill and foresight in affairs may lead to the restoration of the worship of the true God and to the restoration of the sovereign authority of the king (due to him both by divine and human law), and that so the subversion of all things human and divine which has been brought into the Low Countries may by God's aid be checked and at last ended, and that the whole of the Low Countries may be restored to their former happy estate (*De jure et officiis bellicis*: dedication).

In the chapter of his work entitled "Of Just War and Just Causes of War" Ayala spelled out in some detail a theoretical position on the problem of civil rebellion. He was at pains to deny both that revolution was morally legitimate and that military action against rebellious subjects was "war" in the technical sense. Indeed, he argued that the laws of war did not, strictly speaking, apply to the suppression of insurrections. It seems clear that the Dutch-Spanish conflict was foremost in his thinking as he wrote:

> And then a prince has a most just cause of war when he is directing his arms against rebels and subjects who abjure his sovereignty; for it is a heinous offense, against both God and the prince, for subjects to resist his authority, all power being from God above; and St. Paul tells us "whosoever resisteth the power, resisteth the ordinance of God" . . .

> Now rebels ought not to be classed as enemies, the two being quite distinct, and so it is more correct to term the armed contention with rebel subjects execution of legal process, or prosecution, and not war. . . .
>
> For the same reason, the laws of war and of captivity and of postliminy, which apply to enemies, do not apply to rebels, any more than they apply to pirates and robbers (these not being included in the term "enemy" [hostes]). . . . But all the modes of stress known to the laws of war may be employed against them, even more than in the case of enemies, for the rebel and the robber merit severer reprobation than an enemy who is carrying on a regular and just war, and their condition ought not to be better than his (*De jure et officiis bellicis*: I, 2, 12-15).

For Alberico Gentili the major question concerning the Dutch-Spanish war was whether Queen Elizabeth had been morally justified in lending military assistance to the Dutch. Within the section of *De jure belli* which discussed legitimate causes of war, Gentili devoted an entire chapter to the topic "On Defending the Subjects of Another against Their Sovereign." Gentili argued that such intervention was in principle justifiable. To illustrate his thesis, he cited a contemporary example: "Consider what is just now a burning question, namely, whether the English did right in aiding the Belgians against the Spaniards, even if the cause of the Belgians was unjust and although the Belgians are even now subjects of Spain; both of which statements, however, are considered false" (*De jure belli*: I, 16).

Gentili listed no fewer than eight arguments in favor of English intervention against Spain in the Low Countries. His concluding argument praised the foresight of Robert Dudley, the Earl of Leicester, who had led the contingent of English troops sent to the Netherlands by Queen Elizabeth:

> If my neighbor should collect engines of war in his home and make other preparations directed against my home, should I not be afraid and should I not take steps against my neighbor? It was just in that way that the Belgians made preparations, as wise men have seen, and the great hero Leicester wisely realized that the defence of the Belgians was most expedient and necessary for his own country, and recommended that it be undertaken; for fear that if that bulwark of Europe . . . should be broken down by the Spaniards, nothing would be left as a bar against their violence (*De jure belli*: I, 16).

Grotius, the historiographer of Holland, was thoroughly familiar with the major events in the Dutch-Spanish wars. When he placed these events into the framework of his just war thought, the resulting construct differed radically from Ayala's perception of the same period and diverged (to a lesser extent) from Gentili's perspective as well. In Grotius' view, the Dutch-Spanish struggle was a contest between a venerable, independent nation—the Netherlands—and a conditionally appointed ruler, Philip II, who had repeatedly and deliberately violated the terms of his contract with that nation. The following passage from Grotius' *De jure praedae* argues that the Spanish lacked a just cause for war and that the Dutch campaign against Alva and his successors (presumably including Parma) was a war of legitimate self-defense. In addition, Grotius explicitly criticized Ayala's views concerning appropriate military conduct vis-a-vis rebels and heretics.

. . . Who is ignorant of the fact that the Dutch have now been at war with the Spanish nation for thirty long years, and more? And who does not know that this conflict was begun when Fernando, Duke of Alba [Alva], penetrated with a Spanish army into the then peaceful territory of the Low Countries, after he had been sent out as governor of that region by Philip the Second, King of the Spanish realms and sovereign of the said countries?

Relying confidently upon his armed force, and with no pretext other than the occurrence, prior to his arrival, of a disturbance connected with religious questions (a disturbance for which only a very small number of individuals were to blame, as is acknowledged even by those persons who wish to establish the fact that guilt did exist, since the incident took place against the will of the majority of both magistrates and citizens), Alba proceeded to alter the laws, judicial provisions, and system of taxation. He took these measures in contravention of the statutes which the various princes had sworn to observe and which, by striking a rare balance between princely power and liberty, were preserving both the due measure of imperial sovereignty and the foundations of the local state.

The exigencies created by Alba's conduct drove private citizens, first of all, to set in motion a force whereby they might repel force: for their bodies were being dragged away to punishment, their goods were being seized either for the imperial treasury or for payment of tribute in defiance of the domestic laws above mentioned, and they were cut off from every other means of defence. Next, separate municipalities adopted a similar course of action. Shortly thereafter, the States Assembly of Holland (which had been a true commonwealth for all of seven centuries) added its authority to the movement. . . . Gathered in public assembly, it decreed war against Alba and the Spaniards; and this war, in which other peoples of the Low Countries joined, was continued against the successors of Alba, also, since those successors demanded all that Alba had demanded and penalties for the defensive activities, as well.

It would be too long a story, if we attempted to tell what quantities of blood have been shed from that time on; what plundering on the part of the Spaniards and what expenditures on the opposite side have drained the resources of the Low Countries (expenses so heavy, in fact, that an accurate reckoning would show them to be in excess of those borne by any other people in any age); or, finally, what perfidy characterized the Spaniards whether in the conduct of war or in the simulation of peace. These things can be inferred well enough from the following facts: the Spanish designate as 'heretics' all persons who dissent from the See of Rome in regard to any interpretation of Holy Writ or any accepted religious rite, and as 'rebels' all persons whatsoever not of the opinion that princes should invariably and without exception be obeyed; and at the same time, rejecting every argument in favour of conciliation or clemency, they openly declare that there is no fellowship of good faith[a] to be observed with heretics or rebels (*De jure praedae*: XI).

[a]See Ayala, I. vi. 11.

Unlike the previous two case studies, which dealt with wars on the frontiers of Christendom, this third case study concerns a military conflict in the midst of Christian Europe. Once again political and religious considerations were intertwined. To Ayala the heresy of the Dutch was a significant aspect of their rebellion; Gentili and Grotius, on the other hand, laid primary emphasis upon political factors and sought to minimize the religious element of the conflict.

In our first case study we noted that Vladimiri and his opponents disagreed in their description of past historical events. Similar discrepancies occur in this case. To Ayala it appeared that a "subversion of all things human and divine" had erupted in the Low Countries. Grotius — referring, to be sure, to an earlier stage of the conflict — emphasized the limited character of the "disturbance" and the competence of the local magistrates to take appropriate remedial action. In addition, however, there is in the case study a more fundamental problem, which we might call a difference of *categorization* rather than a difference of *description*. The theorists disagreed on whether the Dutch-Spanish conflict qualified as a "war" in the strict sense of the term. Grotius, emphasizing the traditional independence of the Low Countries, argued that the conflict was indeed a war. Ayala, on the other hand, preferred to subsume the Dutch-Spanish struggle under the rubric "rebellion" — or in modern parlance, "revolution" — rather than to concede any semblance of sovereign status to the subjects of the Spanish Crown.

In their comments on the Dutch-Spanish conflict the three theorists discussed the traditional just war criteria of authority, cause, and means. Each of the theorists employed one or more of the criteria in *apologetic* fashion. To cite three examples, Grotius argued that the States Assembly of Holand possessed full authority to wage war. According to Gentili, there was just cause for England to intervene on behalf of the Low Countries in their warfare with Spain. In Ayala's view the customary code of military conduct could be suspended in a campaign against rebels. In addition, one finds in Grotius an interesting twist which related means to cause in an apologetic argument. Grotius seems to have argued that Spanish excesses in the conduct of war (*jus in bello*) constituted a just cause (*jus ad bellum*) for military counter-action by the Dutch.

Even in these theorists of the late sixteenth and early seventeenth centuries, one finds some evidence for the continuing existence of competing just war theories. The writings of Ayala suggest that he considered heresy to be a just cause for war; Gentili, a religious refugee, and Grotius, a Dutch Protestant, did not share Ayala's view.[8] There was also an apparent disagreement between Ayala and Grotius on the quesion of keeping faith with one's military adversaries.

IV

In 1497 Vasco de Gama of Portugal sailed around the southern tip of Africa in search of India. During the century which followed Portuguese adventurers and traders traveled to the east in relatively large numbers. The East-West commerce prospered, and by the close of the sixteenth century there existed a widespread network of Portuguese trading centers in present-day India, Iran, Sri Lanka, Malaysia, and Indonesia — the so-called *Estado da India*. For much of the century the Portuguese enjoyed a virtual monopoly on commerce between the East and Europe (Harrison, 1970: 644-646).

In 1596 the *status quo* was threatened by the appearance of Dutch ships in Asian waters. In earlier years Dutch traders had taken on Eastern products in the Portuguese port of Lisbon and had distributed them throughout northern Europe. This trade ceased when Philip II of Spain, who had recently annexed Portugal, seized all Dutch shipping in Portuguese ports. Deprived of their traditional source of products, the Dutch sought to establish new commercial contacts in the East.

Predictably, a period of conflict followed. The Portuguese, both directly and indirectly through their Asian trading partners, sought to exclude the Dutch. For their part, the Dutch joined an attack by the Amboinese on the Portuguese. More significantly, in 1602 the Dutch traders organized themselves into a private corporation, the Dutch East India Company, which sought to give teeth to their demand for freedom of the seas (Harrison, 1970: 646-647).

In the year 1604 a Dutch admiral, Jacob van Heemskerck, annoyed at continuing harassment by the Portuguese, seized a richly-laden Portuguese trading vessel, the *Catharina*, claiming it as a prize. When this decisive action was upheld by the Dutch College of Admiralty, the captured booty was sold, the profits being distributed among the Admiral and the members of the Dutch East India Company (Fruin, 1925: 8-32).

The admiral's seizure had serious repercussions in Holland. Orthodox Calvinists generally approved the capture, but some shareholders in the East India Company declined to accept their share of the profits, preferring instead to give them to the poor. Other shareholders, especially the Mennonites and a pacifistic group of Remonstrants, went a step further. They sold their shares and retired from the Company, arguing that it had ceased functioning as a commercial enterprise and had become, instead, a military organization. A twentieth century Dutch historian describes the protest of one shareholder as follows:

> Among the grave Mennonites who did not want to enrich themselves with the booty-money was the chief of a great commercial house at Amsterdam, Pieter Lÿntgens. He had invested more than a ton of gold in the Company, but now that it took to privateering he sold his shares like others of his persuasion. Not content, however, with retiring from the Company as the others and to give up profit for the sake of conscience, he made a plan to found a company for exclusively peaceable trade with the Indies, of which he was to be one of the directors (Fruin, 1925:33-34).

Faced with such defections and the prospect of a commercial rival, the Dutch East India Company quickly retained a twenty-one year old lawyer, Hugo Grotius, to defend the practice of capturing enemy goods. In his role as a sort of "public relations counselor" (Dumbauld, 1969: 25) Grotius sought to demonstrate, on the one hand, that the Dutch seizure of the *Catharina* was morally justified because of previous crimes perpetrated by the Portuguese, and on the other, that neither the NT nor the norms of Christian ethics prohibited such military action. Grotius' brief for the East India Company—and, simultaneously, his first major work on international law—was entitled *On the Law of Prize (De jure Praedae)* (Fruin, 1925:35-46; Van Eysinga, 1952:24-25).[9]

Grotius' most sustained discussion of specific historical events was contained in three chapters of *De jure praedae*. In an extended historical narrative (Chapter XI) Grotius touched upon the Dutch-Spanish conflict (see above, Part III), then detailed numerous offenses of the Portuguese against the Dutch. The two succeeding chapters related the foregoing historical data to traditional just war categories in an effort to demonstrate that the cause of the Dutch war against the Portuguese had been just, whether the war was conceived as a private war between trading companies (Chapter XII) or as a public war between sovereign nations (Chapter XIII).

It is difficult adequately to convey the sense of moral outrage expressed in Grotius' historical narrative. On page after page—for more than forty pages in the Classics of International Law translation—Grotius enumerated Portuguese injustice against the Dutch, often basing his chronicle on first-person accounts or ships' diaries. Two examples must suffice to illustrate Grotius' accusations against Portugal. Grotius noted that there had been a long history of peaceful commerce between Portugal and the Low Countries. According to him, none of the Dutch traders supposed that Philip II's annexation of Portugal would lead to any change in this tradition of international cooperation. Thus, Dutch ships continued to take on goods in Portuguese ports. However, in a sudden, unilateral aciton, Grotius complained, Philip II had broken the "tacit covenant" between the Low Countries and Portugal. In Grotius' words, ". . . when the abundance of merchandise accumulated was adjudged sufficient to make despoliation worthwhile, every one of those ships (the property of entirely unsuspecting persons), was seized, in all Iberian ports and particularly in those of Portugal. Subsequently, the Dutch were compelled to pay the highest conceivable price in order to redeem the vessels seized" (*De jure praedae*: XI).

Grotius' indictment was not confined to the European scene or to the origins of the Dutch-Portuguese conflict. He also accused the Portuguese of atrocious and perfidious conduct in the East Indian phase of the war.

> Six [Dutch sailors], beholding the disaster that had overtaken their comrades [in a sea-battle in the East Indies] and the blood that had been shed on land and sea, took flight in a small boat. . . . The Portuguese, however, called out to these men that they should give themselves up, that the revenge was complete, that their lives and bodies would be safe. An oath was sworn; but an oath is for the Portuguese an instrument for deception as truly as it is for other men a bond of security. When the Dutchmen had been transferred to a small caracore (which is a kind of boat quite common in those regions), a Portuguese officer ordered that they should be drawn up in a row; then, addressing a subordinate who was holding an unsheathed sword in his hand, this officer said: 'Cut off the right arm of the man who is first in line,' to which he added, 'Now cut off his left arm.' The commands were obeyed and in such a manner, indeed, that one might have doubted which was the more barbarous, the person issuing the orders or the person who obeyed them. Moreover, the officer next ordered that the victim's feet should be severed with separate strokes. The

> other captives, whom the same torments awaited, were standing by, more eager for death than they had ever been for life. Yet, as these examples were set before them, one after another, their emotion changed from fear to a mutual compassion. The trunks could be seen surviving their own mutilation and —worst of ills!—deprived of human likeness. Nevertheless, the perpetrators of the deed were much further removed from every semblance of humanity! Lastly, the heads were cut off. Two of the captives, however, were so spirited that they leaped still unharmed into the sea before their turn came at the hands of the swordsman. One of these two was drowned; the other escaped, and bore witness to that most abominable spectacle (*De jure praedae*:XI).

In the just war analysis which followed his historical review, Grotius sought to demonstrate how selected features of the Dutch-Portuguese conflict were related to traditional emphases of the just war tradition. His argument drew upon an empressive list of authorities, and his conclusions and deductions followed from the general principles and descriptive data in almost geometric fashion. At the conclusion of the analysis Grotius summarized his findings in a few terse lines:

> Having thoroughly examined these quesitons, we conclude that the war in which the Portuguese carack and its cargo were captured was just in every respect, not merely for our government but much more so for the East India Company, regardless of whether that war was public or private, and of whether—assuming that it was public—it was waged on behalf of the fatherland or on behalf of allies; and we furthermore conclude that the Company itself become the owner of the above-mentioned prize, from the standpoint of all law (*De jure praedae*:XIII).

Like the first two case studies, this fourth case study concerns a frontier situation. However, the primary conflict in the Dutch-Portuguese war was not between Christians and pagans but rather between professedly Christian nations of different confessions. Thus, this case bears at least a partial resemblance to the third case study as well.

So far as the present author has been able to determine, no other just war theorist has provided us with an alternative account or analysis of the dispute between Portugal and the Low Countries. In this respect, therefore, the fourth case study differs from the first and third examples, where we have examined competing assessments of particular wars, and the second case study, where Vitoria reviewed rival just war arguments at some length.

In our previous case studies we have noted that just war thought can be employed in either an apologetic or a restrictive way. With respect to the Dutch cause Grotius' approach was exclusively apologetic. Indeed, Grotius' writings reveal that, in its apologetic use, the just war theory could be directed either against pacifism or against the claim that one's own side was waging war unjustly.

Once again in this case one sees that the questions of cause and means, or *jus ad bellum* and *jus in bello*, were curiously intertwined. By means of historical narrative and logical analysis Grotius sought to demonstrate that the Dutch *cause* in its war with Portugal was just. However, a significant aspect of this just-cause argument was alleged Portuguese misconduct *in bello.*

V

In this final section we shall attempt to formulate general conclusions on the basis of the foregoing case studies. Two caveats should be noted, however, before we proceed to generalize. First, conclusions about just war thought which are derived from this study apply chiefly to the theorists as commentators rather than to the theorists as systematicians. A much more extended analysis would be required to test whether there were significant differences of emphasis in the theorists' two roles.[10] Second, conclusions based on historical data belong, by definition, to the realm of contingency rather than the realm of necessity. None of our generalizations are logically entailed by the structure of just war thought. At most, such historically-based conclusions may possess a measure of predictive value.

A. A review of the four case studies indicates that just war categories were applied by the theorists to a wide variety of situations. In our small sample alone wars in contemporaneous Western Europe, Eastern Europe, Latin America, and Southeast Asia were analyzed. The just war tradition was also sufficiently broad to include both frontier clashes between Christians and non-Christians and intramural conflicts among professedly Christian peoples.

B. Twentieth century ethicists frequently assume that the phrase "just war" refers exclusively to secular political wars. However, the foregoing case studies clearly demonstrate that major just war theorists of the thirteenth to seventeenth centuries employed just war categories to analyze both political and religious wars. For example, according to Hostiensis and his adherents a war of Christians against infidels was *ipso factor* a just war. Even Vitoria, who rejected numerous religious grounds for war, accepted the defense of Christian missionaries and their converts as a just cause for war. In fact, in the first three of our four case studies the theorists themselves noted the significance of religious factors in the cases under discussion. Thus, we conclude that in an era when religious war was rather prevalent, major figures in the just war tradition assumed that either political or religious wars could be just or unjust, depending on the circumstances.[11]

C. In the introductory section we noted that in their systematic just war treatises Vitoria, Gentili, and Grotius discussed four issues:

1. *Whether* war is ever morally justifiable.
2. *Who* may wage war.
3. *For what reasons* war may be waged.
4. *How* war should be waged.

It seems clear that in their analyses of our four cases, the theorists devoted primary attention to the third of these issues, the just-cause question.[12] The preponderant significance of the cause-question was most clear in the writings of Vitoria and Grotius, both of whom took great pains to gather data concerning the historical background of particular wars. However, Vladimiri, Ayala, and Gentili also examined the causes of the wars which they analyzed.

The issue of authority was seen, for the most part, as an adjunct to the cause-question. Thus, Vladimiri and Vrebach, as well as Vitoria and his intellectual opponents, debated whether papal or imperial grants provided special grounds for war against certain groups. When Ayala refused to acknowledge that the Dutch possessed legitimate authority to wage war, he also denied, by implication, that they possessed a just cause for *war*.

The means-question was clearly a subordinate issue in our four case-studies. In part this question, too, was referred to the cause-question. Grotius, in particular, seems to have considered alleged Spanish and Portuguese excesses *in bello* to be additional grounds for the Dutch struggle against their enemies. Vitoria, however, criticized the cruelty of the *conquistadores* without relating his critique to the question of cause.

Among the theorists treated in this essay, only Grotius discussed the whether-question in commenting on a particular war. The reasons for Grotius' inclusion of this issue are fairly obvious. When he sought to justify the Dutch seizure of the Portuguese vessel, Grotius found it necessary to wage a two-front war—against critics who questioned the justice of the capture and against pacifists who questioned the moral legitimacy of any kind of military action. Grotius' discussion of the whether-question was directed against the pacifist critics.

D. Twentieth century moralists frequently speak of *the* just war theory as if the precise content of the theory were both obvious and relatively constant. However, in the course of examining the four case studies we have noted that there were, within the tradition, *competing versions* of the just war theory vying for preeminence. For example, Hostiensis' just war views were influential in Vladimiri's day and continued to exert influence in the sixteenth century. Again, Vitoria found it necessary to confront and reject a whole series of just-cause arguments, many of which had been advanced by his predecessors and contemporaries within the just war tradition.

A critic of this competing-versions thesis might concede that there had existed, in the past, a variety of just war theories; he might, however, argue that over the course of centuries one can perceive in the tradition a trend toward a single, orthodox just war standard. There is a measure of validity in this counter-argument. Certain positions, like Hostiensis' views on war with the infidels or the conception of the New World Indians as "natural slaves," came to be almost unanimously rejected by the sixteenth and seventeenth century just war theorists. There was also agreement among the theorists that certain formal questions—for example, authority, cause, means—should be included in just war discussions. One can even discover widespread consensus in the theorists' answers to specific sub-questions, for example, the question whether direct attacks on innocent persons were morally justified. However, even among the most recent of the major just war theorists, there always remained a significant measure of theoretical disagreement on questions relating to authority, cause, and means.[13] Thus, we conclude that in historical accounts of just war thought it is imprecise, if not inaccurate, to speak to "*the* just war theory." What one discovers, instead, is a variety of just war *theories* in an ongoing just war *tradition.*

E. In addition to adopting diverse theoretical positions, the just war theorists also differed in their assessments of particular wars. These disagreements at the practical level can be further subdivided into two distinct types of difficulty, which we have called problems of *description* and problems of *categorization.*

There were, at times, sharp contrasts in the various theorists' descriptions of historical events. Vladimiri and Ioannis Vrebach, for example, emphasized different events in explaining the background of the conflict between the Teutonic Knights and Poland-Lithuania. For Vrebach papal and imperial grants of authority to the Knights were the major determinants of subsequent history. Vladimiri de-emphasized the significance of these grants and stressed, instead, the conversion of Lithuania to Christianity. Similarly, Ayala and Grotius described the origins of the Dutch-Spanish conflict in radically different terms. What seemed to Ayala to be a serious general outbreak of heresy was, according to Grotius, a minor religious disturbance which could have been quelled by local magistrates and citizens.

In addition, the theorists sometimes disagreed on the appropriate categories to be applied to a particular war. For example, Vrebach conceived of the struggle between Poland-Lithuania and the Teutonic Knights as a religious war. Vladimiri, however, interpreted the conflict as a war between two political powers. A similar discrepancy in categorization was apparent in two perspectives on the Dutch-Spanish dispute. In Ayala's view, the Dutch were subjects of the Spanish Crown engaged in an unlawful rebellion. According to Grotius, they were the soldiers of an independent nation which was waging a just war.

F. Twentieth century proponents of just war thought frequently argue that it serves as a critical tool and a restraining force. There is some basis for this assertion in the present essay. The second case-study has illustrated how Vitoria employed just war categories to deny numerous alleged causes for war with the Indians and to condemn Spanish excesses in military conduct.

However, the various just war theories were two-edged swords. In addition to performing a restrictive role, they also fulfilled what we have called an apologetic function. A review of the four case studies reveals that *all* of the theorists used just war categories to argue that their own countries had a just cause for war in the cases under discussion. In addition, with the partial exception of Vitoria, the theorists who discussed the means-question asserted either that the means employed by their own countries were appropriately moderate or that the means employed by the enemy were cruel and excessive.

In summary, these four historical vignettes have shown how several pre-modern thinkers wrestled with the moral aspects of wars waged by their contemporaries. The case studies reveal that just war thought was applied to religious and political wars in a wide variety of historical contexts. They also demonstrate that diversity of viewpoint—at both the theoretical and practical levels—has been a recurring phenomenon in the history of the just war tradition. Finally, in the four case studies surveyed in this essay, just war categories and arguments were usually employed to support the policies of the theorists' own governments or countrymen.

As we noted earlier in this concluding section, a historical study deals with the realm of contingency rather than the realm of necessity. Thus, it cannot be assumed that just war thought either must or always will be used as it was in our four case studies. At the same time, however, these case studies are perhaps not entirely irrelevant to twentieth-century just war discussions. In my own view, there are two primary lessons to be learned from these historical applications of just war thought. The first is that careful attention to the complex problems of description and categorization is crucial to any attempt at fair-minded analysis of a particular conflict. The second lesson is in some respects the negative side of the first. The past theorists' preponderant use of just war thought as an apologetic instrument can be viewed as a warning—a caution against the possibility of self-deception in moral reasoning when matters of critical importance to one's own nation are at stake.[14]

NOTES

[1] For more detailed analysis of the major questions discussed by the classic just war theorists see Walters (1971:6-8, 59, 276-280).

[2] I am aware that the manner of narrating the historical background for each case study may seriously affect readers' assessments concerning the justice of particular wars. Insofar as possible, I have tried to present a balanced and accurate perspective on each theorist's socio-political context.

[3] It seems probable that Ioannes Vrebach de Bamberga was also called Ioannes Urbach. The latter, a professor at Erfurt, was a canonist of some renown. However, this identification is not certain (Belch, 1965:1110-1111). What is clear is that Ioannes Vrebach was associated with a German city and a pro-German point of view.

[4] This quotation and all succeeding quotations from works by Vitoria, Ayala, Gentili, and Grotius are taken from the Classics of International Law translations cited in the bibliography under "Primary Sources."

[5] Already in 1510 John Major, a Scottish professor in Paris and the teacher of several of Vitoria's teachers, had applied the Aristotelian doctrine of natural slavery to the Indians. Within a few years of Vitoria's death there was a major public confrontation between Las Casas and Sepúlveda at Valladolid concerning the moral appropriateness of regarding the New World Indians as natural slaves (Hanke, 1959:p. 14, chaps. 3-7).

[6] The original title of Grotius' work was *Annales et historiae de rebus belgicis, 1560-1609.*

[7] Only one chapter of *De jure praedae* was published during Grotius' lifetime. The remainder

of the work was lost for several centuries and was only re-discovered, edited, and published in the late nineteenth century (Dumbauld, 1969:23-24).

[8] For further documentation of this point see Walters (1971:345-348).

[9] This early work formed the basis for Grotius' classic treatise *On the Law of War and Peace (De jure belli ac pacis)*, which was published in 1625. The latter work included much new material and was systematically purged of references to sixteenth and seventeenth century history.

[10] In my study of five classic just war theorists—including Vitoria, Gentili, and Grotius—I was unable to discover any fundamental contradiction between the theorists' two roles. There was, however, relatively greater emphasis on the cause-question in the theorists' assessments of particular wars and relatively greater attention paid to the means-question in their systematic treatises (Walters, 1971:278-279).

[11] For a more detailed discussion of the relationship between political and religious wars in the just war tradition see Walters (1973).

[12] Writing as systematicians, Vitoria, Gentili, and Grotius concentrated primary attention on the cause- and means-questions, laying slightly greater emphases on the latter. See fn. 10 above.

[13] For an attempt to list areas of consensus and dissensus within the just war tradition see Walters (1971:418-419).

[14] I wish to thank the editors of this volume and Dr. André E. Hellegers for their helpful comments on an earlier version of this essay.

REFERENCES

A. Primary Sources

Ayala, Balthasar

1581 *De jure et officiis bellicis.* Reprinted and translated in *De jure et officiis bellicis et disciplina militari libri III.* Edited by John Westlake. 2 vols. Washington, D.C.: Carnegie Institution of Washington, 1912.

Gentili, Alberico

1598 *De jure belli.* Reprinted and translated in *De iure belli libri tres.* 2 vols. Oxford: Clarendon Press, 1933.

Grotius, Hugo

1604-1606 *De jure praedae.* Reprinted and translated in *De iure praedae commentarius.* 2 vols. Oxford: Clarendon Press, 1950.

Vitoria, Francisco de

1539 *De Indis.* Reprinted and translated in *De Indis et De iure belli relectiones.* Edited by Ernest Nys. Washington, D.C.: Carnegie Institution of Washington, 1917.

Vladimiri, Paulus

1415a *De potestate papae et imperatoris respectu infidelium.* Edited and published in Belch (1965:792-844).

1415b *Opinio Hostiensis.* Edited and published in Belch (1965:864-884).

Vrebach, Ioannes de Bamberga

1416 *Tractatus de statu Fratrum Ordinis B. Mariae Virginis Teutonicorum et pugna eorum adversus infideles. . . .* Edited and published in Belch (1965:1116-1180).

B. Secondary Sources

Belch, Stanislaus

1965 *Paulus Vladimiri and His Doctrine Concerning International Law and Politics.* 2 vols. The Hague: Mouton.

Beltran de Heredia, Vicente

1967 "Personalidad del maestro Francisco de Vitoria y transcendencia de su obra doctrinal." In Francisco de Vitoria, *Relectio de Indis: o libertad de los Indios*. Edited by L. Perena and J. M. Perez Prendes. Madrid: Consejo Superior de Investigaciones Cientificas.

Dumbauld, Edward

1969 *The Life and Legal Writings of Hugo Grotius*. Norman: The University of Oklahoma Press.

Fruin, Robert

1925 "An unpublished work of Hugo Grotius's." *Bibliotheca Visseriana* 5 :3-71.

Hanke, Lewis

1959 *Aristotle and the American Indians: A Study of Race Prejudice in the Modern World*. Chicago: Henry Regnery.

Harrison, J. B.

1970 "Europe and Asia." *The New Cambridge Modern History*. Vol. IV: *The Decline of Spain and the Thirty Years' War, 1609-48/59*. Edited by J. P. Cooper. Cambridge: University Press.

Hoffner, Joseph

1947 *Christentum und Menschenwurde: das Anliegen der spanischen Kolonialethik in goldenen Zeitalter*. Trier: Paulinus-Verlag.

Holland, Thomas Erskine

1898 "Alberico Gentili." In *Studies in International Law*. Oxford: Clarendon Press.

Koenigsberger, H. G.

1968 "Western Europe and the Power of Spain." *The New Cambridge Modern History*. Vol. III: *The Counter-Reformation and Price Revolution, 1559-1610*. Edited by R. B. Wernham. Cambridge: University Press.

Prescott, William H.

1847 *History of the Conquest of Peru with a Preliminary View of the Civilization of the Incas*. 2 vols. London: Richard Bentley.

Ramsey, Paul

See the bibliography of Ramsey's works in this volume. Capital letters (e.g. 1950A) denote books and occasional papers; lower case letters (e.g. 1968a) denote articles.

Scott, James Brown

1934 *The Spanish Origin of International Law*. Vol. I: *Francisco de Vitoria and His Law of Nations*. Oxford: Clarendon Press.

Van der Molen, Gesina

1968 *Alberico Gentili and the Development of International Law: His Life and Times*. 2nd ed., revised. Leyden: A. W. Sijthoff.

Van Eysinga, W. J. M.

1952 *Hugo Grotius: eine biographische Skizze*. Translated by Frau Plemp Van Duiveland. Basel: Benno Schwabe.

Vreeland, Hamilton

1917 *Hugo Grotius: The Father of the Modern Science of International Law*. New York: Oxford University Press.

Walters, LeRoy

1971 "Five Classic Just-war Theories: A Study in the Thought of Thomas Aquinas, Vitoria, Suarez, Gentili, and Grotius." Ph.D. dissertation, Yale University.

1973 "The just war and the crusade: antitheses or analogies?" *The Monist* 57 (October):584-594.

Westlake, John

1912 "Introduction." In Balthazar Ayala. *De jure et officiis bellicis et disciplina militari libri III*. Vol. II: *The Translation*. Washington, D.C.: Carnegie Institution of Washington.

CHAPTER VII

The Structure of Justification in the Political Ethics of Paul Ramsey

DAVID LITTLE

Paul Ramsey's attempts to think morally about politics provide an occasion for observing not only his conclusions about politics, which are interesting in themselves, but also the general way he reasons morally, the way his "moral system" works. This essay has the following objective: to analyse and criticize Ramsey's way of reasoning morally, with special reference to his political reflections.

The analysis of moral reasoning, whether Ramsey's or anyone else's, involves discerning and plotting out the structure of justification characteristic of the figure in question. To think morally is (sooner or later) to give justification for practical prescriptions, or action-guides, and to give justification is to do at least three things.

1. First, and preliminarily, it is to specify the kinds of actors and the range of actions to which the norms of an ethical system are to be particularly applied, an aspect of justification I shall call *situational relevance*. Deter-

mining the situational relevance does not indicate how the norms are, or ought to be, applied, but simply to whom and to what they are to be applied. Consequently, Ramsey's attempt to develop a "political ethics," or, as he says, a "Christian theory of politics" (1968A: 12), leads him to concern himself with *political* situations. In doing this, he must, as he does, try to (a) define what will count as "political" circumstances, as distinguished from other circumstances, (b) describe the special character of those circumstances (1972c: 44).

2. Second, in relating moral reflection to certain kinds of situations, one will be required to appeal to a hierarchy of increasingly general and abstract rules and principles, and, finally, to an ultimate or basic principle(s) or standard(s). This process of referring, in an appellate fashion, to principles or standards of justification, I shall call *validation*. Especially in his more recent work, Ramsey has been self-conscious about how the structure of validation functions in his own moral reasoning, as well as in that of others. "Our model of the component stages in moral reasoning can, therefore, be stated as follows: ultimate norm (*agape*, utility, self-realization, etc.); general principles; *defined*-action principles, or generic terms of approval and *generic* offense-terms; definite action rules, or moral-*species*-terms; then the subsumption of cases" (1968a: 75). What Ramsey calls the "ultimate norm" we shall refer to as the *basic validating norm*, and we shall have to see how, in Ramsey's case, it works in relation to lower-order principles and rules, in political situations.

Analysis of validation involves two special concerns. One concern is determining what *type* the basic validating norm is—whether it is teleological or deontological in character or, as Ramsey seems to suggest, a third type. Investigation at this point means figuring out how Ramsey actually employs terms like "teleological" and "deontological" in relation to his basic norm. It will also mean pointing to some problems here and there. Ramsey, as we shall see, has a view of teleological and deontological reasoning in political ethics that is, in several senses of the word, peculiar. The second concern here has to do with what I shall call the *mode of validation*. Having indicated the situational relevance of a moral position, as well as its validating principles and rules, there is still the question, in concrete cases, of *how* to determine what specifically ought to be done. This is what Ramsey calls, in his model of moral reasoning, the "subsumption of cases," or the stipulation of "application-governing rules" (1968a: 103-105), if there are any. Ramsey's procedure for making concrete decisions on the basis of his moral position—his mode of validation—is, to an extent, intentionally discretionary for reasons that relate directly to some of his general assumptions about political and moral reasoning.

3. Last, the basic validating norm(s), as well as the procedures for relating and applying the norms to practical (for our purposes, political) life themselves invite a final kind of support or authentication, which I shall call

the *vindication* of a moral position. Vindication describes *how* one perceives and is convinced of the particular validating norms he has adopted (along with the procedures for relating and applying norms). It is the aspect of justification normally denominated "metaethics." Because of limitations of space, we shall be able to address here only the questions of *situational* relevance and *validation*.

I.
SITUATIONAL RELEVANCE: RAMSEY'S DEFINITION AND DESCRIPTION OF POLITICS

A. Toward a Definition of Politics

In identifying the situational relevance of his moral position, Ramsey undertakes to "examine the nature of the political act" and thus to define politics.

> [P]olitics is defined by both its *genus* (community) and its *specific difference* (the use of power). What political community has in common with other communities (friendship, economic associations, professional and cultural groups transcending national boundaries) within the *genus* to which they belong may comprise the higher human qualities. Every community pursues a common good, or a good in common. But the legitimate use of decisive physical power distinguishes political community from these other communities in the formation of the life of mankind. Generic social values are the matter of politics; but so also is the *specific* use of power. You can say that the former comprise the higher values to which the latter is a conditional value; but not that the latter is a merely extrinsic instrument that can be dropped. In fact, in the *definitional* sense of "primary" and "secondary," *generic* community values are the secondary (i.e., the distinctly human) purpose of politics while the use of power comprises the differentiating *species* of the primary (i.e., the distinctive) modality of politics (1968A: 7).

At other points, he uses the following characteristic language: What is "primary" in politics is "the exercise [presumably by the magistrates of a state] of a monopoly of power" (1968A: 85); or, "the general point, however, is that government's enforcement powers are never interrupted, [namely] its monopoly of power, its political use of coercion—and possibly of violence" (1972c: 61).

Two things call for clarification and scrutiny.

1. First, the phrase which appears several times in Ramsey's writings, "the use of power, and possibly the use of force, is of the *esse* of politics . . . ," is ambiguous. It could mean that the use of power is certainly of the *esse* of politics, while the use of force (read also "decisive physical power," "armed force," "coercion," "violence," all of which Ramsey seems to use interchangeably) *might also be* of the *esse* of politics, though whether it *is* or not remains uncertain.

But that is not what Ramsey means. He intends to say, rather, that the use of power, *backed up by the capacity to use force* (impose physical compulsion and/or injury) *in extreme circumstances*, is of the *esse* of politics.

This is an important point to be clear on, for it helps to bring out the centrality of the control or ordering of force in Ramsey's definition of politics.

> The crux, the essential element of government—whatever other good and more positive purpose it may serve—is said to be this: "Whoever sheds man's blood, by man shall his blood be shed, for in the image of God made he man" (Gen 9:6 RSV). That alone holds the waters back from ever again becoming a flood, in a world history in which, we can be sure, God does not mean ultimately to yield to man's propensity to destruction and self-destruction. The Flood was once an emergency remedy; government is a remedy for all time (1972c: 60).

The "primary" purpose of government, then, is to control or order the sort of force that appears in the form of "man's propensity to destruction and self-destruction." Governments do that by monopolizing force, since only a monopoly can guarantee that force will be met effectively by force.

For Ramsey this basic function of government is crucial, in part, because it is preconditional to all other human activities. However, the ordering of force is not only an instrumental or "menial" requirement. To order force is an activity that is *constitutive* of politics and political decisions, whatever other interests may also be operative. For Ramsey, politics is inconceivable apart from what we might call a primary concern for order.

It follows that "political situations" have unavoidably, though not exclusively, to do with the control of force. Moreover, political actors can best be understood by dividing them into those who *initiate* action on the basis of the effective control of force (magistrates and citizens, in certain contexts) and those who are *recipients* of such action (subjects and citizens, in different, more passive, contexts).

2. Second, the role of values in Ramsey's definition of politics is confusing. There are at least two possible interpretations of the words quoted above. First, Ramsey might mean to define politics purely descriptively, along the lines of Weber's famous definition of the state. An organization "will be called a 'state,' " said Weber, "if and in so far as its administrative staff successfully upholds a claim to the *monopoly* of the *legitimate* use of physical force in the enforcement of its order" (Weber, 1968: I, 54, author's italics). Ramsey's words, "the legitimate use of decisive physical power distinguishes political community . . . ," are obviously close to Weber's meaning. Weber's understanding is descriptive because, while it includes reference to values as an unavoidable aspect of authorizing or legitimating governments, it says nothing about what particular normative appeals will constitute the criteria of legitimacy in specific cases. Indeed, Weber explicitly allows for a plurality of possible appeals. In no way does he suggest which appeals "ought" to count in order to make a government "really" legitimate. Such suggestions would infringe his famous maxim regarding the value-freedom of scientific work.

The second interpretation of Ramsey's words is that, contrary to Weber's maxim, he has insinuated into his definition a particular normative appeal of his own. "*Generic* social values are the matter of politics; but so also is the *specific* use of power. *You can say that the former comprise the higher values to which the latter is a conditional value; but not that the latter is a merely extrinsic instrument that can be dropped*" 1968A: 7, italics supplied). One is driven to ask Ramsey *why*, among the possible justifications for governments, it is not conceivable to legitimate a government precisely by regarding it as "a merely extrinsic instrument" to some "higher" goal. I fail to see that having to legitimate governments entails anything about how, or for what reason, governments must be valued.

By means of this language about how the use of power "must be" valued, Ramsey may be smuggling in a favorite point of his, that the ordering and exercise of power is a "terminal value," "a good in itself" (1967A: 116), or, what is apparently the same thing, an intrinsic rather than an extrinsic value. But to do this is to advance a value-claim of his own about what will count, at least in part, as an acceptable legitimating belief concerning political power. It is to construe the relation between the use of power—the "*esse* of politics"—and the legitimating of power—the "*bene esse*"—in a particular normative way.

B. Describing or Prescribing?

These two interpretations of Ramsey's definition of politics are very different. The first is close to what Weber called a "conceptual minimum" for the concept of politics, and, as such, comprises a satisfactory *reportive* definition. However, the second, which is closer, I believe, to Ramsey's normal understanding, constitutes a *persuasive* definition. A persuasive definition is one which "gives a new conceptual meaning to a familiar word without substantially changing its emotive meaning, and which is used with the conscious or unconscious purpose of changing, by this means, the direction of peoples' interests [what they prefer or value]" (Stevenson, 1963: 32). In other words, persuasive definitions "load" a common and fuzzy-edged term like politics with a particular normative significance, and then aim at converting users of the term to espouse the same normative significance, and to take that to be the "real meaning" of the term.

The second interpretation of Ramsey's definition actually turns on a normative view of what is "good" politics. The reason Ramsey does not favor a political doctrine in which order is purely "menial" is because of his own moral and religious beliefs, and that ought to have been made clear. He ought to have said, because that is all he is entitled to say, that a doctrine which views political order purely instrumentally is not a *good* doctrine, from his point of view, though it *is* a political doctrine.

The trouble with persuasive definitions is not only that they obscure certain unconfessed and undefended normative ingredients, though that is a serious problem. Another difficulty is that while persuasive definitions give the impression of being *reportive*, they are actually *reformative*. They recommend for adoption one preferred meaning over competing definitions commonly in use. I have the impression that Ramsey is not clear on which sort of definition he is advancing though he would probably like to think he is advancing a reportive definition.

The same sort of confusion exists in regard to Ramsey's description of the "political act" and "political decision." Is he, in his discussion of these things describing or prescribing? In his essay, "Force and Political Responsibility," it is true that he provides a description of these phenomena only after pointing out his normative orientation. He admits that he is a "religious thinker," who can only say some things that seem, "as a theological ethicist, right to say about politics" (1972c:44). But when Ramsey goes on to describe a political act and decision he writes as though he is doing more than simply proposing a theologically-grounded prescription for political action. He appears to be reporting what people are "really doing" or what they "really understand themselves to be doing" (if they think about it), when they make political decisions and perform political acts.

> The political act calls the things that are into being from things that are not. *In a very real* sense an exercise of statecraft is a creation ex nihilo. For all the doctrine and the policy research that went before, a statesman shapes events by decisions or indecisions that go beyond doctrine, that launch out into the unknown and the not-yet, and that do not pop out of research, game playing or systems analysis . . . To prove after the event that political decisions were right is rather like speculating what world history would have been if Cleopatra's nose had been longer, or like asking whether God should have created this world and not some other. . . . I conclude from this that government—the political act and the statesman's, the politician's, the magistrate's, the citizen's office—is a matter of the risk-filled venture of creatively doing something, not primarily making, engineering, manipulating, composing, or arranging anything at all. In this view, the political actor is not a mere maker of schemes that can be quantified, but rather a doer of deeds that bring-out of nothing, beyond all rational calculation, the things he hopes to be. . . . [The statesman] lives in a world of doing; he is going to encounter other doings that are coming upon him and to which he must respond with some risk-filled, unmeasurable, creative decision which shapes the future in a way that cannot be definitely demonstrated to have been wise (1972c: 47-49).

Whatever Ramsey intends in this passage, if these observations are meant to report "in a real sense" what people generally mean by a political act and decision, they are unacceptable. In practice, people constantly evaluate the wisdom and adequacy of political acts and decisions, according to various standards, and, for the life of me, I do not see how they could do otherwise. Some of these standards or "measures" are rational in a loose sense. Wise policies could hardly be made up of ends and means that contradict each other, or that claim to produce results they cannot produce, or that claim to have considered a relevant set of circumstances that has not in fact been considered, etc. There may be exceptions in particular political decisions to the applicability of these rational standards, but if there are, we normally request to know the reasons why.

Indeed, Ramsey himself seems to waver between saying that political acts and decisions are of such a sort that they cannot be measured or evaluated *at all*, and that they cannot be "*definitely* demonstrated to have been wise." Perhaps the latter, weaker claim is closer to a general understanding of political decisions, as the result of the irreducible complexity of such decisions, as well as of the difficulties of calculating and weighing the consequences of decisions. Nevertheless, to admit that it is difficult to demonstrate "definitely" the wisdom of a policy is *not* to say that standards of appraisal are irrelevant. It is clear that people often hold political leaders accountable according to whether their policies turn out to have been wise or not: It is also clear that people often hold their standards of criticism to be reasonably objective and binding, and to be capable of being applied with a fair amount of certainty in some cases. For example, many people, such as the "liberals" Ramsey delights in attacking, have frequently adjudged policies, both foreign and domestic, to have been "definitely" unwise. To keep things clear, therefore, Ramsey ought to say that when the liberals apply their special standards of evaluation to political decisions, they are, to be sure, thinking politically. But they are not thinking politically in the *right* way.

There are good reasons, then, to suspect that Ramsey's exposition of the situational relevance of his moral position is normatively laden, though Ramsey in his writings is not as self-conscious about that as he should be. This brings us to the explicit normative position which stands behind so much of his analysis and description of politics. In terms of the analytical scheme introduced earlier, we are coming to a consideration of the *validational* aspects of Ramsey's moral system, and how he relates those aspects to political matters.

II

THE VALIDATION OF RAMSEY'S POLITICAL ETHICS: 1. THE BASIC VALIDATING NORM

Ramsey's political ethics is but one aspect of his general moral system, and it is justified accordingly. We must therefore attend first to the structure of that system before turning to its relevance for politics.

Ramsey's basic validating norm is agape. It functions as the ultimate logical justification (standard of validity) for the lower-order principles, rules and particular judgments. Ramsey frequenty identifies other principles alongside agape as having substantial justificatory weight in his scheme, principles like order, law, justice, and covenantal fidelity. These principles, however, in no way compete with agape. "In Christian ethics, at least, agape works by many a principle through principle and to defined principles in its ceaseless endeavor to unfold the meaning of the life of charity. These are always feature-relevant specifications of love" (1968a: 91). In various ways, it is in the notions of justice, order, law, and covenantal fidelity that love becomes "in-principled," in a favorite, if awkward, Ramsey expression.

Ramsey does not elaborate or clarify very well the precise character of these basic notions. Nor does he elucidate very successfully the relations among the specifying principles, nor between each of them and agape. Nevertheless, the following reconstruction is at least plausible.

The basic concept of agape has two "sides" or dimensions for Ramsey: a *discretionary* and a *formalistic* side. Everything in Ramsey's system is keyed directly to this distinction. On the one hand, agape is, to a certain extent, *in*expressible in the form of principles, if "principle" is taken to mean an abstract and general set of rationally determinable characteristics or features which can be practically applied with a high degree of certainty. This aspect of agape is, therefore, indeterminate and incalculable, which is to say "discretionary." On the other hand, agape is also, to a certain extent, expressible in principles; it has a rational form. This is naturally the "formalistic" side.

A. The Discretionary and the Formalistic: Distinction

So far as the discretionary aspect goes, Ramsey suggests that "the Christian . . . starts with people and not rules" (1967A: 112), and that the principles and rules which specify agape and guide action in relation to it are "subordinate to agape" (1968a: 74). This way of looking at agape implies that it possesses a "plus-factor" above and beyond whatever rationally determinable characteristics can be designated. Ramsey illuminates this "plus-factor" by likening it to the legal notion of "equity." If equity is understood, in the words of C. K. Allen (1961: 368) as "a discretionary or moderating influence . . . superadded to the rigour of formulated law," then that is just the role agape, in its fullest sense, plays for Ramsey. Agape always involves a disposition to attend to the "multiple claims and needs" (1967A: 112) of "concrete persons" (1961A: 28) in specific situations, and benevolently to reconcile those claims and needs *in a discretionary way*. In other words, the manner of adjustment and application cannot be anticipated or formulated in fixed rules and principles. It is for this reason that Ramsey suggests, at one point, that discretionary determinations, which are situational or circumstantial in character, can be understood in relation to the categories of "act-agapism" and "summary rule-agapism" (1967A: 121; cf. 106ff.). A person filled with the spirit of agape "has discretion" in the sense that he has, and must be allowed to exercise, an authority to make creative, unpredictable and "unmeasurable" decisions. In this way he brings about what Ramsey loves to call "a new creation." So far as the discretionary side goes, Ramsey is unabashedly a "situation ethicist."

But there is also the formalistic side of agape, which, to borrow Allen's words again, supplies "the rigour of formulated law." Here situationism does not obtain. For there is, Ramsey believes, a range of specifications for right and wrong actions that is rationally determinable and unexceptionable and about which rational certainty is possible. These specifications constitute the "outer limits" within which discretion takes place. Agape itself "dictates" the specifications, though they are also made available by natural rational perception.

The formalistic side of agape is illuminated most clearly in Ramsey's discussions of the "principle" of covenantal fidelity or fellow humanity.

> . . . [B]ecause [human] creatureliness is from the beginning in the form of fellow humanity and because the creation in him is in order to covenant, and because this means he has real being only by being *with* and *for* fellow man, we have to reckon with this in everything that is said about justice and the rights of man. His rights have their being in, with, and for covenant (1961A: 31).

Covenantal fidelity or fellow humanity expresses a crucial aspect of agape. That is because a pledge of fidelity, or a promise, expresses the true character of "steadfast love," by guaranteeing loyalty in the face of future adversity. ". . . [I]t is what makes for fidelity, which permits or calls for actions that embody righteousness in the relations of man to man and which define the essence of practices that are genuinely human" (1968a: 126).

What is so signal about fidelity, and the reason it is so illuminative of the second "side" of agape is that it excludes, in certain important respects, *consequential calculation*. "The consequences of individual and of joint action are, of course, not unimportant; but what holds us together in the communications of life does not consist of ways to secure certain consequences" (1968a: 126). Fidelity obligations determine the rightness of actions, not according to some standard for evaluating good or bad ends and consequences, but according to the qualities and characteristics of actions themselves (1967A: 108); that is, according to the *form* the acts take.

Agape *requires* certain sorts of actions with certain definite features. These actions are to be done because they express and specify agape, or fellow humanity, and not because doing them makes more probable some future balance of good over bad results. In other words, the formalistic side of agape entails certain "defined action principles" and "definite-action rules" as "the floor below which love cannot and may not and must not fall" (1967A: 113). This side of agape yields the "rule-agapist" aspect of Ramsey's position. It accounts for the *moral prohibitiva* he discusses so often.

As is well-known, Ramsey puts special emphasis on the formalist or "deontological" side of agape. "*Agape* defines for the Christian what is right, righteous, obligatory to be done among men; it is not a Christian's definition of the good that better be done and much less is it a definition of the right way to the good. . . . The Christian understanding of righteousness is therefore radically nonteleological" (1967A: 108). But despite this emphasis, Ramsey is not fully comfortable describing his basic validating norm, agape, in exclusively deontological terms. The reasons for his discomfort, as well as for the prominence he gives to "deontology" in his moral system, can be traced to the central distinction between the two "sides" of agape.

B. The Two Aspects of Agape Combined

At several points, Ramsey flirts with the idea that "agapism [may be] . . . a third and distinctive type of normative theory which is neither *teleology* . . . nor *deontology* . . ." (1967A: 108-109), but, presumably, some combination of the two. He wishes to make room for a teleological approach, though only insofar as it is "in the service of [a formalistic] definition of righteousness, and subordinate to [a formalistic] view of obedient love" (1967A: 109). This apparently means two things: first, that to the extent that agape functions *with rational determinateness* as a validating norm, it is deontological or formalistic in character. It requires certain "feature-specific" actions to be done and to be avoided. These actions constitute, as we have seen, the outer limits of right moral action. Second, there is a "plus factor," the discretionary side of agape, which has the role of relating the requirements of love to the ends and consequences of action. It involves a teleological procedure.

Teleological reflection is for Ramsey a form of reasoning only in a special sense. It is reasoning under conditions of what we might call "systematic indeterminateness." That phrase can probably be applied in two ways. First, Ramsey's understanding of the discretionary side of agape means that there are no rationally determinate standards of assessment according to which agape can finally be measured, and that rational certitude is, on that account, conceptually excluded. Second, the activity of calculating and predicting consequences is invariably uncertain and therefore indeterminate, because consequences are, to an important degree, uncontrollable or unforseeable. While teleological reflection, then, has a role in Ramsey's position, and while it constitutes a form of reasoning in a certain sense, it is "transrational" in that it is finally governed by something other than rational standards. That something may be a kind of intuition or special religious insight, though I remain unclear about that.

Ramsey seeks to link together the deontological (or formalistic) and teleological (or discretionary) sides of his position in the following way. Teleological "reasoning" is conditioned by the formalistically determined requirements of agape, and in that way it is "in their service" or "subordinate" to them. As one thinks teleologically, he may not properly violate the fixed or determinate outer limits of agape. But within the limits set by these requirements, the teleological task is "systematically indeterminate" and incalculable. That means that in the matter of teleological judgments, rational certitude must give way to some other kind of intuitive or possibly religiously inspired certitude.

This way of understanding validation applies directly to Ramsey's political ethics, though not without raising some serious difficulties. As we

would expect, the formalist side of agape yields certain pri
rules—like order, justice, and law—that are of special significanc
political behavior. Each of these is, in its own way, independently requir
love, and each specifies a range of politically relevant actions that have a certain definite and unmistakable form. Yet each principle is by itself only a partial expression of agape, and each must be balanced and reconciled with the others in concrete political situations, if agape is truly to be manifested.

C. *Order, Justice and Law as Requirements of Agape*

For Ramsey the principle of *order* is central to his definition of politics. The ordering of force by means of monopolization is not only a necessary condition of government, it is by itself a necessary expression of agape in a fallen world, and thus is something independently validated in relation to agape. "Order is a good in itself, in that the orders [including the political monopolization of force] provide the fabric in which men may dwell" (1967A:116). Order, in other words, is one of the direct requirements of agape.

The principle of *justice* is also of great significance in Ramsey's scheme, though the meaning and role of this principle is anything but precise, consistent, or clear. At one point, Ramsey defines justice in a bewildering way: it refers, he says, "to the regulative ideal of all political action summed up, I suppose, in the word 'humanitarianism,' and to political judgments that are made in terms of the national and world common good" (1968A:12). This is, to say the least, a broad definition. Very little in the sphere of social and political values and ideals is excluded. The definition is even more peculiar since it is not employed consistently. Elsewhere (1968A:29-30), Ramsey distinguishes justice from national and international common good, as well as from humanitarianism, although he does not identify the residual meaning of justice. In a moment, we shall see that there are still further puzzles about Ramsey's understanding of justice. But, whatever it means, justice is "dialectically related" to order.

> Order and justice are both 'values'; both are rules of love. Order may be a conditional value and justice a higher value; but order is not merely menial in the service of justice (1967A:116). Both are in some respects conditional to the other. . . . Order is for the sake of justice, since the only real political order in which men may dwell in community and peace is one that is just enough to command the love and allegiance of men, or at least their acquiesence and their compliance. Order and justice are ever in tension yet in interrelation, and both are terminal goals in politics' act of being *proper* politics (its *bene esse*) (1972c:71-72; cf. 1967A:115-116).

The third relevant political principle is *law* (*lex*). With respect to international politics, it refers to "the current state of international law and the treaties and agreements between governments and the United Nations with the nation-state system it is built upon" (1968A:12). As we indicated, law must be balanced in relation to the other requirements of agape, namely, justice and order.

The *lex* of international agreements and institutions may be understood as an effort to impose coherence upon the order of power, but this coherence also flows from the *justitia* that may be preserved, beyond the legalities, in the relative power positions of nations (the order of power): and there is also a (fluctuating but still definite) coherence inherent in the powers themselves in their encounters and in the mutual limitation of one nation's power of being by that of another. . . . This is a world in which injustice may have the power and/or it may be legal. The use of power should not always stick by the legal boundaries, else the erosion of the order of power and of realized justice may make worse befall than a violation of the legalities (1968A:12).[1]

Order, justice and law are all requirements of agape, entailed by the *formalistic* side of agape. This means that in political situations (essentially concerned with the monopolization of force, as defined), the requirements of order, justice and law act as independent constraints upon political decisions; they create a "field of forces" within which a political decision must ("properly") be rendered. Force must be ordered; it must be ordered in keeping with the perceptions of national and international good; and it must be regulated by honoring legal covenants and agreements and other legal institutions. Any political actor who acts morally, according to Ramsey's validational scheme, will perceive the moral weightiness of each of these three decisional constraints, and act on them to the extent of his ability.

At the same time, these three political ethical principles must be reconciled and harmonized in specific decisions. As we have seen, order, justice and law—all forms of love—must be *con*figured in order to do what agape truly demands. *How* is this configuration to be achieved in specific cases? How ought a magistrate to decide so as properly to combine the principles of order, justice and law? Ramsey's answer, an answer derived from the *first* side of agape, is that the configuring of these principles in concrete political situations is achieved *in a discretionary way*. There is absolutely no principle by which to subsume concrete cases under these principles; there is no "application-governing rule" (1968a:103). "An application-governing rule would be a project for putting out of commission the actual production of particular deeds by absorbing them utterly into the principles."

The discretionary side of political ethical reasoning is *prudential* or teleological for Ramsey. It has regard for the ends and consequences of action, and determines the right political action with respect to an evaluation of "the best outcome," namely the best achievable balance or configuration of order, justice and law.

A [political] decision-maker contemplating, for example, some interventionary or non-interventionary action *should reckon order and justice both as ends or the effects of responsible action*, and not justice only. . . . He will know that order and justice both are *consequences* of his decision to do or to forbear. *He will count the cost of one effect upon the other.* He will ask how much disorder is worth a calculable preservation or extension of justice . . . , or he will ask how much of the injustice of the world . . . it is his responsibility to expunge politically, at the cost of disordering the political system in which alone political justice obtains embodiment (1968A:29; italics added).

Ramsey is firm and consistent about arguing that this matter of balancing and weighing the future consequences of political decisions in relation to order, justice and law must be left to the discretion of the political magistrate. That is to say, there is no abstract principle or rational standard, no "political doctrine," by which to determine the application of moral principles in relation to the *future* ends and consequences of action.

III
The Validation of Ramsey's Political Ethics: 2. The Mode of Validation

The above conclusion puts into perspective Ramsey's definitions of the political act and decision that we scrutinized earlier. He has applied directly and unflinchingly to politics conclusions drawn from his understanding of agape. The formalist side identifies the various requirements within the context or the "moral situation" in which the politician operates, but that is the extent of the efficacy of the formalistic side. Beyond that all is discretion; all is the "doing" as opposed to the "making" of a "new creation"; all is the configuration of future events that is "beyond all rational calculation."

It is also for this reason that Ramsey frequently counsels the church, for one, to "stand in awe before people nowadays called political 'decision-makers,' or rather before the majesty of topmost political agency" (1968A:19). The church's business is exclusively "clarifying and keeping wide open the legitimate options for choice." The church, and presumably other citizens, may reflect and evaluate with respect to the *formalistic* side, that is, the rules of agape or the *prohibitiva* of the political ethical context of decision, but that is all. "Their task is not the determination of policy," a claim at the heart of Ramsey's normative system.[2] This is not, as it may superficially seem, an assertion about the superior factual knowledge of policy-makers or some such. It means that in the nature of moral decision-making in general, a decision-maker *ought* to be allowed to exercise discretion as he calculates and evaluates the future ends and consequences of policy (within the formal limits circumscribed by the principles of justice, order and law), since, by hypothesis, a "good" decision must be made discretionarily. In his political ethics Ramsey has made room for teleological or prudential "reasoning" by identifying it with the discretionary aspect of political decision-making. He has intentionally placed teleological determinations beyond the reach of all rational principles and rules, and, hence, beyond all rational evaluation.

There might seem to be one exception to this conclusion, though upon reflection that turns out not to be the case. It concerns the role in political reasoning of what Ramsey calls "those summaries of political wisdom known as 'the principle of proportion' and 'the rule of double effect.' This may not tell [the political decision-maker] what to think, but it is how he will think" (1968A:11). These two principles, which Ramsey spends much time applying in his discussions of just war, are *rules of rational procedure* that do regulate directly "purposive political action; they specify the moral economy governing the use of force, which must always be employed in politics . . ." (1968A:85). As politicians go about the business of calculating the future ends and effects of action, these two principles are normatively operative in their thinking in the same way that the rules of logic are operative in ordinary thinking. The rules "cannot be repealed; [they] can only be violated" (1968A:164). Examining Ramsey's use of these rules will tell us much about his mode of ethical validation.

A. *Ramsey's Use of Proportion and Discrimination*

The principle of proportionality dictates simply that "there should be a proportion among the good and evil effects of an action; the good accomplished or the evil prevented must be sufficient to justify (in comparison of effects) the evil that is also done" (1968A:430). This is another way of stating what it means to be prudent. In the nature of Ramsey's position, of course, we could have no external abstract standards for evaluating the balance of good over evil, for knowing whether a policy is in fact prudent or not. That must be left to the value commitments, the value-judgments and the creative activity of the magistrate. It is not surprising, therefore, that Ramsey does not have a great deal to say about how this principle applies in practice. To understand the principle properly is to disallow any attempt to restrict the discretion of the magistrate. Thus, on examination, Ramsey's view of the principle of proportionality does not in any way go beyond what he has already said about the limits of rationality in political decision-making.

The "principle of double effect" is used "to determine when a person may lawfully perform an action from which two effects will follow, one bad, and the other good" (*New Catholic Encyclopedia*, 1967:1021). An act justified with respect to this principle must meet at least two basic conditions: the act itself must be morally good, or at least indifferent, and the agent must not positively will the bad end, but may permit it if it is unavoidable. When Ramsey applies this principle to politics, it leads to "the principle of discrimination" or "the moral immunity of noncombatants from direct attack" (1968A:429). There are two interesting things about Ramsey's treatment and application of this principle. First, whereas the principle of proportionality corresponds, as we saw, to the *discretionary* emphasis in Ramsey's moral position, this principle corresponds to the *formalistic* emphasis. It is a *deontological* principle defining abstractly the features of action which are taken to be wrong in themselves, regardless of consequences. It clearly imposes rational restrictions, but it does so only with respect to the *means* of action, and *not* to the ends. Ends are still open to political discretion.

Second, discrimination is at the heart of Ramsey's political ethics. In fact, it is the *only* regulative principle of decision-making that can specify abstractly a set of exceptionless features of permissible action, which are *not* relative, as is the principle of proportionality, to the particular value-commitments and -judgments of given decision-makers. For this reason, Ramsey makes his surprising claim that "the *ends* for which wars may legitimately be fought are not nearly so important in the theory of the just war as is the moral and political wisdom contained in its reflection upon the *conduct or means* of warfare" (1968A:152; italics added; cf. 130-33).

Ramsey is arguing here that the ends of political action, including warfare, may not be regulated by fixed, exceptionless standards. While ends are certainly as important as means in Ramsey's total moral position, they are not "so important" from the perspective of the general moral evaluation of political action. Those who are "outsiders," who are not decision-makers, are not entitled to evaluate the ends of political action with the sort of rational certitude they may have when they evaluate the means of action. Similarly, outsiders have nothing particular to contribute with respect to the application of the principle of proportionality. As we mentioned, the application of that principle depends on the specific value-commitments, value-judgments and creative activity of the magistrates, all of which are discretionary. The only point at which outsiders "have a right" to evaluate or pass judgment on decisions regarding warfare is with respect to the application of the principle of discrimination. That is because the principle is readily available to all rational agents in a way that does not vary with circumstance or value-commitment. On the contrary, the principle of discrimination itself conditions all circumstances and value-commitments.

In discussing the legitimate grounds for selective conscientious objection, Ramsey (1968A:130 ff.), explicitly excludes all the "teleological tests" and allows only the test of the means or conduct of warfare. He stresses that the evaluation of the ends of war is a moral matter, to be sure, and a matter in which each citizen, particularly in a democracy, is bound to engage. *But* it is precisely in respect to the evaluation of ends that, says Ramsey, "men may [legitimately] disagree who are exercising the same conscience. . . ." ". . . [C]onscientious moral objection [on questions of the ends of a policy] *cannot be distinguished from serious political objection to that particular policy*" (italics added). The place for the interplay of conscience on *these* points "is and must remain in the public forum" in such a way that the authority of the magistrates to make prudential judgments is respected. An objector to the ends of a policy must either persuade the magistrates to change their objectives, or he must "bear the burden of refusing to serve," which is to acknowledge the right of the magistrates to punish him for his disobedience. In either case the *right* of the magistrates to discretionary judgment on ends of action goes unchallenged.[3] In other words, questions of the ends of policy, which are the fit subject of political prudence or discretionary judgment, may only finally be settled by the constituted political process.[4] This is the case because, from a rational point of view, they are not "definitely" resolvable in any other way.

B. *Validation of the Rules of Proportion and Discrimination*

The way the two principles of political decision-making are themselves validated deserves further scrutiny. Since these principles of "just war doctrine" are normally understood as regulating warfare according to the dictates of justice, one would expect them to be derivatives of the principle of justice, in Ramsey's view. But that is not the case, nor could it be.[5] For justice, it will be remembered, is only one of the "terminal values" to be figured into a political decision, along with other values. What makes for justice is by no means all-determinative of a political decision. Therefore, if these two "just war" principles were simply specifications of justice, they would, like justice itself, be only one set of considerations among others. But they are decidedly not that in Ramsey's hands. They are normative constituents of the moral thinking process itself.

For principles Ramsey believes to be so powerful he needs a more powerful validation. Thus, by-passing the principle of justice altogether, he "goes right to the top," that is, to agape itself. He is, in fact, very explicit about deriving these two principles *directly* from agape (1968A:144-145, 164; 1961A:59). Indeed, as we mentioned, the two principles are suggestive of the two sides of agape, the discretionary and the formalistic side. They are, then, *two more* directives of agape, the one pointing to and guaranteeing a discretionary sphere of decision-making, and the other supplying a "feature-specific" designation of certain proscribed forms of action.

IV

Ramsey's Mode of Validation: A Critical Interpretation

A. *Validation as Interpretation*

We are now in a position to summarize and criticize Ramsey's mode of validation, or procedure for applying moral principles and rules to concrete cases. Ramsey has what we may call a *mode of interpretation*, a mode which is rather more flexible and open-ended than some other options. A mode of interpretation presupposes one basic validating norm, such as agape, with specifiable and derivative principles and rules, such as order, justice and law, but it also allows for the discretionary interpretation and application of these principles and rules to concrete cases. For example, Ramsey writes:

> If one has, upon proper moral warrants, established that just conduct in war is governed by the principle of discrimination and the principle of proportion, one then has only to get to know the meaning of these principles or "laws of war" and get to know certain stipulations governing the relation between them—that discrimination is the primary of the two, the fact that only proportion admits the possibility of significant reference to consequences while discrimination does not, etc. This can all be made pretty clear in its bearing upon conduct, although this clarity in ethical judgments does *not* remove the question; What then is required in *this* case? and certainly no specification within the meaning of these principles takes the place of many a "policy-decision" (1968a:102).

If I understand Ramsey's argument, "primary" principles like discrimination are exceptionless in that they designate a definite range of action characteristics to which there are no exemptions (1968a:132). In practical decisions, however, "interpretation" is required at two points. First, there is always the "secondary" range of teleological judgments (indicated by the principle of proportionality), which are discretionary, and in that sense "interpretive." For Ramsey, as we know, there is no way to subject teleological judgments to fixed, exceptionless standards.

Second, even the primary, formalistic principles, like discrimination, often have to be interpreted in concrete circumstances. This means, apparently, that there is allowed a certain "deepening" and "enriching" of the formalistic principles and rules by creatively redescribing their meaning in specific situations. Ramsey provides several examples that help to clarify the procedure, even though they do not apply exclusively to political ethics. Given, for instance, that there is a formalistically derived definite-action rule against lying, Ramsey states that "there could be no charitable reason for saying that . . . mere verbal inaccuracies of speech to save a life belong among the meanings of 'lying' " (1968a:91-92). Similarly, he writes:

> If anyone proposed as an *exempting* condition that it would be right to commit a "forgery" if by signing someone else's name to an official document he could save a large number of Jews from extermination in Hitler's "final solution," would not a proper reply be that this was not what was meant by forgery; that forgery means to do the physical action for selfish personal gain, etc. This occasion only drew our attention to what was meant by forbidding forgery (1968a:100-101).

Ramsey is adamant that this kind of interpretation, which would of course also apply to politics, is not the same as tolerating exemptions to formalistic principles and rules. It is more like coming to understand their "true" meaning as expressions of agape, a meaning which was there all along. This aspect of his mode of interpretation allows Ramsey some leeway in working with the formalistic side of agape, although there are some difficulties. Can nothing be said about the limits of interpretation? Ramsey assumes, I believe, a conformity of interpretation among rational men with respect to understanding the "true meaning" of the formalistic principles and rules. But we need to hear more about that, particularly in the light of conceivable conflicts of interpretation. For instance, suppose someone accepts Ramsey's interpretation that forgery "really means" signing someone else's name for selfish personal gain. Is it then not among the meanings of forgery to sign someone else's name in order to acquire new band uniforms for the high school, so long as the signer enjoys no selfish personal gain from the action, and thinks only of the "needs" of the high school? (cf. Evans, 1971:192-198 and reprinted here Chapter II). That would be a curious conclusion to draw, but I do not see how it is excluded by Ramsey's method of creative redescription.

In any case, whatever the particular difficulties, it is important to bear in mind the *two* kinds of interpretive activity operative in Ramsey's procedures for applying ethical norms to concrete situations, though I do not believe Ramsey has clarified the distinction sufficiently. The distinction is, as we would expect, keyed directly to this fundamental distinction between the two sides of agape. Thus, interpretive application of agape to *the ends and consequences* is obviously discretionary or, in our words, "systematically indeterminate," from the point of view of rational criteria and certitude. On the other hand, the interpretive application of agape to *the means* of action—or, at least to those means covered by the formalistic principles like discrimination—is rationally determinate, even though "creative" insight is sometimes required to perceive the "true" implications of a principle or rule.

B. Criticism of Ramsey's Method

There are some general difficulties with Ramsey's way of validating moral judgments, particularly in relation to political ethics. These difficulties come into focus in the remarkable discussion of "deferred repentance" found in an early work (1961B:11-12, cf. 163, 311). Ramsey gets himself into an unusual position in this discussion. He allows that a magistrate, in developing effective military deterrents *vis-a-vis* an enemy, may find himself unable to "escape from the evil necessities" of intending and preparing "to kill another man's children directly as a means of weakening *his* murderous intent." Such action, says Ramsey, "is intrinsically a grave moral evil," because it infringes the principle of discrimination: "readiness and preparation to kill the 'innocent' partake of the crime of actually doing so."[6] He goes on to admit that the magistrate in such a position perhaps ought to stay in office and continue taking part in grave moral evil in order "to engage in negotiation directed to the end [sic!] of limiting war to justifiable means and ends through a period of time in which [he] may have to defer [his] nation's repentance" (1961B:11-12).

We have here, from Ramsey's own pen, an example of its being *in some sense* reasonable or tolerable for a magistrate to make a decision by disregarding, temporarily, the application of the principle of discrimination to the *means* of action in favor of considering its application to the *ends* of action! Notice several things about this. First, Ramsey does *not*, in this case, avail himself of the "interpretive" procedure. According to that procedure, an agent, in concretely applying a "rule of agape," may well be driven to redescribe the features of the rule so as to "deepen" its meaning and applicability. But that is not open to a magistrate in the present context. In fact, Ramsey contends that magistrates caught in the sort of bind he mentions should be fully conscious of the grave moral evil implicit in the course of action he permits. They ought not in any way to minimize the gravity of the matter, but they simply ought to postpone doing something to rectify it.

Second, while it appears that the formalistic or deontological side of Ramsey's position has, in this instance, totally given way to the teleological side, that is not the case. What Ramsey has actually done is of the utmost importance. *He has "deferred" not only repentance, but also the application of the principle of discrimination from the means to the ends and consequences of action.* The deontological requirement of agape, in the form of the principle of discrimination, now controls or regulates the ends of action: the magistrate may acceptably stay in office toward "the end of limiting war [in the future] to justifiable means and ends." He may knowingly, if regretfully, intend to use indiscriminate means in the present so as to create conditions in the future in which the principle of discrimination will be more widely observed. We thus have what Ramsey is usually unwilling to provide, a particular standard or test or measure for making future-oriented calculations. And that standard is precisely derived from the formalistic side of agape.

Third, Ramsey implies in this example that an action in which a magistrate waived the principle of discrimination in the present in order to extend the jurisdiction of that principle in the future is a relatively better act, in moral terms, than one in which the magistrate waived the principle in the present *and also* disregarded the question of its jurisdiction in the future. In other words, the former case is excusable, if not fully justifiable, whereas the latter case is certainly wrong.

Ramsey may have gone back on his account of deferred repentance, at least with respect to admitting the moral excusability of violating the principle of discrimination in the present, the better to serve it in the future. But whether he has or hasn't, he should not have, in my opinion. I can easily imagine a case (somewhat analogous to Ramsey's forgery example) which would appear conceivably to excuse, if not to justify, killing another man's children "as a means of weakening his murderous intent." Let us suppose that an Eichmann is getting ready to put to death thousands of men, women, and children in a German prison camp. One is informed on excellent authority that this individual has twin five-year-old daughters whom he cherishes above all else in the world. As a last resort, one might hold those children hostage, threaten their lives, and, in the face of the father's skepticism, actually kill one of the daughters, all in order to save the lives of thousands of prisoners and, in the future, to prevent the further exercise of this man's murderous intent. This strikes me as a candidate for an excusable, if repulsive, act.

If I am right, we have here a case in which we would decidedly *not* want one of Ramsey's redescriptions or "deepenings" of meaning. To threaten the lives of two innocent children, and to take the life of one of them, is "a grave moral evil," no matter how it is described, and the perpetrator ought to know that. To do such an act with a clear conscience would be the gravest moral offense of all. Furthermore, to threaten the lives of the youngsters, and to take the life of one, and yet at the same time to be aware of the gravity of the act, is to acknowledge a *conflict* in the application of the moral requirement to protect the innocent. As such, it is very similar to the conflict Ramsey alludes to in applying the principle of discrimination. On the one hand, one ought himself to refrain from directly intending and committing harm to the innocent (the twin five-year olds), and, on the other, one ought to do all one realistically and proportionately can to protect the innocent (the thousands of prisoners) from harm directly intended against them by others. This aspect of the requirement includes creating future conditions in which the innocent have a better chance of being protected because the murderous intent of Eichmann-like people is restrained.

Finally, to threaten the children would be to decide to protect the innocent prisoners from harm directly intended against them by threatening harm to the innocent children. While it is true that such a decision involves a calculation of future consequences, it is also true that the consequences are calculated and evaluated according to the *same* moral requirement as applies to one's present responsibility to the little girls, namely to protect the innocent. It so happens that the only realistic means available for carrying out the application of the principle in respect to the thousands of prisoners is to disregard the application of the requirement to the little girls. This is exactly like the dilemma pictured to us by Ramsey regarding the magistrate and the principle of discrimination.

I am aware that being prepared to excuse such an act suggests troubling implications about the general use of terrorism: if this act is excusable, is it also excusable to threaten and perhaps take the lives of innocent airplane passengers in order to prevent the imprisonment of twenty captives considered to be innocent? Without delving into this complicated matter, let me state that I believe it would be possible to draw limits. It would seem reasonable to draw them on the basis of such things as *the moral enormity* of the situation being prevented (the murdering of thousands versus the imprisoning of twenty captives); *the realistic probability* that, in a given case, one's action would produce the desired effect; and the degree of *symmetry or proportion* between the action to be prevented and the action to be engaged in (killing one innocent to prevent the murder of thousands of innocents versus killing several innocents to prevent the imprisonment of several innocent captives).

Whatever the nature of the calculus involved, and however it is employed in regulating acts of terrorism, we may suggest two fundamental propositions as the result of our foregoing observations. First, the same determinate moral requirement (e.g., the principle of discrimination or the principle of protecting the innocent) will often apply *both* to the means *and* to the ends and consequences of an action; and, second, it may sometimes do so in such a way that the two applications contradict each other, and a choice between them may not eliminate the contradiction.

Generally speaking, to avoid adopting means of action that directly intend harm to noncombatants may, as a direct consequence, seriously decrease chances of creating a world in which noncombatants are respected. Similarly, to avoid adopting means of action that directly intend harm to innocent children may allow as a direct consequence the unrestrained exercise of murderous intent upon the lives of thousands, as well as the perpetuation of a system permitting such unrestrained exercise. In neither of these examples will (or should) a particular decision eliminate awareness of intense moral contradiction. To try in any way to "redescribe" the cases so as to remove the contradiction is to miss the point of the cases.

Ramsey shows some signs of accepting these propositions in his discussion of "deferred repentance," but his general moral position and his political ethics run counter to such acceptance. He resists both propositions by generally restricting the application of principles and rules to *the means* of action. Correspondingly, he weakens, if he does not undermine altogether, their efficacy as rational standards of evaluation regarding *the ends and consequences* of action. As we already know, to try to apply rational measures to the ends and consequences is forbidden on Ramsey's view, because the calculation of consequences is a discretionary affair. This conclusion is the result of his "split" view of agape. But whatever the reasons for it, the view seems seriously amiss.

Conclusion

As I indicated earlier, Ramsey's outlook flies in the face of what we actually, and, I believe, inescapably, do when we think morally about politics. I, for one, am uncomfortable when I am told that the moral evaluation of the ends and consequences of a policy is an altogether different sort of thing from the evaluation of the means. I am therefore uncomfortable when I am told, on the basis of this distinction, that I must manifest my "awe" of magistrates, and honor their discretionary prerogative, by refraining on principle from subjecting the ends and consequences of their politices to the same sort of definite moral standards to which I may subject the means of their policies.

To be more specific, I have always been surprised by Ramsey's relative indifference to the question of "the ends for which wars may legitimately be fought." In the debate over United States policy in Vietnam, I have not, and do not, share the judgment of many critics of that policy that the cause for and the end of United States military effort there was unambiguously "unjust and immoral." But I have always believed, against Ramsey, that the critics were right to bring up the questions of cause and end, and to consider those questions subjects for moral evaluation. These questions are every bit as important, though not more important, than the conduct of war. That it is difficult definitively to settle debate on the questions of cause and end, which it assuredly is in the case of Vietnam, does not render those questions any less salient or significant from a moral point of view.

For example, for Ramsey to call the test of just cause for war a "teleological test," and thus to construe it as properly a political or discretionary, rather than a distinctively moral, matter (1968A:130-131) is misguided. It is of course true, as Ramsey argues, that in our plualistic world the apprehensions of justice of one nation do not ordinarily reflect a common, universal apprehension of justice (1968A:130). But I do not see that this fact in any way alters the necessity of making judgments about the justice and injustice of the use of physical force in the world community. And if judgments must be made, determinate standards must logically be presupposed, and there is no reason not to think of these standards as moral in character. Moreover, if such standards must be presupposed, political decision-makers can make mistakes with respect to them, and, when they do, they ought to be called to account. Did Hitler misuse physical force or not? Did the North Vietnamese commit aggression or not? Sometimes questions of this sort are easily answered, sometimes not. And it is also true that precisely what a nation will do in response to perceived violations does not follow directly from taking a stand on the issue of just cause. That is a "political" problem (though not, for that reason, excluded from moral scrutiny). But neither the difficulty of settling the issue of just cause, nor the political complexity of deciding what to do in response to perceived violations means that passing judgment on the question of just cause should be exclusively "up to" the magistrates, or that they may not be held accountable for their judgments according to determinate and generally available standards of moral evaluation. In this respect, I see little difference between the moral evaluation of the means of warfare employed and the ends for which the war is fought.

The basic difficulty, then, is Ramsey's inclination to restrict the category of determinate moral requirements to decisions regarding the means of action. If we extend the applicability of this category to cover ends and consequences as well (as, I believe, an adequate moral position must do) then we will reverse Ramsey's position and *restrict* the wide range of moral discretion he permits to political decision-makers. At the same time, we will become aware of the ways moral principles and rules apply to ends and consequences of action as well as to means, and we will come to appreciate that conceivable contradictions in application constitute some of the irreducible moral dilemmas *faced by magistrates and citizens in the same way.*

In short, what we need, if we are to develop an adequate political ethics, is a set of standards for measuring, as best we can, the ends as well as the means of political policy. At times and on particularly complex and difficult issues, we may feel the need to "stand in awe" before our magistrates. But at other times, and on other issues, we may be called upon, as Calvin said, "to spit on the heads of magistrates." We need a set of criteria for enabling us to tell when to do one and when the other with respect to *both* means *and* ends.

NOTES

[1] It is surprising that Ramsey, in his too cursory discussion of "law," does not stress the moral significance that "treaties and agreements" should be supposed to have within his position. Given his emphasis on promise-keeping as one of the forms and rquirements of love, legal agreements or "covenants" between nations would have to have great moral weight in and of themselves. However, although legal covenants are undoubtedly weighty, they are by no means absolute or unbreakable for Ramsey, when it comes to making practical political decisions.

[2] See 1967B for an extended defense of this point of view.

[3] On the other hand, I do not see how, logically, Ramsey could argue that a magistrate had a moral right deliberately to infringe the principle of discrimination, since "it is never right to do wrong that good may come of it" (1968A:250). It is true that he flirts with such a prospect in his discussion of "deferred repentance" (see below, pp. 156ff.) but he has consistently backed off from such a conclusion in developing his position. Given, then, the superiority and priority of discrimination in moral reasoning for Ramsey, it would have to follow that there could be no moral justification for a clear and intentional violation of discrimination. Moreover, given the rational determinateness of the principle, all rational agents, and thus all eligible citizens, must conceivably be able to pass judgment on policy decisions relevant to discrimination. They will of course need reliable evidence of violation, but *that is an empirical, not a logical, condition.* Finally, it follows from this that citizens have a moral right to stand in judgment on magistrates regarding subjects covered by the principle of discrimination, and therefore ought to be allowed to exercise that right. Whence the grounds for a restricted form of selective conscientious objection. In the absence of such a provision, is there in Ramsey's thought a moral basis for a right to resistance?

[4] In a democracy every eligible citizen becomes a "lesser magistrate" who may participate "in the public processes," according to which the *ends* of military policy, for example, are determined. He may use his influence and cast his vote in accord with his own subjective view of the proper ends of policy. But since the matter of settling the issue of ends and consequences is "systematically indeterminate" on Ramsey's position, it may only be settled *procedurally*. If the constituted political procedures have been observed, so far as the determination of ends goes, then those whose recommendations are not adopted must, from a moral point of view, go along with the policy until they can overturn the decision by means of the political process (1968A:274-276).

[5] Ramsey frequently speaks of the just-war principles as principles for determining the "justifiedness" rather than the "justice" of a military operation. This is very significant in the light of our analysis.

[6] By his own testimony, Ramsey later "corrects" this view of deterrence (1968A:147, fn. 4: 248-258). In rethinking the matter, Ramsey contends that "deterrence sufficient to keep war limited and just need *not* rest on the intention to do murder," as he here assumes it does. It is also true that he is moving toward this "corrected" view even in *War and the Christian Conscience* (1961B:163ff.). I want to emphasize that however Ramsey later revises his views on the morality of deterrence so as to make them conform to the restrictions imposed by the principle of discrimination, I find that the above passage introduces, if only tentatively, considerations that raise some fundamental problems for Ramsey's ethical position, as I try to show below.

REFERENCES

Allen, C. K.
1961 *Law in the Making*. London: Oxford University Press.

Evans, Donald
1971 "Paul Ramsey on exceptionless moral rules." *American Journal of Jurisprudence* 16: 184-214. Also Chapter II in this volume.

Ramsey, Paul

See the bibliography of Ramsey's works in this volume. Capital letters (e.g., 1950A) denote books and occasional papers; lower case letters (e.g., 1968a) denote articles.

Stevenson, Charles L.

1963 *Facts and Values*. New Haven: Yale University Press.

Weber, Max

1968 *Economy and Society*. Vol. I. New York: Bedminster Press.

CHAPTER VIII

Morality and War: The Contribution of Paul Ramsey

WILLIAM V. O'BRIEN

As war, deterrence and revolution persist as prominent forms of international relations, the questions posed by just-war doctrines continue to be of primary importance. Few modern moralists have treated these questions with the wisdom, erudition, imagination and personal commitment of Paul Ramsey. It is the purpose of this essay to give an evaluation of Ramsey's effort to develop and apply just-war doctrine in terms of the problems of modern war, deterrence and revolution.

My evaluation will be undertaken from a background that includes three perspectives:

(1) traditional Roman Catholic just-war doctrine and its contemporary formulations by popes, councils and moralists;

(2) the international law of war;

(3) contemporary strategy.

I will first summarize and comment briefly on Ramsey's understanding of just-war in terms of his "twin-born" justification and limitation on war, i.e., in terms of his integrated concept of just cause (the *jus ad bellum*) and just conduct (the *jus in bello*). The greater part of the essay will then be devoted to

Ramsey's treatment of the *jus in bello* and its specific application in nuclear deterrence, counter-insurgency, and the use of incapacitating gases. I will conclude with an analysis of the *jus ad bellum* and its relation to problems of the *jus in bello*, particularly the problem of defining the concept of proportionality of permissible means to permissible ends.

I

Central Elements in Ramsey's Thought on War

A. *The "Twin-born" Justification of and Limitation on War*

Ramsey finds the justification for war in charity. A "love-informed reason" finds a duty in charity to protect the innocent from the depredations of aggressors. The same source limits intrinsically the permissible means of such protection by excluding attacks upon other innocents. Thus there is a simultaneously "twin-born" justification and limitation for just war. In this rationale, Ramsey explicitly excludes "abstract 'natural' justice" (1968A:142-143).

In broad outline Ramsey's just-war concepts unfold as follows:

Jus ad bellum—just war derives from the right and duty in social charity (love) of the strong to defend the weak and threatened from aggressors.

Jus in bello—just war must be conducted in accordance with two principles derived from the nature of the undertaking, namely, *discrimination* and *proportion.* The principle of discrimination prohibits direct, intentional attacks on non-combatants (innocents), the very category of persons whose protection justifies recourse to arms. The principle of proportion limits the force employed in defense of the innocent to that which is proportionate to the just end.

It is a distinctive feature of Ramsey's approach that his "love-informed" reason finds the object of defense against injustice to be not the "self" but another person who is victim. He says:

> While Jesus taught that a disciple in his own case should turn the other cheek, he did not enjoin that his disciples should lift up the face of another oppressed man for *him* to be struck again on *his* other cheek. . . . It is the work of love and mercy to deliver as many as possible of God's children from tyranny, and to protect from oppression, if one can, as many of those for whom Christ died as it may be possible to save. When choice *must* be made between the perpetrator of injustice and the many victims of it, the latter may and should be preferred—even if effectively to do so would require the use of armed force against some evil power. This is what I mean by saying that the justice of sometimes resorting to armed conflict originated in the interior of the ethics of Christian love (Ramsey, 1968A:143, original emphasis).

It is to be observed that the usual Catholic just-war formulations do not insist upon the concept of "love-informed" reason but are content with reason as a reflection of God's natural law. Within this natural law tradition "self-defense" is accepted as natural and morally justified (O'Brien, 1967a;1969:21-29). However Christians may have borrowed "subsequently to elevate and refine the Stoic concept of natural justice" (Ramsey, 1968A:143), it appears that natural law teaching within the Catholic scholastic tradition is closer to "natural justice" than to love-informed reason on this point.[1] As an adherent of the Catholic natural law tradition, I cannot accept Ramsey's insistence that one may never defend oneself but that one is entitled and obliged to defend others, because of love. But it is clear that Ramsey's love-informed reason aspires to a higher, more altruistic level of behavior than that accepted by natural law and the near-universal standards of domestic positive laws (Ramsey, 1968A:145).

It is not apparent, however, whether or in what respects it makes any difference to Ramsey's *jus ad bellum* if the right of defense of others includes the right of defense of self. Ramsey's concept of defense is corporate, not a collection of individual defenses of individual threatened innocents. He concludes the passage justifying participation in war by referring to the requirement "to serve the needs of men in the only concrete way possible, and maintain a just endurable order in which they may live" (Ramsey, 1968A:143). This is a corporate, public order version of the love-informed reason imperative, as contrasted with the formulation that precedes it, *viz.* disciples of Jesus are not to lift up the face "of another oppressed man for *him* to be struck again. . ." (Ramsey, 1968A:143).[2]

We have here what the literature on international relations calls the level of analysis problem (e.g., Singer, 1969). One can approach the problem of just defense at the level of individual men, some of whom are to be protected from oppression by those capable of doing so. Those latter may justly employ armed force and even take the lives of the oppressors because of the right and duty in social charity to resist injustice. Or, more pertinent to the problem of public war, one can take the perspective of the soldier who is called upon to use armed force and take enemy lives—not for the defense of specific individuals but for the protection of "a just endurable order" (Ramsey, 1968A:143).

In the case of the individual, the strong man who perceives threats of violence and oppression against the innocent makes up his own mind about the justice of resistance on their behalf. In the case of the same strong individual, serving in the public forces of his country, he must normally take it on the authority of this government that recourse to public armed force meets the specifications of a just war.[3]

But Ramsey consistently steers clear of second-guessing the *raison d'état* decisions of political authorities. In so doing he concedes a great deal. For, as I will attempt to explain in the last section of this essay, no adequate judgment on the *jus in bello* issues can ultimately be made without considering the causes for which public war is waged.

The transfer of the focus of moral decision from the individual strong man protecting the innocent to the collective authority which legitimately orders many strong men to engage in public war on behalf of the innocent and for a just endurable order brings us to the issue of just cause. What goals or values are sufficient to warrant recourse to war? In the few typical passages quoted, Ramsey refers to "resisting injustice," "tyranny," "oppression," "some evil power." But, precisely because war is a collective, political act, the focus of inquiry should be sharpened with respect to the question of defining goals or values warranting armed defense into the age-old question, "Who decides?" I understand (but cannot accept) the idea that although I may not kill an armed felon in self-defense, I may kill him if he is threatening others. When we move to the level of determining whether one political society is justified in taking up arms against another for reasons other than self-defense against armed attack, i.e., to protect the innocent from injustice, tyranny, oppression and some evil power, however, I require a more detailed elaboration with respect to the presumptions for authoritative decision within the contemporary world public order.

B. *Discrimination and Proportion*

On the face of it, modern total (i.e, conventional) war, nuclear war and deterrence, revolutionary war and counter-insurgency all appear to involve violation of the principle of discrimination. As Ramsey has often pointed out, this apparent "fact" has driven some into pacifism and others, who suppose war to be an inescapable, evil institution into the realist minimization-of-evil approach. But Ramsey does not want to take either of these paths. He is persuaded that there continues to be a need for defense of others rooted in love-informed reason. Although he never really works out the "threats" to human life and freedom—as, for example, John Courtney Murray (1958) attempted to do—he appears to take such threats as given and as engendering challenges which strong and righteous men and nations cannot ignore.

Ramsey therefore assumes the task of helping guide the consciences of these strong and righteous men and nations by showing them *how* they can in Christian charity accomplish their mission of assisting victims of aggression and injustice while maintaining their fidelity to the twin-born justification and limitation of just war. The heart of this guidance is the explanation and elaboration of the principles of discrimination and proportion.

Ramsey is insistent that the principle of discrimination always comes first in moral analysis of war and defense. If an act or policy does not pass the test of discrimination, there is no warrant for discussing its alleged proportionality. If an act passes the test of discrimination, it still must pass the test of proportion.

It will be useful to have a typical statement of these points before us. The following passage provides a concise summary:

> The principle of discrimination is shorthand for "the moral immunity of non-combatants from direct attack." This does not require that civilians never be knowingly killed. It means rather that military action should, in its primary (objective) thrust as well as in its subjective purpose discriminate between directly attacking combatants or military objectives and directly attacking non-combatants or destroying the structures of civil society as a means of victory. . . . The latter is the meaning of murder, which is never just even in war; while the former is the meaning of the killing in war which can be justified, including the collateral and forseeable but unavoidable destruction of non-combatants in the course of attacking military objectives (Ramsey, 1968A:429).

On proportion and its relation to discrimination Ramsey says:

> . . . the ends justify the means, since nothing else can; but they do not justify *any* means. The means which no ends can justify have to be determined by the principle of discrimination. The statement that only the ends justify the means is a statement falling under the principle of proportion; so understood, it is unquestionably correct. The statement that the ends do not justify the means (or are not capable of justifying any and all means) is a statement falling under the principle of discrimination; so understood it too is unquestionably correct. The principle of proportion is regulative of all actions that are finally *to be done*; prudence governs in determining the effects or consequences that ought never to be let loose in the world. Especially in politics, only the ends justify the means (Ramsey, 1968A:430-431).

In the world of moralists and experts concerned with war, Ramsey is virtually alone in this understanding of and emphasis on the principle of discrimination. This does not prejudice his case. As a sympathetic critic, however, I must point out that his isolation on this point walls him off from positions that otherwise are consonant with his effort to revive just-war doctrine, namely, the positive international law of war and the social teaching of the Catholic Church.

II

Two Other Sources of Limits on War

A. *International Law*

From c.1648 to 1914, positive international law developed the principle of non-combatant immunity from intentional direct attack. While this principle of positive law may have owed something to Scholastic and other earlier just-war doctrines, its more influential source appears to have been in secular political theory, summed up in the Rousseau-Portalis doctrine that war is a relationship of states, not men, and that only the public forces of warring states are proper belligerents and proper objects of attack (O'Brien, 1960a:83-86 and authorities therein cited; O'Brien, 1960b:134-138).

The demise of this version of non-combatant immunity in modern total war was already recognized after World War I. It was a controverted, hen-and-egg question whether the real reason for this demise lay in the indiscriminate character of modern weapons systems and economic warfare or in the fact that mobilization of whole nations for total war was seen by Sherman and others who followed him as an invitation for and justification of carrying war to the "home front." In any event, contemporary positive international law reflects the destruction by modern war of the once-honored principle of non-combatant immunity from direct intentional attack. Today, there are provisions to protect non-combatants as part of the "humanitarian" international law of war (O'Brien, 1972a:653-658). But contemporary international law, viewed as a reflection of the values, authoritative decisions and expectations of the holders of power in the world public order, does not hold as binding the principle of discrimination as formulated by Ramsey.

The historic distinction between combatants and non-combatants once provided what John Bassett Moore (1924:viii) called "the vital principle of the modern law of war." But by the post-World War II period the great English publicist Lauterpacht (1952:364-365) was writing that the only "unchallenged" principle in this regard is the "rule that non-combatants, whether in occupied territory or elsewhere, must not be made the object of attack unrelated to military operations and directed exclusively against them." Judge Lauterpacht found that it was a "clear rule of law" that "international terrorisation—or destruction—of the civilian population as an avowed or obvious object of attack" was prohibited. Lauterpacht observed that "admission of a right to resort to the creation of terror among the civilian population as being a legitimate object *per se* would inevitably mean the actual and formal end of the law of warfare." He concluded that "the prohibition of terror not incidental to lawful operations must be regarded as an absolute rule of law." In a grim, ironic understatement summing up the state of positive international law with respect to the principle of discrimination, McDougal and Feliciano (1961:80) observe: "The essentially modest character of this 'absolute rule' needs no underlining."

Indeed, aside from the principle of proportion as the heart of the principle of legitimate military necessity, positive international law cannot be said to prescribe *any* general limitation on the means of destruction in war (O'Brien, 1960a:82-100; 1972a:613-616, 638-641). Limitations on chemical-biological warfare are a special case (O'Brien, 1962a; 1972a:641-647). Efforts to outlaw weapons under the so-called St. Petersburg Principle (Declaration of St. Petersburg of 1867) prohibiting weapons causing "superfluous suffering" remain confused and unsuccessful (O'Brien, 1960a:87-88; 1972a:637-638).

Positive international law does not coincide with international morality. But it is important to know the state of a question in a normative discipline that stands between morality and raw international politics. In short, pre-World War I positive international law provided evidence for Ramsey's characterization of the principle of discrimination as part of our Western just-war tradition. But since World War I, the virtual demise of the principle of non-combatant immunity in positive international law suggests that Ramsey may be attempting an impossible task when he attempts to maintain both the option of some form of effective modern defense and the principle of discrimination.

B. *Catholic Social Teaching*

Appraisal of Ramsey's principle of discrimination in terms of the social teaching of the Catholic Church is complicated by the fragmentation and imprecision of that body of thought (O'Brien, 1967a, 1969). Ramsey recognizes that most recent official Catholic pronouncements on war, including its effects on non-combatants, are based primarily on opposition to illegal acts of aggression or on the actual or potential disproportion of modern war to any stated goals. Ramsey's principle of discrimination is not explicitly invoked in most official Catholic statements on war.

Ramsey, however, professes to be heartened by Vatican II's *Pastoral Constitution on the Church in the Modern World*, wherein it is laid down (Article 80) that "Any act of war aimed indiscriminately at the destruction of entire cities or of extensive areas along with their population is a crime against God and man himself," which "merits unequivocal and unhesitating condemnation" (Abbott, 1966:294; Ramsey, 1968A:372-373). But Ramsey's interpretation of this passage as supporting his version of the principle of discrimination is questionable. The *Pastoral Constitution* of Vatican Council II does not offer a *specific* restatement of the principle of discrimination. The passage quoted from Article 80 would seem to combine the principles of discrimination and proportion. The act of war condemned is "the destruction of entire cities or of extensive areas along with their population." The literal characterization of this condemnation would appear to be something like the immunity of entire cities — or population centers — from direct, intentional attack.

This is a different characterization from that of Ramsey's more formal principle of non-combatant immunity (discrimination). Since Article 81 of the Vatican II document, which follows the passage quoted, deals with nuclear deterrence, it is reasonable to conclude that the Council is talking in Article 80 about nuclear war and condemning the counter-city character of most forseeable forms of such war. This is an important judgment by the Council. But, as is too often the case with Catholic social doctrine, the judgment is unsupported by a rationale which would justify the claim that the Council has reaffirmed a principle as formal as Ramsey's principle of discrimination.

Vatican II has been put on notice that Christians and men of good will wanted clarification of the components of just-war doctrine as well as of the rationale underlying those components (Finn, 1965). A very substantial body of opinion rested its opposition to nuclear war (and, indeed, to modern conventional war) on the principle of non-combatant immunity. Unlike Ramsey, I cannot consider Article 80 to be responsive to these demands for clarification. This is a pity, particularly in view of the general trends away from the disposition of Catholics to give official social teachings the benefit of the doubt. In the post-*Humanae Vitae* era, Catholics want to scrutinize the reasons *why* an act is considered immoral. Unsupported or unelaborated judgments are not presently carrying sufficient authority to convince those who disagree with the results of the moral determination of issues. The conclusions asserted in Article 80 are an unfortunate instance of such judgments.

One other point should be made regarding the *Pastoral Constitution* as a reinforcement of Ramsey's position on discrimination. Although the Vatican Council recognized the continued necessity for defense, it continued the line of modern popes in calling for "the time when all war can be completely outlawed by international covenant" (Article 82, Abbott, 1966:295). This is not, of course, a possibility seriously envisaged by either Ramsey or this writer. On the contrary, our whole approach is predicated on the assumption that war is a perennial feature of the international system and that just-war doctrine is, accordingly, a perennial necessity. It would seem that to the extent the "entirely new attitude" called for in Article 80 of the *Pastoral Constitution* (Abbot, 1966:293) is pursued literally, just-war doctrine will continue to be ignored. This need not be the case, but that has been our experience.

III

Ramsey's Jus in Bello Applied

It is unfortunately not possible in this essay to undertake the detailed analyses of Ramsey's applications of the principles of discrimination and proportion that a full critique requires. I will restrict myself to a brief summary of Ramsey's three principal applications of these principles to contemporary problems and offer some general critical observations.

A. *Nuclear Strategy*

Ramsey's struggle with U.S. nuclear war and deterrence policies has turned on his efforts to reconcile efficacious deterrence with his principle of discrimination. He manages to find proposals for counter-force deterrence which can be interpreted as meeting the limits of discrimination. Ramsey is, however, confronted with the prevailing counter-value threat deterrent system summed up in the prevailing concept of Mutual Assured Destruction (MAD), according to which deterrence rests upon the credible threat of unacceptable counter-value attacks in response to nuclear aggression.

Ramsey is not prepared to endorse any deterrent that depends on credible threats to take actions violative of the principle of discrimination, no matter what necessities are claimed by strategists. In developing his own position he has moved two ways. First, he has sought the assistance of strategists who hold out the prospect of adequate deterrence based on some form of counter-force (only) warfare.[4] Second, he has explored the risky idea that one might obtain deterrence from possessing means capable of delivering either counter-force or counter-value attacks, with the resolution to use such means only for counter-force, hoping that the opponent would not be willing to exceed such auto-limitation by threatening counter-value escalation (Ramsey, 1968A:253).

The first approach, as Ramsey frequently acknowledges, puts the fate of morally permissible nuclear deterrence in the hands of the strategists. It is up to them to find efficacious forms of counter-force deterrence, as some have claimed to do, e.g., McNamara's 1962 Ann Arbor initiative and Schlesinger's current proposals. In this approach Ramsey, like John Courtney Murray elsewhere, is addressing a moral imperative to strategists to find morally permissible and efficacious means of defense and deterrence.[5]

The second approach, has, in my view, been unfortunate and has reduced Ramsey's credibility. Rather than review it, it is sufficient to welcome Ramsey's recent admission that "I now think that an input of deliberate ambiguity about the counter-people use of nuclear weapons is not possible unless it is (immorally) meant, and not a very good idea in the first place" (Ramsey, 1973j:142).

B. *Insurgency and Counter-Insurgency*

Turning to insurgency and counter-insurgency, "modern war" in the writings of many military experts, we find another firm application of the principle of discrimination by Ramsey. Once again, a form of warfare is unable to reach the test of proportionality because it cannot clear that of discrimination. Ramsey observes that insurgency avoids direct battle with the government's military forces. "Instead, it deliberately strikes the civil population, or a selected number of the civil population, in order to subvert a whole country's traditions and institutions and to bring down the government" (Ramsey, 1968A:432). Ramsey equates "the moral quality of such action" with "fire-storms" or "city-busting" as integral conventional or nuclear warfare strategies (Ramsey, 1968A:432).

In Ramsey's moral analysis, the "morality of the conduct of insurgency" is not dependent on "the program of 'national liberation.' " Typically placing the *jus in bello* principle of discrimination before just cause, Ramsey insists that "instead we must focus attention upon what happens when insurgency resorts to arms," irrespective of what insurgency accomplishes by political, psychological and other means. The invariable use of terror, even selective terror, might fit some standards of proportion, but it cannot help violating unacceptably the principle of discrimination, even if "only a comparatively few among the non-combatant population" are the direct object of attack.

Ramsey's judgment is that to the extent that "the strategy of contemporary insurgency" is "to strike selectively the civil population in order to subvert government," it "is an inherently immoral plan of war, no matter how many benefits are supposed to accrue from it" (Ramsey, 1968A:433).

This judgment may well be more far-reaching than Ramsey's condemnation of counter-value nuclear war and deterrence. Whereas his interpretation of discrimination questions the morality of the seemingly *most effective* forms of nuclear deterrence, his interpretation of that principle precludes *any* form of revolutionary warfare following the strategies and methods that have become universal with modern revolutionaries from Vietnam to the Middle East and from Uruguay to Northern Ireland. Unable in virtually every case to match incumbent forces and their allies with conventional strength, rebels today tend to find revolutionary warfare along the Maoist-Ho Chi Minh-Giap model to be the only serious option. Whereas the great issues of nuclear war and deterrence affect all mankind only to some degree, the perceived right of and necessity for revolution is a universal phenomenon. It is a hard saying that the principal means of exercising that right must involve "an inherently immoral plan of war, no matter how many benefits are supposed to accrue from it" (Ramsey, 1968A:433).

With respect to counter-insurgency, as with the case of nuclear deterrence, Ramsey remains opposed to any use of counter-value means. He is inclined to believe that the counter-insurgents' best chance lies in political-economic rather than in military measures, a judgment which may be sound although it has not been sufficiently tested. It is to be regretted that such an approach was either not sufficiently feasible or was simply not pressed adequately in Vietnam. It should also be remembered that it is precisely the revolutionaries' interest to prevent at all cost the success of positive programs of political-economic-social reform—by terrorist tactics if necessary.

Ramsey recognizes the inevitability of military encounters in revolutionary conflicts. Such encounters challenge the principle of discrimination because the revolutionaries habitually blend in with the people (Mao's sea in which the guerilla fish swim) and present objectives and targets involving inevitable injury to non-combatants and to the social infra-structure (Ramsey, 1968A:435, 502-503).

As an attempt to show that counter-insurgency war is not necessarily indiscriminate, Ramsey compares air and ground attacks against Viet Cong strongholds and areas of control with the catapults sanctioned in medieval sieges wherein the innocent suffered with the combatant defenders. He finds that such air attacks are capable of meeting the requirements of discrimination, something that neither counter-value nuclear deterrence and war nor revolutionary insurgency of the Maoist model are, in his opinion, able to do. (This generalized judgment would have to be reviewed in particular cases and does not address the problems of strategic bombing of North Vietnam.)

If the test of discrimination can be passed, what of the second of Ramsey's principles? The proportionality of counter-insurgency war such as was waged by the Republic of Vietnam and the United States and its allies is not really the object of extended analysis by Ramsey. However, he has recently observed that:

> . . . a chief lesson to be drawn from Vietnam is that, when an industrial power like the United States gets involved in counter-insurgency in a traditional and preindustrial society, *disproportionate violence is bound to be done*. Indeed, that is the one proper way to condemn the U.S. involvement . . . (Ramsey, 1973c:37, original emphasis).

It should be noted that Ramsey does not state that it is *his* conclusion that the Vietnam War was disproportionate and to be condemned accordingly. Note further that by October 1973 Ramsey still does not consider that the counter-insurgency war in Vietnam involved *necessary* violations of the principle of *discrimination.* He refers only to proportionality.[6]

C. Incapacitating Gases

It remains to say a word about Ramsey's discussion of non-lethal, incapacitating gases. Ramsey, in contrast to moralists for whom chemical warfare as such is disallowed, displayed an interest in incapacitating gases as a weapon capable of discrimination and very possibly preferable to existing weapons in counter-insurgency wars (wherein it is difficult to attack combatants without great collateral damage to the innocent and coerced). He faced, in this inquiry, the objection that chemical warfare of all kinds has been proscribed by international law, because *inter alia*, as a category it represents a practical "firebreak" which, the nations have decided, should not be breached. (This is the problem which I have discussed, as have others, in terms of the dangers of opening a Pandora's box [O'Brien, 1962a:63; 1969:247, 1972a:641-647].)

Ramsey assimilates this objection into the principle of proportion. That is, it would be disproportionate to "create a peril of escalation" to lethal, possibly indiscriminate gases (Ramsey, 1968A:476). He formulates the issue in terms of disproportionate escalation beyond an established firebreak, notwithstanding his characterization of the firebreak as "a non-rational boundary" (Ramsey, 1968A:477).

IV

Ramsey's Jus in Bello: An Assessment

Before returning to some issues related to the *jus ad bellum* and its role in assessing proportionality under *jus in bello*, an assessment of Ramsey's *jus in bello* is in order. The following propositions summarize my reaction to Ramsey's attempt to formulate a firmly principled and effective basis for moral deterrence and defense.

(1) The principle of discrimination as interpreted by Ramsey rests on moral grounds that, while overwhelmingly clear and sufficient to him, are not

convincing to me and to many others who write in the broad just-war tradition.

Ramsey's principle of discrimination is not based on the authority of the traditional just-war doctrine but only on an interpretation of Augustine's contribution to that doctrine (Curran, 1973:61-66, 72-76; Hartigan, 1966a, 1966b). One may be an adherent of the traditional just-war doctrine without accepting Ramsey's version of the principle of discrimination. Moreover, in my view, Ramsey's principle of discrimination is inconsistent with the requirements of adequate deterrence and defense, as recognized by international law. This principle is an obstacle to the proper exercise of the moral rights of deterrence and defense indispensable to political life. Ramsey's use of discrimination likewise appears to preclude meaningful exercise of the right of revolution, a fundamental human right.

Ramsey's principle of discrimination, then, bars recourse to certain reasonably efficacious means of deterrence, defense, and revolution for men, nations, and groups having fundamental moral rights to use such means. It would require extremely persuasive arguments and impressive authorities to sustain Ramsey's restrictions on these moral rights. In my view Ramsey has not offered such arguments or cited such authorities with sufficient force to overcome my presumption against limitations on legitimate deterrence, defense and revolution which doom them to failure.

(2) If principled restrictions, "firebreaks," ought to be imposed on moral belligerents, they will have to be more pragmatically conceived. Not only do I reject the logic and authority of Ramsey's "twin-born" justification and limitation of war, I question the utility of choosing "non-combatants" or "innocents" as the immune or protected category. Prescinding from supposed immutable first principles and viewing the interpretation of discrimination as a pragmatic exercise in finding reasonable "firebreaks" or "thresholds" in the *jus in bello*, one would focus on "cities" or "population centers" rather than categories of individuals, unless individuals *per se* were the targets, as in some terrorist attacks. As earlier remarked, just-war defense, even in Ramsey's version, is a corporate proposition, not the defense of discrete innocents. If one moves away from the "twin-born" justification-limitation concept based on individual innocents insofar as justification is concerned, there is good reason to view the limitations in broader fashion, rather than in terms of individual immunities.

In any event, it appears more possible to reconcile effective corporate defense with somewhat looser formulations of restrictive protected categories of targets than is possible under Ramsey's interpretation of just war. The task of making deterrence and defense both moral and effective is still formidable, but I suspect a shift of focus in the restricted categories of the *jus in bello* will produce a more reasonable balance between moral limitation and military necessity. The development of a realistic *jus in bello* becomes more a matter of suggesting and encouraging useful limitations on the conduct of war and less a matter of attempting to interpret intractable prescriptions deduced from immutable first principles in ways that permit the strategist to get out of the corner into which the moralist has painted him.

Ramsey himself recognizes the utility of such pragmatic restrictions in his treatment of non-lethal chemical means. The pragmatism, perhaps the arbitrariness, of thresholds or firebreaks such as, e.g., prohibition of direct, intentional attacks on population centers, or prohibition against *first* recourse to counter-value warfare, is reflected in the existing prohibition of chemical-biological warfare. As Ramsey points out, these prohibitions may not be logical, but they may be effective in building the *jus in bello* and reducing the destruction of war.

(3) *Any* categories established as immune from direct, intentional attack under the principle of discrimination, or any other principle, will endanger the effectiveness of deterrence and defense, since they will delineate areas of efficacious military action which an enemy may undertake without fear of retaliation in kind, or which the enemy may write off as a bonus to himself, even if he lacks the capability to take such actions himself.

Accordingly, any just-war *jus in bello* that places a high value on effectiveness in deterrence and defense (i.e., that is to be more than a rationale for patently inadequate deterrence and defense or for abandoning the attempt altogether) must find some formula for accepting *present* recourse to possibly immoral but effective means of deterrence and defense, provided that reasonable efforts are made to bring about fundamental changes in the international system. This seems to be the line preferred by Vatican II. Despite its condemnation of counter-value war (Article 80), the main thrust of the *Pastoral Constitution on the Church in the Modern World* is that the "terrible trap" of the arms race, war and deterrence must be escaped through vigorous efforts to change the system. This approach seems to leave room for retaining the means necessary to deal with opponents who would escalate beyond moral limits—provided sufficiently forceful steps are being taken to change the system that puts moral men and nations in such dilemmas.

If, on the other hand, it is believed that war is a perennial fact and a moral necessity (in effect, that the international system is not likely to be changed in the ways enjoined by the Church), the dilemmas of reconciling effective deterrence and defense with firm moral principles (e.g., discrimination) cannot be avoided by calls for "an entirely different attitude towards war." They can, under this more pessimistic view, only be resolved by the ingenuity of the theorists and practioners of military strategy and technology in answering the normative appeal for effective limited war and deterrence doctrines and capabilities.

(4) If the firebreak provided by the principle of discrimination will not hold against the pressures of effective deterrence and defense requirements, the remaining moral constraint is the principle of proportion.

With all of its weaknesses of subjectivity and relativity, but with the advantages of its indispensable emphasis on weighing competing values and producing working models of "reasonableness," the principle of proportion is the ultimate source of whatever realistic restrictions are possible in deterrence, defense, and revolution. A retreat, as it were, to the principle of proportion as the main firebreak manifests a failure in Ramsey's gallant stand at that of discrimination. But this is preferable to renouncing efficacious legitimate deterrence, defense and revolution on the one hand and moral restraint in war on the other. As I have argued elsewhere (O'Brien, 1957; 1960a; 1960b; 1967a; 1969 and 1972a), the principle of proportion may be rendered more manageable and stable by realistic efforts to formulate material-normative typologies of actions which, in specified contexts, are *prima facie* "reasonable" or "unreasonable." This, of course, is the path followed by domestic law (e.g., lethal traps for chicken thieves are unreasonable and unlawful) and in international law (chemical and biological warfare are *prima facie* unreasonable and unlawful even though not necessarily *mala in se*).

These comments on the *jus in bello* could be extended, but it is necessary now to return to the just cause element of the *jus ad bellum* which furnishes a central referent for the calculus of proportionality.

V

The Jus ad Bellum Again — Proportionality to What?

It has been earlier observed that Ramsey provides little elaboration on his *jus ad bellum* categories. He appears to take as given that, in the modern world, there are aggressors, very often totalitarians, who would impose unjust *regimes* on innocent people by unjust armed force. Accordingly, the problem is to find moral — and effective — means of preventing these unjust aggressors from carrying out their manifest designs.

As to the concrete decisions necessary to identify just causes of this kind and to calculate the proportion between probable good resulting from defense of the victims of totalitarian aggression and the probable evil to be anticipated from recourse to war, Ramsey is loath to second-guess the responsible decision-makers. Indeed, he seems disposed to question only their decisions on the means employed in presumptively just deterrence and defense.

Ramsey's critics include some who are so anxious to question Western values and intentions and so eager to understand, excuse and condone the values and intentions of others, notably Communists, that they either reject outright his whole estimate of the situation in terms of threat assessment of totalitarian tyranny and aggression or take it as evidence of adherence to perspectives now discredited among the revisionist *elites* of the post-Cold War World. As one who is not of those *elites*, I find Ramsey's handling of the question of just cause in terms of credible threats to peace, order and justice to be valid. Like Ramsey (1968A:448-449), I am "not antecedently convinced of the single overriding absolute principle that the triumph of Titoist types of communism is in general the greater good" in revolutionary situations like Vietnam.

Thus, my dissatisfaction with Ramsey's handling of the *jus ad bellum* does not arise from essential disagreements with his political-ideological assumptions or prudential judgments about the present world situation. To be sure, a complete just-war analysis in the manner of Ramsey would require a thorough re-examination of the threats to peace, order and justice that persist in the world. But it is no more unreasonable for Ramsey to posit an essentially Cold War model of the international system than it is for others to assume a *detente* model which may or may not survive the Middle East conflict, possible heating up of the arms race, the energy crisis, and the permutations of Soviet-Chinese relations.

Although Ramsey's position on contemporary just causes is not unreasonable, it is far from satisfactory. It is not satisfactory, in particular, because of the integral, "twin-born" character of Ramsey's *jus ad bellum—jus in bello*. Even if one is willing to excuse Ramsey from elaboration of the *details* of the *jus ad bellum* because of his principled disinclination to meddle in the prudential realms of statecraft and strategy, he cannot avoid more serious attention to this category than he provides because the principle of proportionality is meaningless without a referent in the category of ends.

The principle of proportion is applicable to both components of just-war doctrine, *jus ad bellum* and *jus in bello*. The *jus ad bellum* requirement that the probable good from a war will exceed the probable evil is, of course, a requirement of proportionality (McCormick, 1967:803,804; Curran, 1973:75-76; O'Brien, 1967a:41-43). The *jus in bello* also has its principle of proportion. The question arises as to the referent of the proportionality of means under the *jus in bello*. Do all means of war have to be judged in terms of proportionality to the ends of war? Or, are there intermediate ends that should be consulted in judging the proportionality of means?

In dealing with this question from the perspectives of international law, I have elsewhere distinguished judgments of proportionality of acts of war in terms of *military* necessity (*raison de guerre*) from judgments in terms of ultimate *state* necessity (*raison d'état*) (O'Brien, 1957:111-136, 160-176; 1960a:49-58; Huber, 1913). My analysis was strongly influenced by the attempted development in international law of an aggressor-legal defender distinction which, if pushed to extremes, would brand all acts of war by "aggressors" as automatic, inherent "war crimes" (O'Brien, 1960a:49-50). It would not follow that all acts of war taken by a just defender (or, if one ever appeared, a United Nations or other international "enforcement" force under collective security) would automatically be legally permissible. Nevertheless, there was in World War II a decided psychological disposition to accept without question all sorts of acts by just defenders against Axis "war criminals," e.g., strategic bombing of cities.

Since I was interested in mitigation of the conduct of war and adherence to just intention, concerned with the *jus in bello* from the perspectives of military commanders and troops, and anxious that the agressor/just-defender distinction not go the way of older just-war excesses clothed in overriding just causes, I defined proportionality in the *jus in bello* in terms of *military*, not ultimate political, ends.

For example, German Field Marshal Erich von Manstein was tried as a war criminal after World War II, accused of violation of the principle of proportion in his employment of "scorched earth" policies as his armies retreated out of Russia. Should the referent in this case be the *military* necessities of a commander in von Manstein's situation—*any* commander in a comparable situation? Or should the measures be judged in terms of the referent of Hitler's war aims and genocidal policies with respect to Russia—and the world? If the latter, then nothing done by von Manstein would be proportionate to a just (legitimate, permissible) end. On the other hand, the fact that the bombing of Dresden was ordered by the victims of aggression and the liberators of Europe from totalitiarian tyranny and genocide raises the question of the *military* disproportion of measures taken by a just defender. I would conclude that von Manstein's military measures were proportionate and acceptable and that the Allied bombing of Dresden was disproportionate and unacceptable (Paget, 1951:49-53, 102-104, 175-177; Manstein, 1958:Chapters 16-22; Liddell Hart, 1948:63-67; Irving, 1963).

Borrowing from my professor Ernst H. Feilchenfeld, I adopted the concept of a "reasonable colonel," symbolic of a standard of reasonableness for conduct in war, comparable to the "reasonable man" standard in domestic criminal and tort law. It is clear that many acts of war are not proportionate in terms of military utility as it would be judged by a competent military professional, e.g., the Mylai massacre.

In my own comprehensive concept of legitimate military necessity, I also included normative "firebreaks" for acts violative of the natural law and for acts violative of the positive law of war, *viz.*:

> Military necessity consists in all measures immediately indispensable and proportionate to a legitimate military end, provided that they are not prohibited by the laws of war or the natural law, when taken on the decision of a responsible commander, subject to judicial review (O'Brien, 1957:138).

As to the requirements of the natural law, I had in mind restrictions such as those claimed by Ramsey in his interpretation of the principle of discrimination, although I was then and remain now unclear as to the sources and imperative character of that principle. In the case of genocide there is a convergence of positive international law and natural law (O'Brien, 1969:19).

I still maintain that it is preferable to judge as many military actions as possible by a standard of proportionality to agreed legitimate military ends rather than to the political-ideological-strategic ends of belligerents. A major argument for this approach is that it limits military command responsibility to the military dimension of acts of war. It does not require the soldier to attempt to judge the ultimate just causes, a requirement which might be impossible for him to meet — or which might be an invitation to license and arrogation of authority and control from civil superiors. Even if this approach is followed, however, it is clear that some actions will be typical of broad strategies which in turn will be so central to the calculus of *raison d'état*-level means and ends that they will span both the realms of *jus ad bellum* and *jus in bello*. All forms of nuclear war and deterrence appear to be in this category, as do most strategies that are viewed as indispensable to particular forms of war, e.g., conventional counter-value strategic bombing policies, commitment of large-scale modern conventional forces to combat in populated areas, and the forms of revolutionary guerrilla warfare advocated by Mao, Ho Chi Minh, Giap and others, on the one hand, and counter-insurgency experts such as Sir Robert Thompson (1970), on the other.

Thus, to the extent that the *jus in bello* must rely on the principle of proportion, it would be useful to produce typologies of military actions and recurring military contexts in order to break down the spectrum of military ends and means which is so vast as to impede or obscure analysis, even if the calculus of proportionality is limited to some arbitrarily established boundary between *raison de guerre* and *raison d'état*. If, however, it is thought imperative to go beyond that imaginary line and to include *raison d'état*-level goals in the judgment of *raison de guerre*-level means, it will be necessary to attempt some typologies of causes which could furnish the starting point for analyses of proportionality in terms of *raison d'état* and *raison de guerre*. Having said this, I should emphasize that all of these proposed typologies of ends and means would be sufficient only to order the *normative* evaluation of military acts or policies. The *final* evaluation would have to be made in terms of the specific context. Lasswell and McDougal have provided a matrix for such analyses (most relevantly in Myres McDougal and Norbert A. Schlei, "The Hydrogen Bomb Tests in Perspective," [McDougal and Associates, 1960:763-843] and in McDougal and Feliciano, 1961). While these attempts have been criticized for their complexity, they have not been challenged by anything remotely as comprehensive and elaborated in the literature of international law, morality or politics. (I disagree however, with the apparent propensity of the Lasswell-McDougal model to judge all issues of proportionality or reasonableness in terms not only of the ultimate *raison d'état* of belligerents but in transcendent perspectives that could be called "*raison du monde*.")

Elaborate as it is, the Lasswell-McDougal normative matrix comes down to value judgments with respect to just ends or causes that are substantially the same as those which Ramsey posits without much ado. Essentially these values are the "minimum world public order" presumption against aggression (i.e., first recourse to armed coercion in violation of the U.N. Charter collective security system) and a "fundamental human dignity" presumption in favor of the kinds of human rights that exist in what some of us can still call the Free World and against *regimes* that deny those rights.

It is my belief that Ramsey, Lasswell and McDougal are essentially right in positing these *jus ad bellum* values. In Ramsey's case, greater elaboration is called for if he is to have an acceptable, comprehensive *jus ad bellum*. As for the *jus in bello*, I think that Ramsey will have to acknowledge what Lasswell and McDougal and other international lawyers have learned, namely, that the principle of discrimination will not hold up as an absolute limit and that the principle of proportion must be taken more seriously. It must be given a more prominent role in the *jus in bello* (I would say the preeminent role) and it must be developed through typologies, precedents, formulas of reasonableness, etc., so as to be more manageable and effective.

Conclusion

A colonel said to me recently, "We in the Army have nothing but moral problems." He meant that the military can succeed more often than not in dealing with technical military problems but that the human, moral, problems have proved intractable, yet central to real success in the proper use of the military instrument. These colonels and their civilian superiors need help from moralists. They do not need the kind of help, against which Paul Ramsey has written, that would negate the military instrument by creeping pacifism and surrender. Responsible military commanders and statesmen need moralists who understand the legitimacy of their military missions—and thereby the limits to such legitimacy. And they need much more concrete guidelines than have hitherto been provided by moralists as to the kinds of things that are, generally speaking, permissible or impermissible in just war, as well as special guidance for the controverted areas in the middle.

While Paul Ramsey has been adamant in putting moral principles ahead of facts or alleged necessities, he has been outstanding in his application of his principles to facts and claimed necessities. Moreover, his work has been characterized by recognition of the changing nature of the factual aspects of just-war problems and the need to keep abreast of them. As indicated, I do not share his conviction with respect to the character and practical potential of the principle of discrimination or his skepticism about the principle of proportion. But it remains clear to me that our quest for just-war doctrine, both *jus ad bellum* and *jus in bello*, must go on, indeed, ought to be accelerated and deepened. To the extent that the maxim *inter arma silent leges* remains true, a pressing remedial task confronts those moralists who believe that resort to arms will continue to be a social fact that cannot be wished away, but must be dealt with by the perennial just-war doctrine.

NOTES

[1] Curran (1973:59-63) traces Ramsey's treatment of this subject and distinguishes the Catholic natural law elements emphasizing reason. McCormick (1967:803) states: "In his explicit treatment of war (ST 2a2ae, 40) St. Thomas added little to what Augustine had written . . . However, Thomas' more important contributions would appear to consist in his stress of the natural law and his reintroduction of the Aristotelian concept of the perfect society, a notion that complicated the identification of the authority competent to declare and wage war."

[2] It seems to me that these two levels of analysis have been inadequately developed in Ramsey's writing and that he moves back and forth too quickly between them.

A brief summary of the *jus ad bellum* requirements in the Catholic tradition will indicate whole areas which Ramsey eschews. I have elsewhere attempted to synthesize the traditional Catholic teaching on this point (O'Brien, 1967a:22-25) as follows:

(1) *Competent authority*—war must be fought for public, not private purposes and must be ordered by the highest public authority. This requirement is challenged in cases of civil or revolutionary war, a form of conflict on which Catholic teaching both traditional and contemporary is highly unsatisfactory (O'Brien, 1969:27-29, 185-215).

(2) *Just cause* is broken down into three categories:

(a) *Grave wrong*—a real and grave wrong to be righted or defended, including:

(1) wars of self-defense;

(2) offensive wars to obtain cessation of wrongs, restitution for past wrongs, and assurances against recurrences;

(3) offensive wars of vindictive justice (e.g., against infidels and heretics).

(b) *Proportionality*—reasonable expectation that the evil effects of war will be outweighed and justified by the action taken to remove the grave wrong. This raises the complex issue of the probability of success for the just party. It appears that the tradition concedes the right of self-defense, however, irrespective of the probability of success for the just party.

(c) *Exhaustion of peaceful remedies*—every reasonable effort must be made to avoid war by submission of differences to international negotiations, arbitration, adjudication or resolution by an international organization such as the United Nations or a competent regional organization such as the Organization of American States.

In terms of positive international law, the *jus ad bellum* is even more restrictive. Recourse to armed force in the sense of Article II (4) of the United Nations Charter may only be justified as:

(1) collective security enforcement action under Chapter VII of the Charter;

(2) individual or collective self-defense in the sense of Article 51 of the Charter.

All of these *jus ad bellum* requirements of the traditional just-war doctrine and of contemporary international law invite discussion, interpretation and controversy. But these issues of *corporate* morality and of public international law receive scant attention from Ramsey, who really seems to rely on a simple analogy: just nations like just men must protect the innocent victims of aggression.

[3] Indeed, this presumption has been so strong in the Roman Catholic tradition that it was not until Vatican II's *Pastoral Constitution on the Church in the Modern World* (notably in Article 79) that the "official" teaching of the Church acknowledged rights of conscientious objection and disobedience to "criminal" orders by public authorities engaged in war. Ramsey (1968A:91-137) has advocated enactment of provisions for selective conscientious objection for "a man who forms his conscience in terms of *jus gentium*, and not only in terms of his conscience's own inner demands or in terms of political disagreement with his nation's policy. . . ." (Ramsey, 1968A:136).

[4] In an important paper in 1965, Ramsey rejected as immoral all forms of counter-value warfare. "Only counterforce-plus-avoidance may be called a just way to conduct war, since traditional and acceptable moral teachings concerning legitimate military targets require the avoidance of civilian damage as much as possible even while accepting this as an unavoidable indirect effect."

"Counter-force nuclear war is the upper limit of rational, politically purposive military action. . . ." (Ramsey, 1968A:215).

[5] Murray asserted that, "the terms of public debate are set in two words, 'limited war.' He insisted that all objections that limited war is not possible today must be overcome. "In the face of this position [that limited war is impossible] the traditional doctrine simply asserts again, 'The problem today is limited war' " (Murray, 1960:88).

Ramsey appeals to strategists in similar terms. See Ramsey, 1973j. In my review of McDougal and Feliciano (1961) I say: ". . . there is another central point on which the reviewer must remain in disagreement with McDougal and Feliciano. They state quite rightly that the operative concept in the application of the principle of military necessity is proportionality of means to ends. (McDougal and Feliciano, 1961:524-530) The question then occurs as to whether proportionality should be calculated in terms of ultimate, political ends (*raison d'etat*) or proximate, military ends (*raison de guerre*). McDougal and Feliciano state that, 'It is not easy to see how military objectives could be evaluated as legitimate or nonlegitimate save in terms of their relation to some broader political purpose postulated as legitimate.' (McDougal and Feliciano, 1961:526) This may possibly be true at the level of ultimate evaluation by authoritative decision-makers of a record of coercive action. However, at the level of tactical commanders it is generally impossible to judge or to control significantly the whole political-military picture. The commander is faced with a series of military problems which he should attempt to solve by the use of appropriate means which are proportionate to accepted military ends. The legitimacy of his policy choices should be judged solely on that basis unless, as is sometimes the case, his powers and responsibilities extend into the area of higher political policy. This approach, admittedly, still does not address itself to the problem of normative evaluation of the legitimacy of the ultimate political, stragetic ends which, true enough, engender the military ends. It seems clear that this complex subject warrants additional thought and the perspectives furnished by McDougal and Feliciano will be invaluable to those who take up this task" (O'Brien, 1962b:420).

The classic survey remains that of Huber, 1913.

[6] In this article Ramsey encourages Richard Neuhaus' initiative in probing the moral requirements of just revolution and characteristically laments the "hash" made of the "small beginnings" achieved in developing a moral *jus in bello* as a result of the "necessities of advocacy" to which moralists bowed in the great stop-the-war debate over Vietnam (Ramsey, 1973c:40).

REFERENCES

Abbott, Walter M. S. J., (ed.)

1966 *The Documents of Vatican II.* New York: Guild Press, American Press, Association Press.

Curran, Charles E.

1973 *Politics, Medicine, and Christian Ethics: A Dialogue with Paul Ramsey.* Philadelphia: Fortress Press.

Finn, James (ed.)

1965 *Peace, the Churches, and the Bomb.* New York: Council on Religion and International Affairs.

Getler, Michael

1974 "U.S. studies re-targeting of missiles." Washington *Post*, January 11, 1974, pp. Al, Col. 4; A16.

Hartigan, Richard Shelly

1966a "St. Augustine on war and killings: the problem of the innocent." *Journal of the History of Ideas* 27 (April-June):195-204.

1966b "Noncombatant immunity: reflections on its origin and present status." *Review of Politics* 29:204-220.

Huber, Max

1913 "Die kriegsrechtliche Verträge und die Kriegsraison." *"Zeitschrift für Völkerrcht und Bundesstaatsrecht* (Breslau, 1913), 7, 351-374.

Irving, David
1963 *The Destruction of Dresden.* New York: Holt, Rinehart & Winston.
Lauterpacht, H.
1952 "The problem of the revision of the law of war." *British Year Book of International Law* 29:360-382.
Liddell Hart, B. H.
1948 *The German Generals Talk.* New York: William Morrow & Co.
McCormick, R. A.
1967 "War, morality of." *New Catholic Encyclopedia.* New York: McGraw-Hill. 14:802-807.
McDougal, Myres S. & Associates
1960 *Studies in World Public Order.* New Haven & London: Yale University Press.
McDougal, Myres S. and Feliciano, Florentino
1961 *Law and Minimum World Public Order.* New Haven & London: Yale University Press.
Manstein, Field-Marshal Erich von
1958 *Lost Victories*, Anthony G. Powell, trans. Chicago: Henry Regnery Co.
Moore, John Bassett
1924 *International Law and Some Current Illusions.* New York: Macmillan.
Murray, John Courtney S. J.,
1958 [principal contributor with Walter Millis] *Foreign Policy and the Free Society.* New York: Published for The Fund for the Republic by Oceana Publications.
1960 "Theology and modern war." Pp. 69-91 in William J. Nagle (ed.), *Morality and Modern Warfare.* Baltimore: Helicon Press.
O'Brien, William V.
1957 "The meaning of 'military necessity' in international law." Pp. 109-176 in William O'Brien (ed.), *World Polity*, Vol. I. Utrecht: Spectrum Publishers.
1960a "Legitimate military necessity in nuclear war." Pp. 35-120 in William V. O'Brien (ed.), *World Polity*, Vol. II. Utrecht: Spectrum Publishers.
1960b "Nuclear warfare and the law of nations." Pp. 126-149 in William J. Nagle (ed.), *Morality and Modern Warfare.* Baltimore: Helicon.
1962a "Biological/chemical warfare and the international law of war." *Georgetown Law Journal* 51(No. 1):1-63.
1962b Review of *Law and Minimum World Public Order: The Legal Regulations of International Coercion* by Myres S. McDougal and Florentino P. Feliciano. *Yale Law Journal* 72 (No. 2):413-420.
1963 (co-editor with Ulrich S. Allers) *Christian Ethics and Nuclear Warfare.* Washington, D.C.: Institute of World Polity.
1967a *Nuclear War, Deterrence and Morality.* New York: Newman.
1967b "International law and the outbreak of war in the Middle East, 1967." *Orbis* 11:692-723.
1968 "The Nuremberg principles." Pp. 140-194 in James Finn (ed.), *A Conflict of Loyalties.* New York: Pegasus. Reprinted (pp. 193-247) in Richard A. Falk (ed.), *The Vietnam War and International Law*, Vol. 3. Princeton: Princeton University Press, 1972.
1969 *War and/or Survival.* Garden City, N.Y.: Doubleday.
1972a "The law of war, command responsibility and Vietnam." *Georgetown Law Journal* 60(No. 3):605-664.
1972b Commentary (Pp. 57-70) in Wilson Carey McWilliams, *Military Honor after Mylai.* New York: Council on Religion and International Affairs, Special Studies No. 213.
Paget, R. T.
1951 *Manstein.* London: Collins.
Ramsey, Paul
See the bibliography of Ramsey's works in this volume. Capital letters (e.g. 1950A) denote books and occasional papers; lower case letters (e.g. 1968a) denote articles.

Sherman, George
1974 "Nuclear strategy and Schlesinger." Washington *Star-News*, April 15, 1974, Pp. A1, Cols. 13; A4, Cols. 1-8.
Singer, J. David
1969 "The level of analysis problem in international relations." Pp. 20-29 in Joseph N. Rosenau (ed.), *International Politics and Foreign Policy.* New York: The Free Press.
Thompson, Sir Robert W.
1970 *Revolutionary War in World Strategy.* New York: Taplenger.

Part Three

MEDICAL ETHICS

CHAPTER IX

Social Justice and Equal Access to Health Care[1]

GENE OUTKA

I want to consider the following question. Is it possible to understand and to justify morally a societal goal which increasing numbers of people, including Americans, accept as normative? The goal is: the assurance of comprehensive health services for every person irrespective of income or geographic location. Indeed, the goal now has almost the status of a platitude. Currently in the United States politicians in various camps give it at least verbal endorsement (see, e.g., Nixon, 1972:1; Kennedy, 1972:234-252). I do not propose to examine the possible sociological determinants in this emergent consensus. I hope to show that whatever these determinants are, one may offer a plausible case in defense of the goal on reasonable grounds. To demonstrate why appeals to the goal get so successfully under our skins, I shall have recourse to a set of conceptions of social justice. Some of the standard conceptions, found in a number of writings on justice, will do (these writings include Bedau, 1971; Hospers, 1961:416-468; Lucas, 1972; Perelman, 1963; Rescher, 1966; Ryan, 1916; Vlastos, 1962). By reflecting on them it seems to me a prima facie case can be established, namely, that every person in the entire resident population should have equal access to health care delivery.

The case is prima facie only. I wish to set aside as far as possible a related question which comes readily enough to mind. In the world of "suboptimal alternatives," with the constraints for example which impinge on the government as it makes decisions about resource allocation, what is one to say? What criteria should be employed? Paul Ramsey, in *The Patient as Person* (1970B:240), thinks that the large question of how to choose between medical and other societal priorities is "almost, if not altogether, incorrigible to moral reasoning." Whether it is or not is a matter which must be ignored for the present. One may simply observe in passing that choices are unavoidable nonetheless, as Ramsey acknowledges, even where the government allows them to be made by default, so that in some instances they are determined largely by which private pressure groups prove to be dominant. In any event, there is virtue in taking up one complicated question at a time and we need to get the thrust of the case for equal access before us. It is enough to observe now that Americans attach an obviously high priority to organized health care. National health expenditures for the fiscal year 1972 were $83.4 billion (Hicks, 1973:52). Even if such an enormous sum is not entirely adequate, we may still ask: how are we to justify spending whatever we do in accordance as far as possible with the goal of equal access? The answer I propose involves distinguishing various conceptions of social justice and trying to show which of these apply or fail to apply to health care considerations. Only toward the end of the paper will some institutional implications be given more than passing attention, and then in a strictly programmatic way.

Another sort of query should be noted as we begin. What stake does someone in religious ethics have in this discussion? For the reasonable case envisaged is offered after all in the public forum. If the issue is how to justify morally the societal goal which seems so obvious to so many, whether or not they are religious believers, does the religious ethicist then simply participate qua citizen? Here I think we should be wary of simplifying formulae. Why for example should a Jew or a Christian not welcome wide support for a societal goal which he or she can affirm and reaffirm, or reflect only on instances where such support is not forthcoming? If a number of ethical schemes, both religious and humanist, converge in their acceptance of the goal of equal access to health care, so be it. Secularists can join forces with believers, at least at some levels or points, without implying there must be unanimity on every moral issue. Yet it also seems too simple if one claims to wear only the citizen's hat when making the case in question. At least I should admit that a commitment to the basic normative principle which in Christian writings is often called *agape* may influence the account to follow in ways large and small (see Outka, 1972). For example, someone with such a commitment will quite naturally take a special interest in appeals to the generic characteristics all persons share rather than the idiosyncratic attainments which distinguish persons from one another, and in the playing down of desert considerations. As I shall try to show, such appeals are centrally relevant to the case for equal access. And they are nicely in line with the normative pressures agapeic considerations typically exert.

One issue of theoretical importance in religious ethics also emerges in connection with this last point. The approach in this paper may throw a little indirect light on the traditional question, especially prominent in Christian ethics, of how love and justice are related. To distinguish different conceptions of social justice will put us in a better position, I think, to recognize that often it is ambiguous to ask about "*the* relation." There may be different relations to different conceptions. For the conceptions themselves may sometimes produce discordant indications, or turn out to be incommensurable, or reflect, when different ones are seized upon, rival moral points of view. I shall note several of these relations as we proceed.

Which then among the standard conceptions of social justice appear to be particularly relevant or irrelevant? Let us consider the following five:

I. To each according to his merit or desert.
II. To each according to his societal contribution.
III. To each according to his contribution in satisfying whatever is freely desired by others in the open marketplace of supply and demand.
IV. To each according to his needs.
V. Similar treatment for similar cases.

In general I shall argue that the first three of these are less relevant because of certain distinctive features which health crises possess. I shall focus on crises here not because I think preventive care is unimportant (the opposite is true), but because the crisis situation shows most clearly the special significance we attach to medical treatment as an institutionalized activity or social practice, and the basic purpose we suppose it to have.

I

To each according to his merit or desert. Meritarian conceptions, above all perhaps, are grading ones: advantages are allocated in accordance with amounts of energy expended or kinds of results achieved. What is judged is particular conduct which distinguishes persons from one another and not only the fact that all the parties are human beings. Sometimes a competitive aspect looms large.

In certain contexts it is illuminating to distinguish between efforts and achievements. In the case of efforts one characteristically focuses on the individual: rewards are based on the pains one takes. Some have supposed, for example, that entry into the kingdom of heaven is linked more directly to energy displayed and fidelity shown than to successful results attained.

To assess achievements is to weigh actual performance and productive contributions. The academic prize is awarded to the student with the highest grade-point average, regardless of the amount of midnight oil he or she burned in preparing for the examinations. Sometimes we may exclaim, "it's just not fair," when person X writes a brilliant paper with little effort while we are forced to devote more time with less impressive results. But then our complaint may be directed against differences in innate ability and talent which no expenditure of effort altogether removes.

After the difference between effort and achievement, and related distinctions, have been acknowledged, what should be stressed I think is the general importance of meritarian or desert criteria in the thinking of most people about justice. These criteria may serve to illuminate a number of disputes about the justice of various practices and institutional arrangements in our society. It may help to explain, for instance, the resentment among the working class against the welfare system. However wrongheaded or self-deceptive the resentment often is, particularly when directed toward those who want to work but for various reasons beyond their control cannot, at its better moments it involves in effect an appeal to desert considerations. "Something for nothing" is repudiated as unjust; benefits should be proportional (or at least related) to costs; those who can make an effort should do so, whatever the degree of their training or significance of their contribution to society; and so on. So, too, persons deserve to have what they have labored for; unless they infringe on the works of others their efforts and achievements are justly theirs.

Occasionally the appeal to desert extends to a wholesale rejection of other considerations as grounds for just claims. The most conspicuous target is need. Consider this statement by Ayn Rand.

> A morality that holds *need* as a claim, holds emptiness—nonexistence—as its standard of value; it rewards an absence, a defect: weakness, inability, incompetence, suffering, disease, disaster, the lack, the fault, the flaw—the *zero*.
>
> Who provides the account to pay these claims? Those who are cursed for being non-zeros, each to the extent of his distance from that ideal. Since all values are the product of virtues, the degree of your virtue is used as the measure of your penalty; the degree of your faults is used as the measure of your gain. Your code declares that the rational man must sacrifice himself to the irrational, the independent man to parasites, the honest man to the dishonest, the man of justice to the unjust, the productive man to thieving loafers, the man of integrity to compromising knaves, the man of self-esteem to sniveling neurotics. Do you wonder at the meanness of soul in those you see around you? The man who achieves these virtues will not accept your moral code; the man who accepts your moral code will not achieve these virtues. (1957:958)

I have noted elsewhere (1972:89-90, 265-267) that *agape*, while it characteristically plays down, need not formally disallow attention to considerations falling under merit or desert; for in the case of merit as well as need it may be possible, the quotation above notwithstanding, to reason solely from egalitarian premises. A major reason such attention is warranted concerns what was called there the differential exercise of an equal liberty. That is, one may fittingly revere another's moral capacities and thus the efforts he makes as well as the ends he seeks. Such reverence may lead one to weigh expenditure of energy and specific achievements. I would simply hold now (1) that the idea of justice is not exhaustively characterized by the notion of desert, even if one agrees that the latter plays an important role; and (2) that the notion of desert is especially ill-suited to play an important role in the determination of policies which should govern a system of health care.

Why is it so ill-suited? Here we encounter some of the distinctive features which it seems to me health crises possess. Let me put it in this way. Health crises seem non-meritarian because they occur so often for reasons beyond our control or power to predict. They frequently fall without discrimination on the (according-to-merit) just and unjust, i.e., the virtuous and the wicked, the industrious and the slothful alike.

While we may believe that virtues and vices cannot depend upon natural contingencies, we are bound to admit, it seems, that many health crises do. It makes sense therefore to say that we are equal in being randomly susceptible to these crises. Even those who ascribe a prominent role to desert acknowledge that justice has also properly to do with pleas of "But I could not help it" (Lucas, 1972:231). One seeks to distinguish such cases from those acknowledged to be praiseworthy or blameworthy. Then it seems unfair as well as unkind to discriminate among those who suffer health crises on the basis of their personal deserts. Most people do not suppose that a newborn child deserves his hemophilia or the tumor afflicting her spine.

These considerations help to explain why the following distinction is often made. Bernard Williams, for example, in his discussion of "equality in unequal circumstances," identifies two different sorts of inequality, inequality of merit and inequality of need, and two corresponding goods, those earned by effort and those demanded by need (1971:126-137). Medical treatment in the event of illness is located under the umbrella of need. He concludes: "Leaving aside preventive medicine, the proper ground of distribution of medical care is ill health: this is a necessary truth" (1971:127). An irrational state of affairs is held to obtain if those whose needs are the same are treated unequally, when needs are the ground of the treatment. One might put the point this way. When people are equal in the relevant respects—in this case when their needs are the same and occur in a context of random, undeserved susceptibility—that by itself is a good reason for treating them equally (see also Nagel, 1973:354).

In many societies, however, a second necessary condition for the receipt of medical treatment exists de facto: the possession of money. This is not the place to consider the general question of when inequalities in wealth may be regarded as just. It is enough to note that one can plausibly appeal to all of the conceptions of justice we are embarked in sorting out. A person may be thought to be entitled to a higher income when he works more, contributes more, risks more, and not simply when he needs more. We may think it fair that the industrious should have more money than the slothful and the surgeon more than the tobaccanist. The difficulty comes in the misfit between the reasons for differential incomes and the reasons for receiving medical treatment. The former may include a pluralistic set of claims in which different notions of justice must be meshed. The latter are more monistically focused on needs, and the other notions not accorded a similar relevance. Yet money may nonetheless remain as a causally necessary condition for receiving medical treatment. It may be the power to secure what one needs. The senses in which health crises are distinctive may then be insufficiently determinative for the policies which govern the actual availability of treatment. The nearly automatic links between income, prestige, and the receipt of comparatively higher quality medical treatment should then be subjected to critical scrutiny. For unequal treatment of the rich ill and the poor ill is unjust if, again, needs rather than differential income constitute the ground of such treatment.

Suppose one agrees that it is important to recognize the misfit between the reasons for differential incomes and the reasons for receiving medical treatment, and that therefore income as such should not govern the actual availability of treatment. One may still ask whether the case so far relies excessively on "pure" instances where desert considerations are admittedly out of place. That there are such pure instances, tumors afflicting the spine, hemophilia, and so on, is not denied. Yet it is an exaggeration if we go on and regard all health crises as utterly unconnected with desert. Note for example that Williams leaves aside perventive medicine. And if in a cool hour we examine the statistics, we find that a vast number of deaths occur each year due to causes not always beyond our control, e.g., automobile accidents, drugs, alcohol, tobacco, obesity, and so on. In some final reckoning it seems that many persons (though crucially, not all) have an effect on, and arguably a responsibility for, their own medical needs. Consider the following bidders for emergency care: (1) a person with a heart attack who is seriously overweight; (2) a football hero who has suffered a concussion; (3) a man with lung cancer who has smoked cigarettes for forty years; (4) a 60 year old man who has always taken excellent care of himself and is suddenly stricken with leukemia; (5) a three year old girl who has swallowed poison left out carelessly by her parents; (6) a 14 year old boy who has been beaten without provocation by a gang and suffers brain damage and recurrent attacks of uncontrollable terror; (7) a college student who has slashed his wrists (and not for the first time) from a psychological need for attention; (8) a woman raised in the ghetto who is found unconscious due to an overdose of heroin.

These cases help to show why the whole subject of medical treatment is so crucial and so perplexing. They attest to some melancholy elements in human experience. People suffer in varying ratios the effects of their natural and undeserved vulnerabilities, the irresponsibility and brutality of others, and their own desires and weaknesses. In some final reckoning then desert considerations seem not irrelevant to many health crises. The practical applicability of this admission, however, in the instance of health care delivery, appears limited. We may agree that it underscores the importance of preventive health care by stressing the influence we sometimes have over our medical needs. But if we try to foster such care by increasing the penalties for neglect, we normally confine ourselves to calculations about incentives. At the risk of being denounced in some quarters as censorious and puritannical, perhaps we should for example levy far higher taxes on alcohol and tobacco and pump the dollars directly into health care programs rather than (say) into highway building. Yet these steps would by no means lead necessarily to a a demand that we correlate in some strict way a demonstrated effort to be temperate with the receipt of privileged medical treatment as a reward. Would it be feasible to allocate the additional tax monies to the man with leukemia before the overweight man suffering a heart attack on the ground of a difference in desert? At the point of emergency care at least, it seems impracticable for the doctor to discriminate between these cases, to make meritarian judgments at the point of catastrophe. And the number of persons who are in need of medical treatment for reasons utterly beyond their control remains a datum with tenacious relevance. There are those who suffer the ravages of a tornado, are handicapped by a genetic defect, beaten without provocation, etc. A commitment to the basic purpose of medical care and to the institutions for achieving it involves the recognition of this persistent state of affairs.

II

To each according to his societal contribution. This conception gives moral primacy to notions such as the public interest, the common good, the welfare of the community, or the greatest good of the greatest number. Here one judges the social consequences of particular conduct. The formula can be construed in at least two ways (Rescher, 1966:79-80). It may refer to the interest of the social group considered collectively, where the group has some independent life all its own. The group's welfare is the decisive criterion for determining what constitutes any member's proper share. Or the common good may refer only to an aggregation of distinct individuals and considered distributively.

Either version accords such a primacy to what is socially advantageous as to be unacceptable not only to defenders of need, but also, it would seem, of desert. For the criteria of effort and achievement are often conceived along rather individualistic lines. The pains an agent takes or the results he brings about deserve recompense, whether or not the public interest is directly served. No automatic harmony then is necessarily assumed between his just share as individually earned and his proper share from the vantage point of the common good. Moreover, the test of social advantage *simpliciter* obviously threatens the agapeic concern with some minimal consideration due each person which is never to be disregarded for the sake of long-range social benefits. No one should be considered as *merely* a means or instrument.

The relevance of the canon of social productiveness to health crises may accordingly also be challenged. Indeed, such crises may cut against it in that they occur more frequently to those whose comparative contribution to the general welfare is less, e.g., the aged, the disabled, children.

Consider for example Paul Ramsey's persuasive critique of social and economic criteria for the allocation of a single scarce medical resource. He begins by recounting the imponderables which faced the widely-discussed "public committee" at the Swedish Hospital in Seattle when it deliberated in the early 1960's. The sparse resource in this case was the kidney machine. The committee was charged with the responsibility of selecting among patients suffering chronic renal failure those who were to receive dialysis. Its criteria were broadly social and economic. Considerations weighed included age, sex, marital status, number of dependents, income, net worth, educational background, occupation, past performance and future potential. The application of such criteria proved to be exceedingly problematic. Should someone with six children always have priority over an artist or composer? Were those who arranged matters so that their families would not burden society to be penalized in effect for being provident? And so on. Two critics of the committee found "a disturbing picture of the bourgeoisie sparing the bourgeoisie" and observed that "the Pacific Northwest is no place for a Henry David Thoreau with bad kidneys" (quoted in Ramsey, 1970B:248).

The mistake, Ramsey believes, is to introduce criteria of social worthiness in the first place. In those situations of choice where not all can be saved and yet all need not die, "the equal right of every human being to live, and not relative personal or social worth, should be the ruling principle" (1970B:256). The principle leads to a criterion of "random choice among equals" expressed by a lottery scheme or a practice of "first-come, first-served." Several reasons stand behind Ramsey's defense of the criterion of random choice. First, a religious belief in the equality of persons before God leads intelligibly to a refusal to choose between those who are dying in any way other than random patient selection. Otherwise their equal value as human beings is threatened. Second, a moral primacy is ascribed to survival over other (perhaps superior) interests persons may have, in that it is the condition of everything else. ". . . Life is a value incommensurate with all others, and so not negotiable by bartering one man's worth against another's" (1970B:256). Third, the entire enterprise of estimating a person's social worth is viewed with final skepticism. ". . . We have no way of knowing how really and truly to estimate a man's societal worth or his worth to others or to himself in unfocused social situations in the ordinary lives of men in their communities" (1970B:256). This statement, incidentally, appears to allow something other than randomness in *focused* social situations; when, say, a President or Prime Minister and the owner of the local bar rush for the last place in the bomb shelter, and the knowledge of the former can save many lives. In any event, I have been concerned with a restricted point to which Ramsey's discussion brings illustrative support. The canon of social productiveness is notoriously difficult to apply as a workable criterion for distributing medical services to those who need them.

One may go further. A system of health care delivery which treats people on the basis of the medical care required may often go against (at least narrowly conceived) calculations of societal advantage. For example, the health care needs of people tend to rise during that period of their lives, signaled by retirement, when their incomes and social productivity are declining. More generally:

> Some 40 to 50 per cent of the American people—the aged, children, the dependent poor, and those with some significant chronic disability are in categories requiring relatively large amounts of medical care but with inadequate resources to purchase such care. (A. Somers, 1971a:20)

If one agrees, for whatever reasons, with the agapeic judgment that each person should be regarded as irreducibly valuable, then one cannot succumb to a social productiveness criterion of human worth. Interests are to be equally considered even when people have ceased to be, or are not yet, or perhaps never will be, public assets.

III

To each according to his contribution in satisfying whatever is freely desired by others in the open marketplace of supply and demand. Here we have a test which, though similar to the preceding one, concentrates on what is desired de facto by certain segments of the community rather than the community as a whole, and on the relative scarcity of the service rendered. It is tantamount to the canon of supply and demand as espoused by various laissez-faire theoreticians (cf. Rescher, 1966:80-81). Rewards should be given to those who by virtue of special skill, prescience, risk-taking, and the like discern what is desired and are able to take the requisite steps to bring satisfaction. A surgeon, it may be argued, contributes more than a nurse because of the greater training and skill required, burdens borne, and effective care provided, and should be compensated accordingly. So too perhaps, a star quarterback on a pro-football team should be remunerated even more highly because of the rare athletic prowess needed, hazards involved, and widespread demand to watch him play.

This formula does not then call for the weighing of the value of various contributions, and tends to conflate needs and wants under a notion of desires. It also assumes that a prominent part is assigned to consumer free-choice. The consumer should be at liberty to express his preferences, and to select from a variety of competing goods and services. Those who resist many changes currently proposed in the organization and financing of health care delivery in the U.S.A.—such as national health insurance—often do so by appealing to some variant of this formula.

Yet it seems health crises are often of overriding importance when they occur. They appear therefore not satisfactorily accommodated to the context of a free marketplace where consumers may freely choose among alternative goods and services.

To clarify what is at stake in the above contention, let us examine an opposing case. Robert M. Sade, M.D., published an article in *The New England Journal of Medicine* entitled "Medical Care as a Right: A Refutation" (1971). He attacks programs of national health insurance in the name of a person's right to select one's own values, determine how they may be realized, and dispose of them if one chooses without coercion from other men. The values in question are construed as economic ones in the context of supply and demand. So we read:

> In a free society, man exercises his right to sustain his own life by producing economic values in the form of goods and services that he is, or should be, free to exchange with other men who are similarly free to trade with him or not. The economic values produced, however, are not given as gifts by nature, but exist only by virtue of the thought and effort of individual men. Goods and services are thus owned as a consequence of the right to sustain life by one's own physical and mental effort. (1971:1289)

Sade compares the situation of the physican to that of the baker. The one who produces a loaf of bread should as owner have the power to dispose of his own product. It is immoral simply to expropriate the bread without the baker's permission. Similarly, "medical care is neither a right nor a privilege: it is a service that is provided by doctors and others to people who wish to purchase it" (1971:1289). Any coercive regulation of professional practices by the society at large is held to be analogous to taking the bread from the baker without his consent. Such regulation violates the freedom of the physician over his own services and will lead inevitably to provider-apathy.

The analogy surely misleads. To assume that doctors autonomously produce goods and services in a fashion closely akin to a baker is grossly oversimplified. The baker may himself rely on the agricultural produce of others, yet there is a crucial difference in the degree of dependence. Modern physicians depend on the achievements of medical technology and the entire scientific base underlying it, all of which is made possible by a host of persons whose salaries are often notably less. Moreover, the amount of taxpayer support for medical research and education is too enormous to make any such unqualified case for provider-autonomy plausible.

However conceptually clouded Sade's article may be, its stress on a free exchange of goods and services reflects one historically influential rationale for much American medical practice. And he applies it not only to physicians but also to patients or "consumers."

> The question is whether the decision of how to allocate the consumer's dollar should belong to the consumer or to the state. It has already been shown that the choice of how a doctor's services should be rendered belongs only to the doctor: in the same way the choice of whether to buy a doctor's service rather than some other commodity or service belongs to the consumer as a logical consequence of the right to his own life. (1971:1291)

This account is misguided, I think, because it ignores the overriding importance which is so often attached to health crises. When lumps appear on someone's neck, it usually makes little sense to talk of choosing whether to buy a doctor's service rather than a color television set. References to just trade-offs suddenly seem out of place. No compensation suffices, since the penalties may differ so much.

There is even a further restriction on consumer choice. One's knowledge in these circumstances is comparatively so limited. The physician makes most of the decisions: about diagnosis, treatment, hospitalization, number of return visits, and so on. In brief:

> The consumer knows very little about the medical services he is buying—probably less than about any other service he purchases.... While [he] can still play a role in policing the market, that role is much more limited in the field of health care than in almost any other area of private economic activity. (Schultze, 1972:214-215)

For much of the way, then, an appeal to supply and demand and consumer choice is not quite fitting. Ittt neglects the issue of the value of various contributions. And it fails to allow for the recognition that medical treatments may be overridingly desired. In contexts of catastrophe at any rate, when life itself is threatened, most persons (other than those who are apathetic or seek to escape from the terrifying prospects) cannot take medical care to be merely one option among others.

IV

To each according to his needs. The concept of needs is sometimes taken to apply to an entire range of interests which concern a person's "psycho-physical existence" (Outka, 1972:esp. 264-265). On this wide usage, to attribute a need to someone is to say that the person lacks what is thought to conduce to his or her "welfare"—understood in both a physiological sense (e.g., for food, drink, shelter, and health) and a psychological one (e.g, for continuous human affection and support).

Yet even in the case of such a wide usage, what the person lacks is typically assumed to be basic. Attention is restricted to recurrent considerations rather than to every possible individual whim or frivolous pursuit. So one is not surprised to meet with the contention that a preferable rendering of this formula would be: "to each according to his essential needs" (Perelman, 1963:22). This contention seems to me well taken. It implies, for one thing, that basic needs are distinguishable from felt needs or wants. For the latter may encompass expressions of personal preference unrelated to considerations of survival or subsistence, and sometimes artificially generated by circumstances of rising affluence in the society at large.

Essential needs are also typically assumed to be given rather than acquired. They are not constituted by any action for which the person is responsible by virtue of his or her distinctively greater effort. It is almost as if the designation "innocent" may be linked illuminatingly to need, as retribution, punishment, and so on, are to desert, and in complex ways, to freedom. Thus essential needs are likewise distinguishable from deserts. Where needs are unequal, one thinks of them as fortuitously distributed; as part, perhaps, of a kind of "natural lottery" (see Rawls, 1971:e.g., 104). So very often the advantages of health and the burdens of illness, for example, strike one as arbitrary effects of the lottery. It seems wrong to say that a newborn child deserves as a reward all of his faculties when he has done nothing in particular which distinguishes him from another newborn who comes into the world deprived of one or more of them. Similarly, though crudely, many religious believers do not look on natural events as personal deserts. They are not inclined to pronounce sentences such as, "That evil person with incurable cancer got what he deserved." They are disposed instead to search for some distinction between what they may call the conditions of finitude on the one hand and sin and moral evil on the other. If the distinction is "ultimately" invalid, in this life it seems inscrutably so. Here and now it may be usefully drawn. Inequalities in the need for medical treatment are taken, it appears, to reflect the conditions of finitude more than anything else.

One can even go on to argue that among our basic or essential needs, the case of medical treatment is conspicuous in the following sense. While food and shelters are not matters about which we are at liberty to please ourselves, they are at least predictable. We can plan, for instance, to store up food and fuel for the winter. It may be held that responsibility increases along with the power to predict. If so, then many health crises seem peculiarly random and uncontrollable. Cancer, given the present state of knowledge at any rate, is a contingent disaster, whereas hunger is a steady threat. Who will need serious medical care, and when, is then perhaps a classic example of uncertainty.

Finally, and more theoretically, it is often observed that a need-conception of justice comes closest to charity or *agape* (e.g., Perelman, 1963:23). I think there are indeed crucial overlaps (see Outka, 1972:91-92, 309-312). To cite two of them: the equal consideration *agape* enjoins has to do in the first instance with those generic endowments which people share, the characteristics of a person qua human existent. Needs, as we have seen, likewise concern those things essential to the life and welfare of men considered simply as men (see also Honore, 1968). They are not based on particular conduct alone, on those idiosyncratic attainments which contribute to someone's being such-and-such a kind of person. Yet a certain sort of inequality is recognized, for needs differ in divergent circumstances and so treatments must if benefits are to be equalized. *Agape* too allows for a distinction between equal consideration and identical treatment. The aim of equalizing benefits is implied by the injunction to consider the interests of each party equally. This may require differential treatments of differing interests.

Overlaps such as these will doubtless strike some as so extensive that it may be asked whether *agape* and a need-conception of justice are virtually equivalent. I think not. One contrast was pointed out before. The differential treatment enjoined by *agape* is more complex and goes deeper. In the case of *agape*, attention may be appropriately given to varying *efforts* as well as to unequal *needs*. More generally one may say that agapeic considerations extend to all of the psychological nuances and contextual details of individual persons and their circumstances. Imaginative concern is enjoined for concrete human beings: for what someone is uniquely, for what he or she—as a matter of personal history and distinctive identity—wants, feels, thinks, celebrates, and endures. The attempt to establish and enhance mutual affection between individual persons is taken likewise to be fitting. Conceptions of social justice, including "to each according to his essential needs," tend to be more restrictive; they call attention to considerations which obtain for a number of persons, to impersonally specified criteria for assessing collective policies and practices. *Agape* involves more, even if one supposes never less.

Other differences could be noted. What is important now however is the recognition that, in matters of health care in particular, *agape* and a need-conception of justice are conjoined in a number of relevant respects. At least this is so for those who think that, again, justice has properly to do with pleas of "But I could not help it." It seeks to distinguish such cases from those acknowledged to be praiseworthy or blameworthy. The formula "to each according to his needs" is one cogent way of identifying the moral relevance of these pleas. To ignore them may be thought to be unfair as well as unkind when they arise from the deprivation of some essential need. The move to confine the notion of justice wholly to desert considerations is thereby resisted as well. Hence we may say that sometimes "questions of social justice arise just because people are unequal in ways they can do very little to change and . . . only by attending to these inequalities can one be said to be giving their interests equal consideration" (Benn, 1971:164).

V

Similar treatment for similar cases. This conception is perhaps the most familiar of all. Certainly it is the most formal and inclusive one. It is frequently taken as an elementary appeal to consistency and linked to the universalizability test. One should not make an arbitrary exception on one's own behalf, but rather should apply impartially whatever standards one accepts. The conception can be fruitfully applied to health care questions and I shall assume its relevance. Yet as literally interpreted, it is necessary but not sufficient. For rightly or not, it is often held to be as compatible with no positive treatment whatever as with active promotion of other peoples' interests, as long as all are equally and impartially included. Its exponents sometimes assume such active promotion without demonstrating clearly how this is built into the conception itself. Moreover, it may obscure a distinction which we have seen agapists and others make: between equal consideration and identical treatment. Needs may differ and so treatments must, if benefits are to be equalized.

I have placed this conception at the end of the list partly because it moves us, despite its formality, toward practice. Let me suggest briefly how it does so. Suppose first of all one agrees with the case so far offered. Suppose, that is, it has been shown convincingly that a need-conception of justice applies with greater relevance than the earlier three when one reflects about the basic purpose of medical care. To treat one class of people differently from another because of income or geographic location should therefore be ruled out, because such reasons are irrelevant. (The irrelevance is conceptual, rather than always, unfortunately, causal.) In short, all persons should have equal access, "as needed, without financial, geographic, or other barriers, to the whole spectrum of health services" (Somers and Somers, 1972a:122).

Suppose however, secondly, that the goal of equal access collides on some occasions with the realities of finite medical resources and needs which prove to be insatiable. That such collisions occur in fact it would be idle to deny. And it is here that the practical bearing of the formula of similar treatment for similar cases should be noticed. Let us recall Williams' conclusion: "the proper ground of distribution of medical care is ill health: this is a necessary truth." While I agree with the essentials of his argument—for all the reasons above—I would prefer, for practical purposes, a slightly more modest formulation. Illness is the proper ground for the *receipt* of medical care. However, the *distribution* of medical care in less-than-optimal circumstances requires us to face the collisions. I would argue that in such circumstances the formula of similar treatment for similar cases may be construed so as to guide actual choices in the way most compatible with the goal of equal access. The formula's allowance of no positive treatment whatever may justify exclusion of entire classes of cases from a priority list. Yet it forbids doing so for irrelevant or arbitrary reasons. So (1) if we accept the case for equal access, but (2) if we simply cannot, physically cannot, treat all who are in need, it seems more just to discriminate by virtue of categories of illness, for example, rather than between the rich ill and poor ill. All persons with a certain rare, non-communicable disease would not receive priority, let us say, where the costs were inordinate, the prospects for rehabilitation remote, and for the sake of equalized benefits to many more. Or with Ramsey we may urge a policy of random patient selection when one must decide between claimants for a medical treatment unavailable to all. Or we may acknowledge that any notion of "comprehensive benefits" to which persons should have equal access is subject to practical restrictions which will vary from society to society depending on resources at a given time. Even in a country as affluent as the United States there will surely always be items excluded, e.g., perhaps over-the-counter drugs, some teenage orthodontia, cosmetic surgery, and the like (Somers and Somers, 1972b:182). Here too the formula of similar treatment for similar cases may serve to modify the application of a need-conception of justice in order to address the insatiability-problem and limit frivolous use. In all of the foregoing instances of restriction, however, the relevant feature remains the illness, discomfort, etc. itself. The goal of equal access then retains its prima facie authoritativeness. It is imperfectly realized rather than disregarded.

VI

These latter comments lead on to the question of institutional implications. I cannot aim here of course for the specificity rightly sought by policy-makers. My endeavor has been conceptual elucidation. While the ethicist needs to be apprised about the facts, he or she does not, qua ethicist, don the mantle of the policy-expert. In any case, only rarely does anyone do both things equally well. Yet cross-fertilization is extremely desirable. For experts should not be isolated from the wider assumptions their recommendations may reflect. I shall merely list some of the topics which would have to be discussed at length if we were to get clear about the implications. Examples will be limited to the current situation in the United States.

Anyone who accepts the case for equal access will naturally be concerned about de facto disparities in the availability of medical treatment. Let us consider two relevant indictments of current American practice. They appear in the writings not only of those who attack indiscriminately a system seen to be governed only by the appetite for profit and power, but also of those who denounce in less sweeping terms and espouse more cautiously reformist positions. The first shortcoming has to do with the maldistribution of supply. Per capita ratios of physicians to populations served vary, sometimes notoriously, between affluent suburbs and rural and inner city areas. This problem is exacerbated by the distressing data concerning the greater health needs of the poor. Chronic disease, frequency and duration of hospitalization, psychiatric disorders, infant death rates, etc.—these occur in significantly larger proportions to lower income members of America society (Appel, 1970; Hubbard, 1970). A further complication is that "the distribution of health insurance coverage is badly skewed. Practically all the rich have insurance. But among the poor, about two-thirds have none. As a result, among people aged 25 to 64 who die, some 45 to 50 per cent have neither hospital nor surgical coverage" (Somers, 1971a:46). This last point connects with a second shortcoming frequently cited. Even those who are otherwise economically independent may be shattered by the high cost of a "catastrophic illness" (see some eloquent examples in Kennedy, 1972).

Proposals for institutional reforms designed to overcome such disparities are bound to be taken seriously by any defender of equal access. What he or she will be disposed to press for, of course, is the removal of any double standard or "two class" system of care. The viable procedures for bringing this about are not obvious, and comparisons with certain other societies (for relevant alternative models) are drawn now with perhaps less confidence (see Anderson, 1973). One set of commonly discussed proposals includes (1) incentive subsidies to physicians, hospitals, and medical centers to provide services in regions of poverty (to overcome in part the unwillingness—to which no unique culpability need be ascribed—of many providers and their spouses to work and live in grim surroundings); (2) licensure controls to avoid comparatively excessive concentrations of physicians in regions of affluence; (3) a period of time (say, two years) in an underserved area as a requirement for licensing; (4) redistribution facilities which allow for population shifts.

A second set of proposals is linked with health insurance itself. While I cannot venture into the intricacies of medical economics or comment on various bills for national health insurance, it may be instructive to take brief note of one proposal in which, once more, the defender of equal access is bound to take an interest (even if he or she finally rejects it on certain practical grounds). The precise details of the proposal are unimportant for our purposes (for one much-discussed version, see Feldstein, 1971). Consider this sketch. Each citizen is (in effect) issued a card by the government. Whenever "legitimate" medical expenses (however determined for a given society) exceed, say, 10 per cent of his or her annual taxable income, the card may be presented so that additional costs incurred will be paid for out of general tax revenues. The reasons urged on behalf of this sort of arrangement include the following. In the case of medical care there is warrant for proportionately equalizing what is spent from anyone's total taxable income. This warrant reflects the conditions, discussed earlier, of the natural lottery. Insofar as the advantages of health and the burdens of illness are random and undeserved, we may find it in our common interest to share risks. A fixed percentage of income attests to the misfit, also mentioned previously, between the reasons for differential total income and the reasons for receiving medical treatment. If money remains a causally necessary condition for receiving medical treatment, then a way must be found to place it in the hands of those who need it. The card is one such means. It is designed effectively to equalize purchasing power. In this way it seems to accord nicely with the goal of equal access. On the other side, the requirement of initial out-of-pocket expenses—sufficiently large in comparision to average family expenditures on health care—is designed to discourage frivolous use and foster awareness that medical care is a benefit not to be simply taken as a matter of course. It also safeguards against an excessively large tax burden while providing universal protection against the often disastrous costs of serious illnesses. Whether 10 per cent is too great a chunk for the very poor to pay, and whether by itself the proposal will feed price inflation and neglect of preventive medicine are questions which would have to be answered.

Another kind of possible institutional reform will also greatly interest the defender of equal access. This has to do with the "design of health care systems" or "care settings." The prevalent setting in American society has always been "fee-for-service." It is left up to each person to obtain the requisite care and to pay for it as he or she goes along. Because costs for medical treatment have accelerated at such an alarming rate, and because the sheer diffusion of energy and effort so characteristic of American medical practice leaves more and more people dissatisfied, alternatives to fee-for-service have been considered of late with unprecedented seriousness. The alternative care setting most widely discussed is prepaid practice, and specifically the "health maintenance organization" (HMO). Here one finds "an organized system of care which accepts the responsibility to provide or otherwise assure comprehensive care to a defined population for a fixed periodic payment per person or per family . . ." (A. Somers, 1971b:v). The best-known HMO is the Kaiser-Permanente Medical Care Program (see also Garfield, 1971). Does the HMO serve to realize the goal of equal access more fully? One line of argument in its favor is this. It is plausible to think that equal access will be fostered by the more economical care setting. HMO's are held to be less costly per capita in at least two respects: hospitalization rates are much below the national average; and less often noted, physician manpower is as well. To be sure, one should be sensitive to the corruptions in each type of setting. While fee-for-service has resulted in a suspiciously high number of surgeries (twice as many per capita in the United States as in Great Britain), the HMO physician may more frequently permit the patient's needs to be overriden by the organization's pressure to economize. It may also be more difficult in an HMO setting to provide for close personal relations between a particular physician and a particular patient (something commended, of course, on all sides). After such corruptions are allowed for, the data seem encouraging to such an extent that a defender of equal access will certainly support the repeal of any law which limits the development of prepaid practice, to approve of "front-aid" subsidies for HMO's to increase their number overall and achieve a more equitable distribution throughout the country, and so on. At a minimum, each care setting should be available in every region. If we assume a common freedom to choose between them, each may help to guard against the peculiar temptations to which the other is exposed.

To assess in any serious way proposals for institutional reform such as the above is beyond the scope of this paper. We would eventually be led, for example, into the question of whether it is consistent for the rich to pay more than the poor for the same treatment when, again, needs rather than income constitute the ground of the treatment (Ward, 1973), and from there into the tangled subject of the "ethics of redistribution" in general (see, e.g., Benn and Peters, 1965:155-178; de Jouvenal, 1952). Other complex issues deserve to be considered as well, e.g., the criteria for allocation of limited resources,[2] and how conceptions of justice apply to the providers of health care.[3]

Those committed to self-conscious moral and religious reflection about subjects in medicine have concentrated, perhaps unduly, on issues about care of individual patients (as death approaches, for instance). These issues plainly warrant the most careful consideration. One would like to see in addition, however, more attention paid to social questions in medical ethics. To attend to them is not necessarily to leave behind all of the matters which reach deeply into the human condition. Any detailed case for institutional reforms, for example, will be enriched if the proponent asks soberly whether certain conflicts and certain perplexities allow for more than partial improvements and provisional resolutions. Can public and private interests ever be made fully to coincide by legislative and administrative means? Will the commitment of a physician to an individual patient and the commitment of the legislator to the "common good" ever be harmonized in every case? Our anxiety may be too intractable. Our fear of illness and of dying may be so pronounced and immediate that we will seize the nearly automatic connections between privilege, wealth, and power if we can. We will do everything possible to have our kidney machines even if the charts make it clear that many more would benefit from mandatory immunization at a fraction of the cost. And our capacity for taking in rival points of view may be too limited. Once we have witnessed tangible suffering, we cannot just return with ease to public policies aimed at statistical patients. Those who believe that justice is the pre-eminent virtue of institutions and that a case can be convincingly made on behalf of justice for equal access to health care would do well to ponder such conflicts and perplexities. Our reforms might then seem, to ourselves and to others, less abstract and jargon-filled in formulation and less sanguine and piecemeal in substance. They would reflect a greater awareness of what we have to confront.

NOTES

[1] Much of the research for this paper, which first appeared in *The Journal of Religious Ethics* 2:1 (Spring, 1973): 11-32, was done during the Fall Term, 1972-73, when I was on leave in Washington, D.C. I am very grateful for the two appointments which made this leave possible: as Service Fellow, Office of Special Projects, Health Services and Mental Health Administration, Department of Health, Education, and Welfare; and as Visiting Scholar, Kennedy Center for Bioethics, Georgetown University.

[2] The issue of priorities is at least threefold: (1) between improved medical care and other social needs, e.g., to restrain auto accidents and pollution; (2) between different sorts of medical

treatments for different illnesses, e.g., prevention vs. crisis intervention and exotic treatments; (3) between persons all of whom need a single scarce resource and not all can have it, e.g., Ramsey's discussion of how to decide among those who are to receive dialysis. Moreover, (1) can be subdivided between (a) improved medical care and other social needs which affect health directly, e.g., drug addiction, auto accidents, and pollution; (b) improved medical care and other social needs which serve the overall aim of community-survival, e.g., a common defense. In the case of (2), one would like to see far more careful discussion of some general criteria which might be employed, e.g., numbers affected, degree of contagion, prospects for rehabilitation, and so on.

[3] What sorts of appeals to justice might be cogently made to warrant, for instance, the differentially high income physician receive? Here are three possibilities: (1) the greater skill and responsibility involved should be rewarded proportionately, i.e., one should attend to considerations of *desert*; (2) there should be *compensation* for the money invested for education and facilities in order to restore circumstances of approximate equality (this argument, while a common one in medical circles, would need to consider that medical education is received in part at public expense and that the modern physician is the highest paid professional in the country); (3) the difference should benefit the least advantaged more than an alternative arrangement where disparities are less. We prefer a society where the medical profession flourishes and everyone has a longer life expectancy to one where everyone is poverty-stricken with a shorter life expectancy ("splendidly equalized destitution"). Yet how are we to ascertain the minimum degree of differential income required for the least advantaged members of the society to be better off?

Discussions of "justice and the interests of providers" are, I think, badly needed. Physicians in the United States have suffered a decline in prestige for various reasons, e.g., the way many used Medicare to support and increase their own incomes. Yet one should endeavor to assess their interests fairly. A concern for professional autonomy is clearly important, though one may ask whether adequate attention has been paid to the distinction between the imposition of cost-controls from outside and interference with professional medical judgments. One may affirm the former, it seems, and still reject—energetically—the latter.

REFERENCES

Anderson, Odin
1973 *Health Care: Can There Be Equity? The United States, Sweden and England.* New York: Wiley.

Appel, James Z.
1970 "Health care delivery." Pp. 141-166 in Boisfeuillet Jones (ed.), *The Health of Americans.* Englewood Cliffs, N.J.: Prentice-Hall, Inc.

Bedau, Hugo A.
1971 "Radical egalitarianism." Pp. 168-180 in Hugo A. Bedau (ed.), *Justice and Equality.* Englewood Cliffs, N.J.: Prentice-Hall, Inc.

Benn, Stanley I.
1971 "Egalitarianism and the equal consideration of interests." Pp. 152-167 in Hugo A. Bedau (ed.), *Justice and Equality. Englewood Cliffs, N.J.: Prentice-Hall, Inc.*

Benn, Stanley I. and Richard S. Peters
1965 *The Principles of Political Thought.* New York: The Free Press.

de Jouvenel, Bertrand
1952 *The Ethics of Redistribution.* Cambridge: University Press.

Feldstein, Martin S.
1971 "A new approach to national health insurance." *The Public Interest* 23 (Spring):93-105.

Garfield, Sidney R.
1971 "Prevention of dissipation of health services resources." *American Journal of Public Health* 61:1499-1506.

Hicks, Nancy

1973 "Nation's doctors move to police medical care." Pp. 1, 52 in *New York Times*, Sunday, October 28.

Honore, A. M.

1968 "Social justice." Pp. 61-94 in Robert S. Summers (ed.), *Essays in Legal Philosophy*. Oxford: Basil Blackwell.

Hospers, John

1961 *Human Conduct*. New York: Harcourt, Brace and World, Inc.

Hubbard, William N.

1970 "Health knowledge." Pp. 93-120 in Boisfeuillet Jones (ed.), *The Health of Americans*. Englewood Cliffs, N.J.: Prentice-Hall, Inc.

Kennedy, Edward M.

1972 *In Critical Condition: The Crisis in America's Health Care*. New York: Simon and Schuster.

Lucas, J. R.

1972 "Justice." *Philosophy* 47 (July):229-248.

Nagel, Thomas

1973 "Equal treatment and compensatory discrimination." *Philosophy and Public Affairs* (Summer):348-363.

Nixon, Richard M.

1972 "President's message on health care system." Document No. 92-261 (March 2). House of Representatives, Washington, D.C.

Outka, Gene

1972 *Agape: An Ethical Analysis*. New Haven and London: Yale University Press.

Perelman, Ch.

1963 *The Idea of Justice and the Problem of Argument*. Trans. John Petrie. London: Routledge and Kegan Paul.

Ramsey, Paul

See the bibliography of Ramsey's works in this volume. Capital letters (e.g. 1950A) denote books and occasional papers; lower case letters (e.g. 1968a) denote articles.

Rand, Ayn

1957 *Atlas Shrugged*. New York: Signet.

Rawls, John

1971 *A Theory of Justice*. Cambridge, Mass.: Harvard University Press.

Rescher, Nicholas

1966 *Distributive Justice*. Indianapolis: The Bobbs-Merrill Company, Inc.

Ryan, John A.

1916 *Distributive Justice*. New York: The Macmillan Company.

Sade, Robert M.

1971 "Medical care as a right: a refutation." *The New England Journal of Medicine* 285 (December):1288-1292.

Schultze, Charles L., Edward R. Fried, Alice M. Rivlin and Nancy H. Teeters

1972 *Setting National Priorities: The 1973 Budget*. Washington, D.C.: The Brookings Institution.

Somers, Anne R.

1971a *Health Care in Transition: Directions for the Future*. Chicago: Hospital Research and Educational Trust.

1971b (ed.), *The Kaiser-Permanente Medical Care Program*. New York: The Commonwealth Fund.

Somers, Anne R. and Herman M. Somers

1972a "The organization and financing of health care: issues and directions for the future." *American Journal of Orthopsychiatry* 42 (January), 119-136.

1972b "Major issues in national health insurance." *Milbank Memorial Fund Quarterly* 50 (April):177-210.

Vlastos, Gregory
1962 "Justice and equality." Pp. 31-72 in Richard B. Brandt (ed.), *Social Justice*. Englewood Cliffs, N.J.: Prentice-Hall, Inc.

Ward, Andrew
1973 "The idea of equality reconsidered." *Philosophy* 48 (January):85-90.

Williams, Bernard A. O.
1971 "The idea of equality." Pp. 116-137 in Hugo A. Bedau (ed.), *Justice and Equality*. Englewood Cliffs, N.J.: Prentice-Hall, Inc.

CHAPTER X

Proxy Consent in the Experimentation Situation[1]

RICHARD A. MCCORMICK, S.J.

It is widely admitted within the research community that if there is to be continuing and proportionate progress in pediatric medicine, experimentation on children is utterly essential. This conviction rests on two closely interrelated facts. First, as Alexander Capron has pointed out (1973), "Children cannot be regarded simply as 'little people' pharmacologically. Their metabolism, enzymatic and excretory systems, skeletal development and so forth differ so markedly from adults' that drug tests for the latter provide inadequate information about dosage, efficacy, toxicity, side effects, and contra-indications for children." Secondly, and consequently, there is a limit to the usefulness of prior experimentation with animals and adults. At some point or other experimentation with children becomes necessary.

At this point, however, a severe problem arises. The legal and moral legitimacy of experimentation (understood here as procedures involving no direct benefit to the person participating in the experiment) is founded above all on the informed consent of the subject. But in, at least, very many instances the young subject is either legally or factually incapable of consent. Furthermore, it is argued, the parents are neither legally nor morally capable of supplying this consent for the child. As Dr. Donald T. Chalkley (1973:41) of the National Institutes of Health puts it: "a parent has no legal right to give consent for the involvement of his child in an activity not for the benefit of that child. No legal guardian, no person standing *in loco parentis*, has that right." It would seem to follow that infants and some minors are simply out of bounds where clinical research is concerned. Indeed, this conclusion has been explicitly drawn by Paul Ramsey. He notes: "If children are incapable of truly consenting to experiments having unknown hazards for the sake of good to come, and if no one else should consent for them in cases unrelated to their own treatment, then medical research and society in general must choose a perhaps more difficult course of action to gain the benefits we seek from medical investigations" (1970B:17).

Does the consent requirement, taken seriously, exclude all experiments on children? If it does, then children themselves will be the ultimate sufferers. If it does not, what is the moral justification for the experimental procedures? The problem is serious. For, as Ramsey notes, the investigation involving children as subjects is "a prismatic case in which to tell whether we mean to take seriously the consent-requirement" (1970B:28).

Before concluding with Shirkey (1968:119f) that those incompetent of consent are "therapeutic orphans," I should like to explore the notion and validity of proxy consent. More specifically, the interest here is in the question: can and may parents consent, and to what extent, to experiments on their children where the procedures are non-beneficial for the child involved? Before approaching this question it is necessary to point out the genuine if restricted input of the ethician in such matters. Ramsey has rightly pointed up the difference between the ethics of consent and ethics in the consent situation. This latter refers to the meaning and practical applications of the requirement of an informed consent. It is the work of prudence and pertains to the competence and responsibility of physicians and investigators. The former, on the other hand, refers to the principle requiring an informed consent, the ethics of consent itself. Such moral principles are elaborated out of competences broader than that associated with the medical community.

I

A brief review of the literature will reveal that the question raised above remains in something of a legal and moral limbo. The *Nuremberg Code* states only that "the voluntary consent of the human subject is absolutely essential. This means that the person involved should have legal capacity to give consent . . ." (this and the following references to codes are from Beecher, 1970:227f). Nothing specific is said about infants or those who are mentally incompetent. Dr. Leo Alexander, who aided in drafting the first version of the *Nuremberg*

Code, explained subsequently that his provision for valid consent from next of kin where mentally ill patients are concerned was dropped by the Nuremberg judges "probably because they did not apply in the specific cases under trial" (1966:62, cf. Ramsey 1970B:26). Be that as it may, it has been pointed out by Beecher (1970:231) that a strict observance of Nuremberg's rule 1 would effectively cripple study of mental disease, and would simply prohibit all experimentation in children.

The *International Code of Medical Ethics* (General Assembly of the World Medical Association, 1949) stated simply: "Under no circumstances is a doctor permitted to do anything that would weaken the physical or mental resistance of a human being except from strictly therapeutic or prophylactic indications imposed in the interest of his patient" (Beecher, 1970:236). This statement is categorical and if taken literally it means that "young children and the mentally incompetent are categorically excluded from all investigations except those that directly may benefit the subject" (Ingelfinger, 1973:791). However, in 1954 the General Assembly of the World Medical Association (*Principles for Those in Research and Experimentation*) stated: "It should be required that each person who submits to experimentation be informed of the nature, the reason for, and the risk of the proposed experiment. If the patient is irresponsible, consent should be obtained from the individual who is legally responsible for the individual" (Beecher, 1970:240). In the context it is somewhat ambiguous whether this statement is meant to apply beyond experimental procedures that are performed for the patient's good.

The *Declaration of Helsinki* (1964) is much clearer on the point. After distinguishing "clinical research combined with professional care" and "non-therapeutic clinical research," it states of this latter: "Clinical research on a human being cannot be undertaken without his free consent, after he has been fully informed; if he is legally incompetent the consent of the legal guardian should be procured" (Beecher, 1970:278). In 1966 the American Medical Association, in its *Principles of Medical Ethics*, endorsed the Helsinki statement. It distinguished clinical investigation "primarily for treatment" and clinical investigation "primarily for the accumulation of scientific knowledge." With regard to this latter, it noted that "consent, in writing, should be obtained from the subject, or from his legally authorized representative if the subject lacks the capacity to consent." More specifically in dealing with minors or mentally incompetent persons the AMA statement reads: "Consent, in writing, is given by a legally authorized representative of the subject under circumstances in which an informed and prudent adult would reasonably be expected to volunteer himself or his child as a subject" (Beecher, 1970:223).

In 1963, the Medical Research Council of Great Britain issued its *Responsibility in Investigations on Human Subjects* (Beecher, 1970:262b). Under title of "Procedures not of Direct Benefit to the Individual" the Council stated: "The situation in respect of minors and mentally subnormal or mentally disordered persons is of particular difficulty. In the strict view of the law parents and guardians of minors cannot give consent on their behalf to any procedures which are of no particular benefit to them and which may carry some risk of harm." Then, after discussing consent as involving a full understanding of "the implications to himself of the procedures to which he was consenting," the Council concluded: "When true consent in this sense cannot be obtained, procedures which are of no direct benefit and which might carry a risk of harm to the subject should not be undertaken." If it is granted that every experiment involves some risk, then the MRC statement would exclude *any* experiment on children. Curran and Beecher have pointed out (1969:77f.) that this strict reading of English law is based on the advice of Sir Harvey Druitt, though there is no statute or case law to support it. Nevertheless it has gone relatively unchallenged.

Statements of the validity of proxy consent similar to those of the *Declaration of Helsinki* and the American Medical Association have been issued by the American Psychological Association (Beecher, 1970:256f.) and the Food and Drug Administration (Beecher, 1970:299f.). The most recent formulation touching proxy consent is that of the Department of Health, Education and Welfare in its *Protection of Human Subjects, Policies and Procedures* (1973). In situations where the subject cannot himself give consent, the document refers to "supplementary judgment." It states: "For the purposes of this document, supplementary judgment will refer to judgments made by local committees in addition to the subject's consent (when possible) and that of the parents or legal guardian (where applicable), as to whether or not a subject may participate in clinical research." The DHEW proposed guidelines admit that the law on parental consent is not clear in all respects. Proxy consent is valid with regard to established and generally accepted therapeutic procedures; it is, in practice, valid for therapeutic research. However, the guidelines state that "when research might expose a subject to risk without defined therapeutic benefit or other positive effect on that subject's well-being, parental or guardian consent appears to be insufficient." These statements about validity concern positive law, in the sense (I would judge) of what is likely to happen should a case determination be provoked on the basis of existing precedent.

After this review of the legal validity of proxy consent and its limitations, the DHEW guidelines go on to draw two ethical conclusions. First: "When the risk of a proposed study is generally considered not significant, and the potential benefit is explicit, the ethical issues need not preclude the participation of children in biomedical research." Presumably, this means that where there is risk, ethical issues do preclude the use of children. However, the DHEW document did not draw this conclusion. Rather its second ethical conclusion states: "An investigator proposing research activities which expose children to risk must document, as part of the application for support, that the information to be gained can be obtained in no other way. The investigator must also stipulate either that the risk to the subjects will be insignificant, or that although some risk exists, the potential benefit is significant and far outweighs that risk. In no case will research activities be approved which entail substantial risk except in the cases of clearly therapeutic procedures . . . ." These proposed guidelines admit, therefore, three levels of risk within the ethical calculus: insignificant risk, some risk, substantial risk. Proxy consent is, by inference, ethically acceptable for the first two levels, but not for the third.

The documents cited move almost imperceptibly back and forth between legal and moral considerations, so that it is often difficult to know whether the major concern is one or the other, or even how the relationship of the legal and ethical is conceived. Nevertheless, it can be said that there has been a gradual move away from the absolutism (represented in the *Nuremberg Code*) to the acceptance of proxy consent, possibly because the *Nuremberg Code* is viewed as containing, to some extent, elements of a overreaction to the Nazi experiments.

Medical literature of the non-codal variety has revealed this same pattern of ambiguity. For instance, writing in *The Lancet*, Dr. R. E. W. Fisher (1953:983) reacted to the reports of the use of children in research procedures as follows: "No medical procedure involving the slightest risk or accompanied by the slightest physical or mental pain may be inflicted on a child for experimental purposes unless there is a reasonable chance, or at least a hope, that the child may benefit thereby." On the other hand, Franz J. Ingelfinger, editor of *The New England Journal of Medicine*, contends that the World Medical Association's statement ("Under no circumstances . . . etc." cf. above) is an extremist position that must be modified (1973:791f.). His suggested modification: "Only when the risks are small and justifiable is a doctor permitted, etc. . . ." It is difficult to know from Ingelfinger's wording whether he means small and *therefore* justifiable, or whether "justifiable" refers to the hoped-for benefit. Responses to this editorial were contradictory. N. Baumslag and R. E. Yodaiken (1973:1247) stated: "In our opinion there are no conditions under which any children may be used for experimentation not primarily designed for their benefit." Ian Shine, John Howieson and Ward Griffen, Jr. (1973:1248) came to the opposite conclusion: "We strongly support his (Ingelfinger's) proposals provided that one criterion of 'small and justifiable risks' is the willingness of the experimentor to be an experimentee, or to offer a spouse or child when appropriate."

Curran and Beecher (1969:81) had earlier disagreed strongly with the rigid interpretation given the statement of the Medical Research Council through Druitt's influence. Their own conclusion was that "children under 14 may participate in clinical investigation which is not for their benefit where the studies are sound, promise important new knowledge for mankind, and there is no discernible risk." The editors of *Archives of Disease in Childhood*

(1973:751f.) recently endorsed this same conclusion adding only "the necessity of informed parental consent." Discussing relatively minor procedures such as weighing a baby, skin pricks, venepunctures, etc., they contend that "whether or not these procedures are acceptable must depend, it seems to us, on whether the potential gain to others is commensurate with the discomfort to the individual." They see the Medical Research Council's statement as an understandable but exaggerated reaction to the shocking disclosures of the Nazi era. A new value judgment is required in our time, one based on a low risk/benefit ratio.

This same attitude is proposed by Alan M. W. Porter (Franklin, 1973:402f.). He argues that there are grounds "for believing that it may be permissible and reasonable to undertake minor procedures on children for experimental purposes with the permission of the parents." The low risk/benefit ratio is the ultimate justification. Interestingly, Porter reports the reactions of colleagues and the public to a research protocol he had drawn up. He desired to study the siblings of children who had succumbed to "cot death." The research involved venepuncture. A pediatric authority told Porter that venepuncture was inadmissible under the Medical Research Council code. Astonished, Porter showed the protocol to the first ten colleagues he met. The instinctive reaction of nine out of ten was "of course you may." Similarly, a professional market researcher asked (for Porter) ten laymen about the procedure and all responded that he could proceed. In other words, Porter argues that public opinion (and therefore, presumably, moral common sense) stands behind the low risk/benefit ratio approach to experimentation on children.

This sampling is sufficient indication of the variety of reactions likely to be encountered when research on children is discussed.

II

The professional ethicians who have written on this subject have also drawn rather diverse conclusions. John Fletcher argues that a middle path between autonomy (of the physician) and heteronomy (external control) must be discovered (1967:620f.). The Nuremberg rule "does not take account of exceptions which can be controlled and makes no allowance whatsoever for the exercise of professional judgment." It is clear that Fletcher would accept proxy consent in some instances, though he has not fully specified what these would be.

Thomas J. O'Donnell, S.J. (1974:73), notes that besides informed consent, we also speak of three other modalities of consent. First, there is presumed consent. Life-saving measures that are done on an unconscious patient in an emergency room are done with presumed consent. Secondly, there is implied consent. The various tests done on a person who undergoes a general checkup are done with implied consent, the consent being contained and implied in the very fact of his coming for a checkup. Finally, there is vicarious consent. This is the case of the parent who consents for therapy on an infant. O'Donnell wonders whether these modalities of consent, already accepted in the therapeutic context, can be extended to the context of clinical investigation (and by this he means research not to the direct benefit of the child). It is his conclusion that vicarious consent can be ethically operative "provided it is contained within the strict limits of a presumed consent (on the part of the subject) proper to clinical research and much narrower than the presumptions that might be valid in a therapeutic context." Practically, this means that O'Donnell would accept the validity of vicarious consent only where "danger is so remote and discomfort so minimal that a normal and informed individual would be presupposed to give ready consent." However, O'Donnell tells us neither what are the criteria, nor what the analysis, that set the "strict limits of a presumed consent."

Princeton's Paul Ramsey is the ethician who has discussed this problem at greatest length (1970B, 1973d). He is in clear disagreement with the positions of Fletcher and O'Donnell. Ramsey denies the validity of proxy consent in nonbeneficial (to the child) experiments simply and without qualification. Why? We may not, he argues, submit a child either to procedures that involve any measure of risk of harm or procedures that involve no harm but simply "offensive touching." "A subject can be wronged without being harmed," he writes. This occurs whenever he is used as an object, or "as a means only" rather than also as an end in himself. Parents cannot consent to this type of thing, regardless of the significance of the experiment. Ramsey sees the morality of experimentation on children to be exactly what Paul Freund has described as the law on the matter: "The law here is that parents may consent for the child if the invasion of the child's body is for the child's welfare or benefit" (Freund, 1965, 1966).

In pursuit of his point Ramsey argues as follows: "To attempt to consent for a child to be made an experimental subject is to treat a child as not a child. It is to treat him as if he were an adult person who has consented to become a joint adverturer in the common cause of medical research. If the grounds for this are alleged to be the presumptive or implied consent of the child, that must simply be characterized as a violent and a false presumption." Thus he concludes simply that "no parent is morally competent to consent that his child shall be submitted to hazardous *or other experiments* having no diagnostic or therapeutic significance for the child himself" (1970B:13). Though he does not say so, Ramsey would certainly conclude that a law that tolerates proxy consent to any purely experimental procedures is one without moral warrants, indeed, is immoral because it legitimates (or tries to) treating a human being as a means only.

A careful study, then, of the legal, medical and ethical literature on proxy consent for non-therapeutic research on children reveals profoundly diverging views. Generally, the pro's and con's are spelled out in terms of two important values: individual integrity, on the one hand; societal good through medical benefits, on the other. Furthermore, in attempting to balance these two values, this literature by and large either affirms or denies the moral legitimacy of a risk/benefit ratio, what ethicians refer to as a teleologial calculus. It seems to me that in doing this, current literature has not faced this tremendously important and paradigmatic issue at its most fundamental level. For instance, Ramsey bases his prohibitive position on the contention that non-beneficial experimental procedures make an "object" of an individual. In these cases, he contends, parents cannot consent for the individual. Consent is the heart of the matter. If the parents could legitimately consent for the child, then presumably experimental procedures would not make an object of the infant and would be permissible. Therefore, the basic question seems to be: why *cannot* the parents provide consent for the child? Why is their consent considered null here while it is accepted when procedures are therapeutic? To say that the child would be treated as an object does not answer this question; it seems that it presupposes the answer and announces it under this formulation. Do we not treat ourselves as "objects" when we allow experiments on ourselves?

III

There is (in traditional moral theology) a handle that may allow us to take hold of this problem at a deeper root and arrive at a principled and consistent position, one that takes account of all the values without arbitrarily softening or suppressing any of them. That handle is the notion of parental consent, and particularly the theoretical implications underlying it. If this can be unpacked a bit, perhaps a more satisfying analysis will emerge. Parental consent is required and sufficient for therapy directed at the child's own good. We refer to this as vicarious consent. It is closely related to presumed consent. That is, it is morally valid precisely in so far as it is a reasonable presumption of the child's wishes, a construction of what the child would wish could he consent for himself. But here the notion of "what the child would wish" must be pushed further if we are to avoid a simple imposition of the adult world on the child. Why *would* the child so wish? The answer seems to be that he would choose this were he capable of choice because he *ought* to do so. This statement roots in a traditional natural law understanding of human moral obligations and calls for a brief explanation.

Here I shall summarize briefly what has been explained at great length by other authors. The first thing that should be said is that moral convictions do not originate from discursive analyses or arguments. Let us take slavery as an example. We do not hold that slavery is humanly demeaning and immoral chiefly because we have argued to this discursively. Rather, first, our sensitivities are sharpened to the meaning and value of human persons. We then *experience* the out-of-jointness, inequality and injustice of slavery. We then *judge* it to be wrong. At this point we develop "arguments" to criticize, modify, and above all communicate this judgment. Reflective analysis or discursive reasoning is an attempt to reinforce rationally, communicably, and from other sources what we grasp at a different level. Discursive reflection does not *discover* the good but only analyzes it. The good that reason seems to discover is the good that was already hidden in the original intuition.

This calls for explanation. How do we arrive at definite moral obligations, moral prescriptions and prohibitions? How does the general thrust of our persons toward good and away from evil become concrete, even as concrete as a code of do's and don't's and caveats? Somewhat as follows—and in this I am following very closely, even verbally at times, the school of J. de Finance, G. de Broglie, G. Grisez, John Finnis and others who have deep roots in Thomistic philosophy. We proceed by asking what are the goods or values man can seek, the values that define his human opportunity, his flourishing? We can answer this by examining man's basic tendencies, for it is impossible to act without having an interest in the object, and it is impossible to be attracted by, to have interest in, something without some inclination already present. What then are the basic inclinations?

With no pretense at being exhaustive, we could list some of the following as basic inclinations present prior to acculturation: the tendency to preserve life; the tendency to mate and raise children; the tendency to explore and question; the tendency to seek out other men and seek their approval—friendship; the tendency to establish good relations with unknown higher power; the tendency to use intelligence in guiding action; the tendency to develop skills and exercise them in play and the fine arts. In these inclinations our intelligence *spontaneously* and *without reflection* grasps the possibilities or good to which they point, and prescribes them. Thus we form naturally and without reflection the basic principles of practical or moral reasoning. Or, as philosopher John Finnis renders it:

> What is spontaneously understood when one turns from contemplation to action is not a set of Kantian or neoscholastic 'moral principles' identifying this as right and that as wrong, but a set of values which can be expressed in the form of principles such as 'life is a good-to-be-pursued and realized and what threatens it is to be avoided' (1970:373).

We have not yet arrived at a determination of what concrete actions are morally right or wrong; but we have laid the basis. Since these basic values are equally basic and irreducibly attractive, the morality of our conduct is determined by the adequacy of our openness to these values. Each of these values has its self-evident appeal as a participation in the unconditioned Good we call God. The realization of these values in intersubjective life is the only adequate way to love and attain God.

Further reflection by practical reason tells us what it means to remain open and to pursue these basic human values. First, we must take them into account in our conduct. Simple disregard of one or the other shows we have set our mind against this good and, in the process, against both the unconditioned Good who is its source and ourselves. Immoral action is always self-destructive in its thrust. Secondly, when we can do so as easily as not, we should avoid acting in ways that inhibit these values, and prefer ways that realize them. Thirdly, we must make an effort on their behalf when their realization in another is in extreme peril. If we fail to do so, we show that the value in question is not the object of our efficacious love and concern. Finally, we must never choose directly against a basic good. For when one of the irreducible values falls immediately under our choice, to choose against it in favor of some other basic value is arbitrary; for all the basic values are equally basic and self-evidently attractive. What is to count as "turning against a basic good" is, of course, a crucial moral question. It need not be discussed here. My only point is that particular moral judgments (e.g., about sustaining life and health, or taking life, what is morally legitimate or illegitimate in dealing with life and health, *etc.*) are incarnations of these more basic normative positions, positions that have their roots in spontaneous, pre-reflective inclinations.

In summary, then, the natural law tradition argues that there are certain identifiable values that we *ought* to support, attempt to realize and never directly suppress because they are definitive of our flourishing and well-being. It further argues that knowledge of these values and of the prescriptions and proscriptions associated with them is, in principle, available to human reason. That is, they require for their discovery no divine revelation.

IV

What does all this have to do with the moral legitimacy of proxy consent? It was noted above that parental (proxy, vicarious) consent is required and sufficient for therapy directed to the child's own good. It was further noted that it is morally valid precisely in so far as it is a reasonable presumption of the child's wishes, a construction of what the child would wish, could he do so. Finally, it was suggested that the child *would* wish this therapy because he *ought* to do so. In other words, a construction of what the child *would* wish (presumed consent) is not an exercise in adult capriciousness and arbitrariness, subject to an equally capricious denial or challenge when the child comes of age. It is based, rather, on two assertions: (a) that there are certain values (in this case life itself) definitive of our good and flourishing, hence values that we *ought* to choose and support if we want to become and stay human, and that therefore these are good also for the child; (b) that these "ought" judgments, at least in their more general formulations, are a common heritage available to all men, and hence form the basis on which policies can be built.

Specifically, then, I would argue that parental consent is morally legitimate where therapy on the child is involved precisely because we know that life and health are goods for the child; that he *would* choose them because he *ought* to choose the good of life, i.e., his own self-preservation as long as this life remains, all things considered, a human good. To see whether and to what extent this type of moral analysis applies to experimentation, we must ask: are there other things that the child *ought*, as a human being, to choose precisely because and in so far as they are goods definitive of his growth and flourishing? Concretely, *ought* he to choose his own involvement in non-therapeutic experimentation, and to what extent? Certainly there are goods or benefits, at least potential, involved. But are they goods that the child *ought* to choose? Or again, if we can argue that a certain level of involvement in non-therapeutic experimentation is good for the child and therefore that he *ought* to choose it, then there are grounds for saying that parental consent for this is morally legitimate, and should be recognized as such.

Perhaps a beginning can be made as follows. To pursue the good of human life means not only to choose and support this value in one's own case, but also in the case of others when the opportunity arises. In other words, the individual *ought* also to take into account, realize, make efforts in behalf of the lives of others. For we are social beings and the goods that define our growth and invite to it are goods that reside also in others. It can be good for one to pursue and support the good of life in others. Therefore, when it is factually good, we may say that one *ought* to do so (as opposed to not doing so).

If this is true of all of us up to a point and within limits, it is no less true of the infant. He would choose to help others because he *ought* to do so. Now, to support and realize the value that is life means to support and realize health, the cure of disease and so on. Therefore, up to a point, this support and realization is good for all of us individually. To share in the general effort and burden of health-maintenance and disease-control is part of our flourishing and growth as humans. To the extent that it is good for all of us to share this burden, we all *ought* to do so. And to the extent that we *ought* to do so, it is a reasonable construction or presumption of our wishes to say that we would do so. The reasonableness of this presumption validates vicarious consent.

It was just noted that sharing in the common burden of progress in medicine constitutes an individual good for all of us *up to a point*. That qualification is crucially important. It suggests that there are limits beyond which sharing is not, or might not be a good. What might be the limits of this sharing? When might it no longer be a good for all individuals, and therefore something that all need not choose to do? I would develop the matter as follows.

Adults may donate (*inter vivos*) an organ precisely because their personal good is not to be conceived individualistically, but socially—that is, there is a natural order to other human persons which is in the very notion of the human personality itself. The personal being and good of an individual does have a relationship to the being and good of others, difficult as it may be to keep this in a balanced perspective. For this reason, an individual can become (in carefully delimited circumstances) more fully a person by donation of an organ; for by communicating to another of his very being he has more fully integrated himself into the mysterious unity between person and person.

Something similar can be said of participation in non-therapeutic experimentation. It can be an affirmation of one's solidarity and Christian concern for others (through advancement of medicine). Becoming an experimental subject can involve any or all of three things: some degree of risk (at least of complications), pain, associated inconvenience (e.g., prolonging hospital stay, delaying recovery, etc.). To accept these for the good of others could be an act of charitable concern.

After making such general statements, there are two qualifications that must immediately be made, and these qualifications explain the phrase "up to a point." First, whether it is personally good for an individual to donate an organ or participate in experimentation is a very circumstantial and therefore highly individual affair. For some individuals these undertakings could be or prove to be humanly destructive. Much depends on their personalities, past family life, maturity, future position in life, *etc.* The second and more important qualification is that these procedures become human goods for the donor or subject precisely because and therefore only when they are voluntary; for the personal good under discussion is the good of expressed charity. For these two reasons I would conclude that as a rule no one else can make such decisions for an individual, i.e., *reasonably* presume his consent. He has a right to make them for himself. In other words, whether a person *ought* to run these risks is a highly individual affair and cannot be generalized in the way the good of self-preservation can be. Thus, if we cannot say of an individual that *he ought* to do something, proxy consent to those acts has no reasonable presumptive bases.

But are there situations where such considerations are not significant and where the presumption of consent is reasonable, because we may continue to say of *all* individuals that (other things being equal) they *ought* to be willing? I believe so. For instance, where organ donation is involved, if the only way a young child could be saved were by a blood transfusion from another child, I suspect that few would find such blood donation an unreasonable presumption on the donating child's wishes. The reason for the presumption is, I believe, that a great good can be provided for another at almost no cost to the donor child. As the scholastics put it, *parum pro nihilo reputatur* ("very little counts for nothing"). For this reason we may say, lacking countervailing individual evidence, that the individual *ought* to run some minimal risks.

Could the same reasoning apply to experimentation? Concretely, when a particular experiment would involve no discernible risks, no notable inconvenience, and yet hold promise of considerable benefit, should not the child be constructed to wish this in the same way we presume he chooses his own life, *i.e.* because he *ought* to? I believe so. He *ought* to want this not because it is in any way for his own medical good, but because it is (a) not in any realistic way to his harm, and (b) represents a potentially great benefit for others. He *ought* to want these benefits for others.

V

If this is a defensible account of the meaning and limits of presumed consent where those incompetent to consent are concerned, it means that proxy consent can be morally legitimate in some experimentations on children. Which? Those (1) that are scientifically well designed (and therefore offer hope of genuine benefit), (2) that contain no discernible risk or undue discomfort for the child and (3) that cannot succeed unless children are used (because there are dangers involved in interpreting terms such as "discernible," and "negligible," and the child should not *unnecessarily* be exposed to these even minimal risks). Here it must be granted that the notions of "discernible risk" and "undue discomfort" are themselves slippery and difficult, and probably somewhat relative. They certainly involve a value judgment and one that it is the heavy responsibility of the medical profession (not the moral theologian) to make. For example, perhaps it can be debated whether venepuncture involves "discernible risks" or "undue discomfort." But if it can be concluded that, in human terms, the risk involved or the discomfort is negligible or insignificant, then I believe there are sound reasons in moral analysis for saying that parental consent to this type of invasion can be justified.

Practically, then, I think there are good moral warrants for adopting the less conservative position espoused by Curran, Beecher, Ingelfinger, the *Helsinki Declaration*, the *Archives of Disease in Childhood* and others. Some who have adopted this position have argued for it in terms of a low risk/benefit ratio. That is acceptable if properly understood, that is, if "low risk" means for all practical purposes and in human judgment "no realistic risk." If it is interpreted in any other way, it opens the door wide to a utilitarian subordination of the individual to the collectivity. It goes beyond what individuals would want because they *ought* to. For instance, in light of the above analysis, I find totally unacceptable the DHEW statement that "the investigator must also stipulate either that the risk to the subjects will be insignificant, or that *although some risk exists, the potential benefit is significant and far outweights that risk*." This degree of risk goes beyond what all of us, as members of the community, necessarily *ought* to do. Therefore it is an inadequate check on proxy consent. Again, for analogous reasons, I would conclude that parental consent for a kidney transplant from one non-competent three-year old to another is without moral justification.

In arguing a position that would not allow even that amount of experimentation on children proposed here, Paul Ramsey has stated that this presumptive consent "must simply be characterized as a violent and a false presumption" (1970B:14). In developing his thought, he states that "a well child, or a child not suffering from an unrelated disease not being investigated, is not to be compared to an unconscious patient needing specific treatment. To imply the latter's 'constructive' consent is not a violent presumption, it is a life-saving presumption, though it is in some degree 'false.' " A careful analysis of this argument will reveal that for Ramsey the presumption is non-violent precisely because it is life-saving for the individual. Furthermore, he would in logic have to argue that any invasion which is not life-saving for the individual concerned is violent, if the individual does not consent thereto. I have attempted to show that this is too narrow. Rather, I would suggest that the presumption of consent to this life-saving therapy is non-violent, not simply because it is life-saving, but more precisely because self-preservation is something the individual would want because he *ought* to want it. I would further propose that there are good warrants for saying that there are other things an individual, as a social being, *ought* to want, and *to the extent that we may say this of him* then presumption of his consent is non-violent, *sc.*, reasonable.

This point is at the heart of the discussion and calls for a rewording. Ramsey does not believe we may "construct" or presume an infant's consent in non-beneficial experimentation because submission to such experimentation pertains to the realm of *charity*; and one may not construe that an individual is consenting to works of charity (1973d:n. 27).

His argument moves in two steps. First, there is "a difference between justice and charity. Charity, of course, is of highest excellence. But the thing one must imply about a child is not that he's charitable. In other words, let's not confuse the realms of nature and grace. You don't imply he's charitable. That comes by grace. That's his moral maturity. Later he can be charitable. Charity is itself not something one can extrapolate and presume to be the good of this child."

Secondly, to buttress this point Ramsey attempts to see where such constructive consent would take us if once we allow it for any non-beneficial experimentation. "Just think of the kind of constructive consents we could imply for children. You can imply, you can construe, that out of all charity this fetus doesn't want to be born because it's the seventeenth. If he's got any sense he doesn't want to fatally increase the poverty of his home. . . . I do not see where one could rationally stop in construing all sorts of works of mercy and self-sacrifice on the part of persons, not themselves capable by nature of grace yet of being the subject of charity."

This is a very strong argument and deserves to be taken with utmost seriousness. However, I believe some qualification is called for. Does *all* non-beneficial experimentation on this infant pertain to what Ramsey calls "charitable works"? By this term Ramsey obviously refers to works of supererogation, works that not all men just by being members of the human race, are held to or *ought* to do. This is the key. It can be argued, and I think successfully, that there are some things that all of us, simply as members of the human community, *ought* to do for others. These are not works of supererogation, nor works of "charity" in this special sense. Here the problem of semantics intrudes. If *any* involvement in non-therapeutic experimentation must be said to be "charitable" (in the strict sense, *i.e.*, beyond what is required of all of us and supererogatory), then Ramsey is correct. But some of the choices about involvement in experimentation seem to pertain to the area of *social justice*, one's personal bearing of his share of the burden that all may flourish and prosper. Therefore, they are choices that all *ought* to make. In other words, these choices do not pertain to charity, or not at least to charity in Ramsey's sense, a sense where ordinary, non-heroic responses get collapsed into and identified with heroic and extraordinary responses.

The distinction I am suggesting, therefore, is that between those works that not all of us can be expected to make and those that all of us can be expected to make. To the former category belong choices involving notable risk, discomfort, inconvenience. Whether it is good for one to make these choices, whether therefore he *ought* to make them, is a highly circumstantial affair and cannot be said of all of us in general. These are the works to which, theologically, the *particular* invitations of the Spirit inspire. They are the works of individual generosity and charity. No presumptive consent is in place here.

But we can establish a baseline and discover other works that involve no notable disadvantages to individuals, yet offer genuine hope for general benefit. It is good for all of us to share in these (unless we are by particular and accidental circumstances so weakened that even trivial procedures would constitute a threat to us) and hence we all *ought* to want these benefits for others. And if that is true, a presumption of consent is reasonable, and vicarious consent becomes legitimate. Thus it would seem that there are some experiments in children that do not pertain to charity in Ramsey's sense—charity as supererogation—and hence do not demand individualization before they can be said to be goods the individual would choose.

Now to Ramsey's second buttressing argument—the slippery slope. "I do not see where one could rationally stop in construing all sorts of works of mercy and self-sacrifice," etc. One stops and should stop precisely at the point where "constructed" consent does indeed involve self-sacrifice or works of mercy, the point beyond which not all of us are called, but only individuals inspired by the Spirit to do "the more," the sacrificial thing. This dividing line is reached when experiments involve discernible risk, undue discomfort or inconvenience.

Ramsey's reluctance or inability to make this distinction is traceable to the fact that he has not analyzed more deeply the validity of proxy consent in *therapeutic* situations. He states: "An 'implied' or 'constructive' consent—proxy consent—clearly is in order in the case of investigational therapeutic trials (beneficial research) when the patient/subject is incapable for any reason of giving actual consent" (1973d). True. But why true? If one answers, as Ramsey does, that it is true because where therapeutic research is involved the patient/subject *would* give consent, he has not gone far enough. The patient *would* give consent because therapeutic research is (or can be) something for his own good and to which, therefore, he *ought* to consent. Reasonable presumption or construction of consent is rooted in this. And it suggests immediately the possibility that there may be other procedures which are not necessarily to the individual's therapeutic good, but still represent a good to others, a good to which he, *like all of us*, ought also to consent. Once, therefore, the validity of proxy consent is traced to its deepest roots, we will see both its further legitimate extensions and its limitations.

These considerations do not mean that all non-competents (where consent is concerned) may be treated in the same way, that the same presumptions are morally legitimate in all cases. For if the circumstances of the infant or child differ markedly, then it is possible that there might be appropriate modifications in our construction of what he ought to choose. For instance, I believe that institutionalized infants demand special consideration. They are in a situation of peculiar danger for several reasons. First, they are often in a disadvantaged condition physically or mentally so that there is a temptation to regard them as "lesser human beings." Medical history shows our vulnerability to this type of judgment. Secondly, as institutionalized, they are a controlled group making them particularly tempting as research subjects. Thirdly, experimentation in such infants is less exposed to public scrutiny. These and other considerations suggest that there is a real danger of overstepping the line between what we all ought to want and what only the individual might want out of heroic, self-sacrificial charity. If such a real danger exists, then what the infant is construed as wanting because he *ought* must be modified. He need not *ought to want* if this involves him in real dangers of going beyond this point.

One test of an analysis is its appeal to common sense. Indispensable as this test certainly is, common sense can occasionally trip us up and turn out to be an appealing but deceptive cover for our own distorted perspectives and enthusiasms. Therefore, the validity of the analysis of proxy consent proposed here needs to be further tested by sampling its connections and consistency with some other issues where consent is an important component. Transplantation of organs between infants seems unjustified as has already been mentioned. But relatively trivial invasions (blood transfusions?) which are life-saving for the recipient would seem to be justified by proxy consent, if the benefit envisaged is otherwise unobtainable. It was suggested that the same is not true where more substantial deprivation is concerned. Case precedent has so far failed either to confirm or deny this analysis since, in allowing a kidney transplant from a non-competent, it has based the decision on the donor's good—the psychological harm he would suffer if the transplant were not done now (Capron, 1973:144).

A more difficult instance is that of parental decision over supporting an infant's life, or allowing the child to die. It would be generally accepted amongst both moral theologians and physicians that not *every* infant need be saved by use of *all* available means. This is but an application to infants of a rather standard and settled moral teaching about the use of ordinary and extraordinary means to sustain life. Some means are extraordinary, or "heroic" as physicians often say, and generally speaking (*per se* or as a general rule, as theologians say) no one is morally bound to preserve his own life by use of such means, though he is free to do so if he wishes. This same reasoning surely should apply to infants. There are contemporary instances, of course, where application of the distinction between ordinary and extraordinary measures becomes extremely difficult and the source of a good deal of controversy. This is especially true of infants in cases involving crippling deformity and/or severe retardation. That need not concern us here. What is important is the general validity of the distinction.

Once it is accepted that one need not *per se* use extraordinary measures to preserve life and that this is true also of infants, it remains only to ask who is to make this decision for the child. It is generally granted that this is a parental responsibility. In other words, just as parental consent is required and sufficient for therapeutic measures in this child, so it is the parents who must decide when this consent to therapy is to be withheld. However, just as parental consent to therapy is not arbitrary and capricious, but represents a reasonable presumption of the infant's wishes because he *ought* to want to preserve his life, so denial of consent must be traced to what the child would not want because it is beyond what he *ought* to want. This is a more difficult construction, of course, because though one need not employ extraordinary measures, he is free to do so. And it is difficult to construct the consent of a child in those areas where anyone is free to accept or reject certain measures. Nevertheless, it seems to be true that the only basis on which to found the moral meaningfulness and validity of parental denial of consent is that the infant is in a situation where we can no longer say that he *ought* to choose to preserve his life. It is because of this that proxy denial of consent makes sense and avoids being simply an exercise of parental utilitarianism. To base this denial of consent on what the child *would* do without further specification hinges the decision to considerations that are both too individualistic and too adult to form the basis of an intelligible generalization.

This thesis is confirmed, it would seem by occasional court overrule of parental denial of consent. Whether this or that overrule was in fact correct is, of course, debatable. But the very fact that we grant that a court can overrule parental denial of consent is instructive. The possibility of legitimate court overrule implies two things. First, it implies that although parental consent or denial thereof ought not be unrelated to the good of the child, it is sometimes judged to be so unrelated. Secondly, it implies that the court recognizes this unrelatedness, knows what is for the good of the child, has criteria for its determination. Otherwise its overrule would be as illegitimate as the decision overruled. But the court cannot know better than the parents (or any of us) what is for the good of the child, and therefore what the child *would* choose unless this *would* roots in what the infant *would* do because he *ought*. If we could not say of the child that life is a good to him and a good he *ought* to choose to preserve, then court overrule of parental denial of treatment would be arbitrary, indeed an exercise of medical vitalism.

The editor of *The Journal of the American Medical Association*, Robert H. Moser, in the course of an editorial touching, among other things, the problem of experimentation, asks whether we are ever justified in the use of children. His answer: "It is an insoluble dilemma. All one can ask is that each situation is to be truly consummate, and if the approach is to be rational and compassionate, then the situation *alone* cannot be the decisional guide." If the situation alone is the guide, if everything else is a "dilemma," then the qualities Moser seeks in the situation are in jeopardy, and along with them human rights. One can indeed, to paraphrase Moser, ask more than that each situation be studied. He can ask that a genuine ethics of consent be brought to the situation so that ethics in the consent situation will have some chance of surviving human enthusiasms. And an ethics of consent finds its roots in a solid natural law tradition which maintains that there are basic values that define our potential as human beings; that we ought (within limits and with qualifications) to choose, support and never directly suppress these values in our conduct; that we can know, therefore, what others would choose (up to a point) because they ought, and that this knowledge is the basis for a soundly grounded and rather precisely limited proxy consent.

NOTE

[1] This paper also appears in a slightly different form in *Perspectives in Biology and Medicine*, Fall, 1974 and is printed here with the permission of the author and editors of that journal.

REFERENCES

Alexander, Leo
1966 "Limitations of experimentation on human beings with special reference to psychiatric patients." *Diseases of the Nervous System* 27: 62f.
Baumslag, N. and R. E. Yodaiken
1973 "Letter to the Editor." *New England Journal of Medicine* 288: 1247.
Beecher, Henry K.
1970 *Research and the Individual.* Boston: Little, Brown and Company.
Capron, Alexander M.
1973 "Legal considerations affecting clinical pharmacological studies in children." *Clinical Research* 21: 141-150.

Chalkley, Donald T.
1973 "Human experimentation." *Medical World News.* June 8: 37-51.
Curran, William J. and Henry K. Beecher
1969 "Experimentation in children." *Journal of the American Medical Association* 210: 77-81.
Department of Health, Education and Welfare
1973 "Protection of human subjects: policies and procedures." *Federal Register* 38 (November 16): 31738-31749.
Editors, *Archives of Disease in Childhood*
1973 "The ethics of research involving children as controls." *Archives of Disease in Childhood* 48: 751-752.
Finnis, John
1970 "Natural law and unnatural acts." *Heythrop Journal* 11: 365-387.
Fisher, R.E.W.
1953 "Letter to the Editor." *The Lancet* (November 7): 993.
Fletcher, John
1967 "Human experimentation: ethics in the consent situation." *Law and Contemporary Problems* 32: 620-649.
Franklin, A. W., A. M. Porter & D. N. Raine
1973 "New horizons in medical ethics: investigations in children." *British Medical Journal* (May 19): 402-407.
Freund, Paul
1965 "Ethical problems in human experimentation." *New England Journal of Medicine* 273: 691.
1966 "Is the law ready for human experimentation?" *Trial* 2: 48.
Ingelfinger, Franz J.
1973 "Ethics of experiments on children." *New England Journal of Medicine* 288: 791-792.
Moser, Robert H.
1974 "An anti-intellectual movement in medicine?" *Journal of the American Medical Association* 277: 432-433.
O'Donnell, Thomas, S. J.
1974 "Informed consent." *Journal of the American Medical Association* 277: 73.
Ramsey, Paul
See the bibliography of Ramsey's works in this volume. Capital letters (e.g. 1950A) denote books and occasional papers; lower case letters (e.g. 1968a) denote articles.
Shine, Ian, John Howieson and Ward Griffen, Jr.
1973 "Letter to the Editor." *New England Journal of Medicine* 288: 1248.
Shirkey, H.
1968 "Therapeutic orphans." *Journal of Pediatrics* 72: 119-120.

CHAPTER XI

Attitudes Toward The Newly Dead[1]

WILLIAM F. MAY

> Maigret suddenly realized that there was one character in the drama about whom nothing was known, the dead man himself. From the outset, he had been to all of them merely a dismembered corpse. It was an odd fact that the Chief Superintendent had often noticed before, that people did not respond in the same way to parts of a body found scattered about as to a whole corpse. They did not feel pity in the same degree, or even revulsion. It was as though the dead person were somehow dehumanized, almost an object of ridicule.
>
> George Simenon
> *Maigret and the Headless Corpse*

I

Just one aspect of the problem of organ transplants surfaces in this passage from Simenon's novel. To extract organs from a corpse is, in a sense, to dismember it. And, if Simenon is to be believed, dismemberment is an act of violence; it dehumanizes, it reduces the body to an object of ridicule.

While living, a person is identified with his body in such a way as to render the dignity of the two inseparable. A man not only *has* a body, he *is* his body; it is the medium of his self-revelation. His behavior betrays the bond between the two: pride expresses itself in his carriage; humiliation leaves his body stricken with shame. Thus, when a man is subject to embarrassment, he wishes that the earth would swallow him up; he averts his face, turns on his heels, or blushes and perspires as though he wished to fabricate for himself a veil.

Apparently this association of self and body does not terminate abruptly with death. Admittedly the corpse is no longer a man. The cadaver is a kind of shroud that now masks rather then expresses the soul that once animated it. And yet—while the body retains its recognizable form, even in death, it commands a certain respect. No longer a human presence, it still reminds us of that presence which once was utterly inseparable from it.

Such is not the case, however, argues Simenon, when the body loses its integrity. The detached organ or member becomes, in a sense, a fit object for ridicule. It has lost its raison d'etre and therefore its centeredness. It has become an eccentricity, an embarrassment, an obscenity. It seems to have committed the indecency of refusing to vanish along with the self, while simultaneously failing effectively to remind us of what has vanished. The severance of death has been crazily compounded by a different order of severance that leaves the community charged with picking up leftovers rather than laying to rest remains.

Proposals, then, for the dismemberment of the body, even if that dismemberment is justified as serving important social purposes, such as organ transplants, awaken certain deep-going reservations that ought not to be ignored. If even in a very preliminary way, we ought to bring them into view and interpret them.

These reservations, of course, may vary considerably according to the specific proposal for salvaging organs; therefore we should keep in mind the several options in their variety:

1. A system of routine salvaging of organs from which exemption may be granted only at the special initiative of the pre-deceased or his family;
2. A program of organized giving of organs which is dependent upon the consent of the donor or his family;
3. Provision for the sale of organs by the pre-deceased or his family; and
4. Provision for the crediting of a family account against the day that some member (of the family) may require an organ.

Advocates of routine salvaging argue that it maximizes the number of organs made available for social purposes and spares citizens the awkwardness of carrying donor cards, or physicians the necessity of making ghoulish overtures to the bereaved at the time of death (Dukeminier and Sanders, 1968). Proponents of organized giving argue that the system will provide some (maybe not so many) organs, while protecting the perceived rights of citizens and their families concerning burial and encouraging a pattern of *giving* that will have positive moral consequences for the society at large (Sadler, Alfred L. and Blair L. Sadler, 1968, 1970; Sadler *et al.*, 1969;

Ramsey, 1970B). In matters so fundamental as the exchange of human organs, it is argued, "giving and receiving" is better than "taking and getting" and certainly to be preferred to "selling and buying." If any bartering is admitted into the process of transplanting organs, a system of family credits for donated organs is to be preferred to the debasing effects of their public sale.

Whether a system of automatic salvaging *alone* will provide a sufficient supply of organs to meet social needs, I would not attempt to resolve. The question of adequate supply cannot be answered until a program of organized giving has been given a fair trial. As advocates of the latter point out, such a trial has not been possible until the recent passage of the Uniform Anatomical Gifts Act in over forty-four states, which, for the first time, removes the legal obstacles in the way of organ donations.[2] More restrictedly, I would argue that human attitudes toward death (and the newly dead) are such that a system of organized giving must be granted a serious test before entertaining the alternative of routine salvaging. In the course of this argument, it will be necessary to examine certain primordial attitudes and basic symbols for death, some further specific convictions about the newly dead as reflected in the funeral practices of both traditional and Christian societies, and, finally, certain resources in belief and practice that give moral warrant for sustaining a program of organized giving.

II

It is convenient to begin with our discussion of attitudes and symbols. Drawing his evidence from both traditional societies and dreams, Edgar Herzog argues (1966) that the most primitive response to a corpse is flight. This phenomenon is more than a matter of the aversion of an individual to a cadaver. Entire villages have been known to move to another location to avoid any further traffic with a corpse. If flight is a primary human response to death, then the development of funeral rites must be interpreted as a secondary response on the part of the community to force itself to be present to death. This presence, of course, does not wholly eliminate the original aversion. The community becomes present, after all, for the purpose of removal. It burns or buries the corpse. The community no longer journeys away from the dead, but it sends the dead on a journey, as it were, away from its presence. Thus, the element of aversion and horror persists even within the form of funeral practice.

The modern humanitiarian, of course, will grow impatient with this kind of analysis. What does a rather primitive, almost subhuman emotion, like horror, have to do with the resolution of modern policy issues? Surely civilized men should not be distracted by such matters. A discussion of organ transplants should focus on the question of the most efficient way of supplying the needs of those dying for the want of vital organs. Let atavistic emotions give way to the central human issue.

Yet the fact of horror may be more germane to the subject of humane procedures for transplants than first appears. It is not advisable in the pursuit of worthy social goals to sidestep or repress the element of aversion with respect to means.

The Grimm Brothers included in their collection of folk tales the intriguing story of a young man who is incapable of horror. He does not shrink back from the dead—neither a hanged man he encounters nor a corpse with which he attempts to play. From one point of view, his behavior seems pleasantly childish, but, from another angle, inhuman. His father is ashamed of him, and so the young man is sent away "to learn how to shudder." Not until he has learned to shudder will he be brought out of his nameless, undifferentiated state and become human. Ingmar Bergman plays with (and complicates) the same theme in his movie *The Magician*, in which the hero—sometime artist, actor, charlatan, magician—contrives to make an apparently detached scientist acknowledge his human capacity for horror. When the magician succeeds in lifting the hair off the head of the scientist, the latter, with an irrecoverable loss of dignity, denies that he has had the experience. At a somewhat more comic level, the modern undertaker has trouble in securing respect for his person and work—because of his overfamiliar association with death. Our laughter and contempt testify to our deep-going sense of connection between human dignity and a capacity for horror.

A policy that institutes the routine cutting up of corpses, even for high-minded, social purposes, may fail precisely at this point; its refusal to acknowledge the fact of human horror. There is a tinge of the inhuman in the humanitarianism of those who believe that the perception of social need easily overrides all other considerations and reduces the acts of implementation to the everyday, routine, and casual. Even the proponents of routine salvaging have to concede indirectly the awkward fact of human revulsion. A system requiring consent, they argue, has two defects. It will fail to produce as many organs as categorical salvaging and it forces upon staff the necessity of making "ghoulish" overtures to the pre-deceased or his relatives. The question remains whether a system that overrides rather than faces up to profound reservations is not, in the long run, more ghoulish in its consequences for the social order.

Human horror before death does not remain a formless, unspecified emotion. The object of horror is associated with certain images and symbols. Specifically, death is identified in language and imagery with the acts of hiding and devouring. An analysis of these two images is required for further appraisal of a system of routine salvaging.

The name of the nymph "Calypso," who encounter Odysseus as the embodiment of death, means literally the one who hides. The death-demon in Indo-Germanic and even pre-Indo-Germanic times, according to Herman

Guntert, is a Hider-Goddess. A "mysterious hiding and shrouding has been experienced as the first essential character-trait of the numinous, hidden power of death from early times" (Herzog, 1966:39).

Eric Neuman has discerned this association of death with devouring, both in archaic myth and contemporary dream life. "Eating, devouring, hunger, death, and maw go together; and we still speak, just like the primitive, of 'death's maw,' a 'devouring war,' a 'consuming disease' " (1970:28). The association appears in the symbol of the *Uroboros*, the dragon that consumes its own tail, and in the mythic representation of the devouring mother. Being swallowed and eaten up is also a pattern that occurs in medieval paintings of hell and the devil. Cannibalism prevails amongst those who are lost in the land of the dead. In the innermost circles of hell, Dante places Judas, Brutus, and Cassius whom Satan devours; and in his modern representations of hell, the American dramatist Tennessee Williams resorts to images of cannibalism—with special emphasis, once again, on the theme of the devouring mother.

Finally, the two activities of hiding and devouring coincide. The corpse, which is hidden in the earth, is thereby swallowed up and absorbed; the flesh, which is devoured by the scavenger, at the same time disappears.

A. *Hider-Goddess and Devourer.* Basic images for death have a way of associating with the institution which deals most with the dying. Traditionally, the hospital was a place of healing and recuperation for the sick and wounded. More recently the hospital, along with homes for the chronically ill and the aged, penal institutions, and mental hospitals, has acquired certain subliminal associations with the Hider-Goddess. Prisoners call themselves the forgotten men. The mentally disturbed and the chronically ill are hidden away from the society at large in preparation for their final disappearance. This process of hiding goes on for all the understandable reasons that pertain in a highly differentiated society and its specialization of functions and services. One would hate to do without these technical services, but they have exacted a high price by imposing upon inmates a kind of premature burial. The institutionalized have forced upon them a loss of name, identity, companionship, and acclaim—an extremity of deprivation of which the ordinary citizen has a foretaste in his complaints about the anonymous and impersonal conditions of modern life. The society at large, of which the hospital is destination and symbol, functions as a kind of Hider-goddess, depriving its citizens of significance.

The development of a system of routine salvaging of organs would tend to fix on the hospital a second association with death—as devourer. In the course of life, a breakdown in health is often accompanied by a sense that one has been exhausted and burned out by a world that has consumed all one's resources. The hospital traditionally offered a respite from a devouring world and the possibility of restoration. The healing mission of the hospital is obscured, however, if the hospital itself becomes the arch-symbol of a world that devours. Categorical salvaging of organs suggests that eventually and ultimately the process of consumption that dominates the outer world must now be consummated in the hospital. One's very vitals must be inventoried, extracted and distributed by the state on behalf of the social order. What is left over is utterly unusable husk.

While the procedure of routine salvaging may, in the short run, furnish more organs for transplants, in the long run, its systemic effect on the institutions of medical care would seem to be depressing and corrosive of that trust upon which the arts of healing depend.

B. *Antigone, Funerals, and Donor-Consent.* A system of salvaging that requires the consent of the donor and/or his family, respects, for want of a better phrase, the "principle of extraterritoriality" in the relations of the person to the social order. This principle of extra-territoriality is already embedded in traditional legal rights concerning burial.

Society traditionally located "quasi-property rights" to the corpse in the family of the deceased. The rights were quasi—in the sense that the cadaver could not be iut up for commercial use or sale. But rights they were in the sense that no other party could normally interpose claims upon the corpse that would interfere with the family's right and obligation to provide for a fitting disposition of the remains. In other words, whatever use and abuse, conflicts and tragedies, a person has been subjected to in the course of his public life, at the deepest level he cannot be reduced to them without remainder. He was a human presence that transcended the world into which he was apparently absorbed.

The principle of extra-territoriality is at issue in Antigone's contest with Creon over the burial of her brother. The king claims the rebel for his own; Polynices, and therefore his body, is wholly at the disposition of the state. In defying the king and insisting on a proper burial, Antigone claims that her brother transcends the social order. His person is not fully exhausted by the claims of the tyrant upon him. In covering him over with the "thirsty dust," she signifies that he is not, and cannot be, devoured by the state.

(A mute recognition of this limit on the power of the state is contained in the symbolism of the modern military funeral. The casket of the fallen soldier is covered with a flag, but when the coffin is lowered into the grave, the flag is neatly folded and withdrawn. The symbolism at once attests to the majesty of the state: A man dies for his country, but a country does not die with the man—long live the country. At the same time the symbolism attests to the limits on the power of the state. The state cannot follow the soldier into the grave. There is a remainder that cannot be remaindered. A human presence that cannot be fully enclosed and devoured.)

The question arises as to whether burial rights and duties pertain to Polynices because he is a *man*, or because he is Antigone's *brother*. Put more generally, does the principle of extra-territoriality adhere to the person or to his family? The issue here is partly exegetical insofar as the proper interpretation of *Antigone* is at stake (a question which I will not attempt to resolve) but also partly symbolic insofar as the significance of a funeral service is at issue. In pursuing the latter question, we will have to cope with further ramifications for the subject of organ transplants.

From one perspective, the funeral service (which includes fitting disposition of the corpse) presupposes and reinforces a certain continuity between the person, his mortal remains, and the family unit. This continuity is particularly prominent while the newly dead body has its recognizable form: it attenuates when the body returns to particles. Thus funeral rites are an expression of the continuity of the soul with its body and with the gathered community of friends, colleagues, and family. From this perspective, the principle of extra-territoriality applies to the family group. The corpse, the deceased, and the family belong, as it were, to a continuum which should enjoy a certain sanctuary against the larger society and the state. Within this context, if one wants to proceed beyond traditional funeral rites to a justification for donating organs, then one will have to interpret the donation as a further and different expression of continuity between the generations. Something like Robert Jay Lifton's—or preceding him, Unamuno's, Soloviev's, or Bulgakov's—concept of symbolic or surrogate immortality is at work in this interpretation of the funeral service and the donation of organs.

From another perspective, the function of the funeral service is not so much to maintain continuity with the deceased as to provide public occasion for the acknowledgment that continuity has been broken by death. The acknowledgment of this separation is a particularly acute problem for those intimates whose lives have been so inextricably intertwined with the deceased. The family therefore has a special need for rites through which it acknowledges and participates in the process of surrender. "Dust thou art and unto dust thou shall return." There is nothing like the rigidity of death and the finality of cremation or burial to force the community to acknowledge that the process of separation has begun. Viewed from this second perspective, if one wants to proceed beyond traditional funeral practice and donate organs to the living, this action will be construed not as a way of achieving symbolic immorality but rather as a finite act in which one mortal human being assists another.

In any event, this second perspective also argues intensively against a system of routine salvaging of organs because the system places the burden of proof on the family if it seeks exemption from the state's right of eminent domain. What is wrong, indecorous, and enraging about placing the burden of proof on the family is that it forces the family to *claim the body as its possession*, only in order to proceed with rites in the course of which it must acknowledge the process of surrender and separation. Antigone has a right to bitterness in her contest with Creon. She is compelled to claim her brother's body as *her* possession, her territory—not Creon's—precisely at the time that death forces all concerned to recognize a human being who is beyond their grasp.

"Quasi-property rights," directed to decent burial, were wisely vested in the family because the family, most of all, has used up and consumed the person in the course of his life, and the family, most of all, must acknowledge that he has moved beyond its effective control. By way of redaction, the rites tacitly acknowledge that the deceased is now, what he has always been, a human presence whose extra-territoriality must be honored.

In summary, the provision of organs for transplants would preferably be based on a system of consent. If the state is granted the categorical authority to dispose of the corpse, packaged it as it pleases, then it goes a long way toward establishing its total and unlimited claim over the person living or dead. Funeral rites, at the center of which are the "remains" attended to by the family and intimates, help establish the principle of a remainder above and beyond the claims of the family and the state. It establishes the principle of extra-territoriality. The person does not belong without limit to his society.

This needs to be acknowledged precisely by those who have most consumed the person in the course of his living—his family, colleagues, and friends—those who have most eaten him alive, who are most torn by guilt and remorse.

III

The crisis of death in primitive culture cannot be adequately interpreted apart from the structure of other crises in the course of life. As Van Gennep (1960) and Van der Leeuw (1963) have observed, life for the primitive is not a straight, unbroken line that terminates in death. Rather, the life-line itself is punctuated by a series of turning points which are themselves an experience of death. Conversely, the event of death is followed by a form of continued life for the deceased that structurally corresponds to the earlier turning points.

Examples of such earlier crises are, of course, puberty rites, marriage, birth, episodes of sickness, coronations, war, departures, and reunions. The puberty rite conveniently illustrates for our purposes the three basic elements of which each turning point consists; that is, the three distinct moments of detachment, transition, and incorporation.

The detachment of an initiate from his past was effected in varying ways, perhaps by a mutilation, a whipping, a disrobing, a tattooing, or the pulling of a tooth. These severities were imposed upon the young as the condition of entrance into adult life. They were all symbolic expressions of dying. The second moment of transition that followed often required the special segregation of young men and women from the society at large. This was a period of great vulnerability for them; hence, their life during this interim was carefully hedged and protected by *tabus*. Finally, the young were assimilated and incorporated into the adult life of the tribe, accepting the sacred duties and powers that characterized adult existence. Clearly these new duties and powers could not be interpreted as casual additions to previous life and identity, the way a modern young person (*e.g.*) might join a club and add it to a long list of his previously defined commitments. The sacred was not in an additive relationship to other matters. That is why this final stage of incorporation had to be preceded by clear rites of detachment. The young, in effect, passed irreversibly from one country into another, from childhood into adult life. Childhood had come to an end; the inauguration of adult life must be preceded by the experience of dying.

Correspondingly, the anthropologists have observed, death is not simply an exclamation point with which an individual life comes to an end. The newly dead have a very special status. Structurally, the event of death includes the three aforementioned moments of detachment, transition, and incorporation. The rituals of detachment and separation associated with the funeral were required not only to break the previously defined ties of the community to the man but also the man to the community. There followed a period of transition (emphasized especially in the work of Robert Hertz, 1960). This is a period of great vulnerability and weakness for the deceased (and perhaps for the community formerly associated with him). Assistance may be offered in the form of closing up the orifices of the body (so the devil cannot break in) or in the provision of food. This period may last for greatly varying lengths of time—four months, six months, one, three, or four years—but, Hertz argues, even when the transition is abbreviated, it symbolically corresponds to the length of time it takes the flesh to decompose, leaving a bare skeleton. Finally, the deceased reaches his destination, as it were, the dwelling place of the ancestors, the blessed isle of the dead. In some tribes, this final rite of incorporation constitutes a distinct funeral service, more joyous than the first.

This mythic and ritual structure for the primitive has its subjective correlate in the experience of the bereaved. The family of the deceased goes through its own social and psychological process of detachment, transition, and final incorporation and return into the society at large. These rites for the bereaved in varying forms persisted in Western society until World War I (argues Geoffrey Gorer, 1956) but rapidly thereafter began to disappear. Wearing widows' weeds did not appeal to the large number of women who lost their husbands in the great war; conventional mourning customs disappeared. Funeral rites meanwhile were removed from the church to the funeral home where the services, detached from the sanctuary and religious tradition, became more vulgar, ostentatious, and meaningless. The way was prepared for the kind of reaction epitomized in Jessica Mitford's book (1969) on vaulting prices. In the place of meaningless rites, Mitford recommended, in effect, no rites. In the place of a vulgar event, there is substituted a non-event.

The social and psychological price exacted by this partial or total elimination of mourning rites may be high. In the absence of specific modes and times for expressing grief, the bereaved run the risk of plunging into what

Geoffrey Gorer has called "limitless grief." "I will never get over his passing," says the widow, in a society without consoling forms. The bereaved (and those who have contact with the bereaved) are in need of clearly defined social occasions and forms in the context of which the work of mourning can go on and reach its completion. If this is true, then the solution to meaningless rites is not the total elimination of ceremonies but the development of meaningful rites for our time.

IV

It helps little to make a general plea for meaningful rites if the absence of meaning is precisely at issue. The bereaved will be little consoled if the sole purpose of an artificially contrived rite is their consolation. Instrumentalist therapy of this kind only produces the smooth efficiency and inanity of current funeral practice.

The Jungian analytic tradition offers a promising basis for investing funeral rites with a meaning. It does so in a form which permits one, additionally, to integrate into traditional practice, provision for the salvaging of organs on a consensual basis.

Funeral rites, the Jungian Edgar Herzog (1966) argues, ultimately permit the family to consent to, even assist in, the death of the deceased. Death, as indicated earlier, is associated with concealing and devouring. The burial service engages the community in both acts. To bury is to conceal. To bury is to *let* the earth devour. The imagery of *Antigone* underscores both elements. Sophocles avers that it is terrible to let a corpse lie exposed to sight, for only living things are to be *seen*; or again, it is mandatory that a body be surrendered up to the "thirsty dust."

Thus human aversion to death is not the last word. Funeral services require the community to appropriate the horror. The living can pass on to mature life only *through* death and through consent to death. Herzog works this out in the context of dream analysis. He concludes, somewhat dramatically, that the *arrested* adult is the one who is unable to participate in the final killing of his parents, an act which carries with it the life responsibility of assuming the parents' role and place. This reluctance on the part of the immature adult is more than a question of general guilt feelings between the generation. In taking his parents' place, he must admit to being an adult who, in his own time and place, will also die. In refusing to "kill," he betrays that he is afraid to die, and, because he is afraid to die, he is unready to live in his own right. The arrested adult must pass through death to life.

This analysis, of course, places weight on the importance of funeral services, the occasion for the appropriation of the death of others and the acknowledgement of one's own dying. At the same time, it also permits, where fitting, a restructuring of those services to give a significant place to the donation of organs destined to be concealed and accepted into the bodies of others. Because, however, the relationship to one's own death and the death of others is not a casual matter, because, indeed, it is a touchstone of the mature life, a system of organ salvage should depend not upon automatic procedures but upon active participation and consent.

Admittedly this kind of justification of funeral rites in its own way is therapeutic, but at least it is therapeutic in a form that requires men and women to face the reality of death instead of disguising the event with pink gels and flesh-colored veils.

V

No paper on the possibility of organ salvage within the context of Western culture would be complete without inquiry into that religious tradition under whose auspices most funerals in the West occur. Not that the Christian tradition could or should be legislatively decisive on the subject. Even if it could be demonstrated that Christian ethics justified a system of routine salvaging of organs, it would be unwise to legislate such a system on that basis alone. The Christian tradition no longer occupies an official regulative position in Western life and culture. Law based on Christian ethics alone would be divisive (and therefore objectionable even on Christian grounds). On the other hand, the Christian Church remains a major institution in the West, with significance for millions; its attitude on the subject could have considerable impact on the acceptance of a system of giving and receiving organs. This paper closes then with a discussion of potential obstacles and warrants for a system of organized giving in the light of Christian thought and practice.

There is an important feature of traditional Christian teaching that would seem to stand in the way of organ transplants, the doctrine of the resurrection of the body. Christian expectations for future life were not dreamy and spiritual. Christians looked forward to a future life which was bodily life together in the presence of God. On this point Catholics and Protestants have recently differed in one important respect. Catholics have carried forward the Greek concept of the immortality of the soul. They have postulated an interim period of future life for the soul without the body. But, even so, the soul would not persist forever in this bodiless state. Final bliss required the graded purgation of the soul and its final unification with the body—in the Apostle Paul's words, a glorified body. Protestants, on the basis of recent biblical scholarship, rejected even this minimal concession to Greek spiritualism. The biblical doctrine of the resurrection of the body had to be radically distinguished from Greek teaching about the immortal soul. The soul, no less than the body, is in need of reconstitution and healing; the soul no less than the body is mortal. Future life therefore depends exclusively on God's final act of resurrection and recreation and not on the soul's own natural immortality or virtue. Despite these differences, however, both Catholics and Protestants have held to what Archbishop Temple called a "holy materialism," the full participation of human existence in eternal life; that is, a future human existence which in some sense is embodied.

Given these views of future life, it is no wonder that early Christians in the funeral customs settled on the convention of burial, rather than the total obliteration of the corpse through cremation. Historical inquiry into the funeral practice in the Roman empire makes it clear that for centuries preceding Christianity cremation had been the prevailing, though not the sole, practice. In the Christian era, burial became the accepted custom. Jocelyn Toynbee (1971) warns us, to be sure, against assuming a cause and effect relationship here. For the centuries immediately preceding the emergence of Christianity, there is evidence of a shift in Roman practice in the direction of burial. But, in any event, the Christians did not reverse this tendency. Quite the contrary, they seemed to set the seal on burial as standard practice in the disposition of the remains.

Our question, then, is whether Christian belief in the resurrection of the body would operate today to place obstacles in the way of a new kind of destruction of the body—not through cremation but through the extraction of organs from the corpse. (The body contains some seventeen salvageable organs, to say nothing of usable tissue and nerves.) I leave aside the sociological question as to how many Christians today would prefer to bypass the question—allowing the traditional doctrine of the resurrection to be demythologized or permitting this once cardinal tenet of the faith to drift from a central to a marginal position in Christian teaching. The question is whether Christian orthodoxy (whose strength ebbs and flows, and may flow again)[3] would find insuperable obstacles to a medical procedure that entailed the human destruction of the integrity of the corpse.

In searching the tradition on this question, I have found most helpful St. Augustine's essay "De Cura Pro Mortuis" (1956). At no point in this defense of burial does Augustine make the practice of burial a *condition* of the resurrection, as though God were somehow prevented from accomplishing his purposes with those who were smashed to pieces or incinerated. Burial is "no aid to salvation" but "an office of humanity." Burial is simply a *fitting* testimony to the resurrection, declaring that the faith does not condemn the body or devaluate it to the position of a disposable cartridge. The full text from St. Augustine reads:

> But as for the burying of the body, whatever is bestowed on that is no aid to salvation, but an office of humanity, according to that affection by which "No man hateth his own flesh" (Eph. 5:29). Whence it is fitting that he take what care he is able for the flesh of his neighbor, when he is gone that bare it. If unbelievers in the resurrection of the flesh do it, how much more beholden to do the same who do believe; that so, an office of this kind bestowed upon a body, dead, but yet to rise again and to remain to eternity may also be in some sort a testimony of the same faith? (1956:550)

Clearly Christian faith in the resurrection does not present an insuperable obstacle to the extraction of organs from the corpse. Must the church, however, merely acquiesce to such procedures reluctantly or does the faith provide positive warrant for the donation of organs and for the institutional mobilization of resources to that end?

My own response to this question is colored by a personal memory which at first glance does not seem too germane to the subject. I recall seeing many years ago in a series of photographs of Northern Renaissance sculpture a sarcophagus, with a statue of the deceased located nearby, a half-erect skeleton. Decomposing flesh hung from the skeletal frame, but the right arm was extended with the hand open, and, in the hand, the figure offered his heart to God. The heart, of course, is the site of the soul in the body; thus the figure offered, in effect, himself under this form. When I saw this figure over twenty years ago, it expressed my understanding of the status of the soul before God. A person could not claim salvation for his own possession or desert, but neither could he face life—or death—as though he were denied communion with God. He could only make his offering. He need not make it anxiously or tentatively, but rather, with some measure of gratitude, confidence, and hope for its acceptance.

The development of a technology for organ transplants, and most dramatically the heart transplant, has opened up now the possibility of another kind of offering of the heart—somatic rather than symbolic—the offering of almost all that remains bodily of the self to the neighbor, in the hope of, and even gratitude for, acceptance and use. This kind of donation, moreover, may actually be closer to the heart of the Christian message than the too-pious Renaissance figure. The statue, even though it denies to itself salvation as a possession, relies still on a certain image of acceptable piety—a sacrificial offering from the human to the divine. It overlooks the self-donative activity of the savior who reportedly freed men from the need to make some kind of saving sacrifice to God and freed them for a donative life toward the neighbor.

There is positive warrant in Christian liturgy and Christian ethics for a system of organ donation. Christ shares, under the form of bread and wine, his body and blood with his disciples. The disciple is invited to share in this life of self-donative service by expending himself for the neighbor. Not many people within Western societies today share these special motivations that would obtain for Christians, but the society at large could benefit from institutional support on this issue from the church. A system of organ donations would shore up and encourage the development of "consensual community in general." For the theologian Paul Ramsey, this is an important reason why organized giving is to be preferred to routine salvaging. "A society will be a better human community in which giving and receiving is the rule, not taking for the sake of good to come. . . . The positive consent called for by Gift Acts, answering the need for gifts by encouraging real givers, meets the measure of authentic community among men" (1970B:210).

While justifying and encouraging organ transplants, the Christian, I would suspect, would have to shy back from the inflationary language of those who would want to interpret such deeds as acts of "symbolic immortality." Such deeds in themselves, for the Christian, cannot be called divine; they are simply signs of a self-donative love which they themselves are not and cannot produce. The language of symbolic immortality is too exaggerated for a monotheist. It would be better to talk simply about the assistance that one mortal renders another.

Coincidentally enough, Augustine had to face this issue of inflation in a different form in the aforementioned essay on the care to be given to the dead. One justification for respectful (and elaborate) funeral services in Augustine's time was the notion that the dead have the power to return to and care for the living. Partial proof of this was offered in the appearance of the dead to the living in dreams. Since the dead are, in effect, both immortal and providential, it behooves the living to treat them right. Augustine undercuts rather matter of factly this proof by pointing out that the living appear to the living in dreams without knowing or caring one whit about them! Why assume that the dead watch over and provide for us as guardians?

Augustine's radical monotheism forced him to be wary of a religious sentimentality that substituted the providence of one's fathers for the providence of God. Consistent with this rejection of ancestor worship, Augustine wanted to eliminate from funerals all suggestion of an immortalizing continuity between the generations. The funeral was an occasion in which the full reality of death had to be acknowledged. Far from continuing to watch over men, the dead have forsaken the living! The funeral is a two-way farewell. The dying man is removed from the care of the community, but also the community, from the care of the dying man.

The fundamental situation is structurally unchanged by procedures for the post-mortem extraction and redeployment of organs. The receiving of an organ does not rescue the living from the need to die. It only defers the day when they will have to do their own dying. Nor does the receiving of an organ, in and of itself, teach the living how to live—unless—the recipient, in receiving the organ discerns a self-donative love of which the giving of the organ may be a modest sign.

This is not the place to take up the further and final question of the Christian warrant for a funeral, but one restricted issue remains.

If there is warrant for the giving of one's organs, nerve, and tissue to unknown recipients, is there also still warrant in such cases for funeral services? Has the liturgy already been held in the hospital? What about the gutted remains? I would suggest that Christians on this point might consider an analogy taken from their chief sacrament—the eucharist. This central liturgical action of the faith is particularly pertinent to the question since it is, after all, an act of devouring—a sacred meal—in which Christians eat bread and wine, as the body and blood, as the symbolic presence of the self-donative activity of their Lord.

In current practice the Catholic and Episcopal churches and others have developed customs for the respectful disposition of the remaining elements—the so-called reserved sacrament. The remaining host will either be taken to the sick, consumed, or poured into the ground. It is held inappropriate to flush it down the toilet. This respect toward leftover bread and wine has some bearing on funeral practices in the cases of bodies from which organs have been extracted. Ritual provision should be made for the respectful disposition of the remains of remains which have been the "matter" of a fraternal action within the human community. Such ritual provision is hardly a condition of salvation, but it is a testimony to the privileged place of the body in acts of love.

NOTES

[1] This essay first appeared in *The Hastings Center Studies* Volume I (1973) pp. 3-13. It is reprinted here with the permission of the author and the Hastings Institute for Society, Ethics and the Life Sciences.

[2] There are additional, non-legal obstacles to organ transplants (such as organ rejection, high costs, logistics, and limits on available medical manpower) that legislation would not solve. These problems have been considered in a paper written for the Freedom and Coercion Project of the Institute for Society, Ethics and the Life Sciences by Alfred M. and Blair L. Sadler (1973).

[3] Who would have predicted at the time of the American Revolution, when Christians dwindled to ten percent of the population, that Christianity would have a significant future?

REFERENCES

Augustine
1956 "De Cura Pro Mortuis" translated by H. Browne in *Nicene and Post Nicene Fathers.* (ed. Philip Schaff) 1st Series, Volume III.

Dukeminier, Jesse and David Sanders.
1968 "Organ transplantation: a proposal for routine salvaging of cadaver organs." *New England Journal of Medicine* 279:413-419.

Gorer, Geoffrey
1956 *Death, Grief and Mourning.* New York: Doubleday.

Hertz, Robert
1960 *Death and the Right Hand.* New York: The Free Press.

Herzog, Edgar
1966 *Psyche and Death, Archaic Myths and Modern Dreams in Analytical Psychology.* London: Hodder and Stroughton.

Mitford, Jessica
1969 *The American Way of Death.* Greenwich, Connecticut: Fawcett World.

Neuman, Eric
1970 *The Origins and History of Consciousness.* Princeton: Princeton University Press.

Ramsey, Paul
See the bibliography of Ramsey's works in this volume. Capital letters (e.g. 1950A) denote books and occasional papers; lower case letters (e.g. 1968a) denote articles.

Sadler, Alfred M. and Blair L. Sadler
1968 "Transplantation and the law: the need for organized sensitivity." *The Georgetown Law Journal* 57:5.
1970 "Transplantation and the law: progress toward uniformity." *New England Journal of Medicine* 282:717-723 (with E. Blythe Stason).
1973 "Providing cadaver organs: three legal alternatives." *The Hastings Center Studies* 1:14-26.
Sadler, Alfred, *et al.*
1969 "Transplantation—a case for consent." *The New England Journal of Medicine* 280:862-867.
Toynbee, Jocelyn M.C.
1971 *Death and Burial in the Roman World.* London: Thames and Hudson.
Van Der Leeuw, Gerardus
1963 *Religion in Essence and Manifestation.* New York: Harper and Row.
Van Gennep, Arnold
1960 *Rites of Passage.* Chicago: University of Chicago Press.

Bibliography of Paul Ramsey's Works

PREPARED BY JAMES T. JOHNSON

This Bibliography lists Ramsey's works in two groups: Books and Occasional papers, and Articles and Chapters. Within each grouping the individual works are listed by year, and within years the ordering is alphabetical. Short book reviews are not included, though some more lengthy review articles are cited.

BOOKS AND OCCASIONAL PAPERS

1950A *Basic Christian Ethics*. New York: Charles Scribner's Sons.

1957A *Faith and Ethics: The Theology of H. Richard Niebuhr* (ed. and contributor). New York: Harper and Brothers.

1957B *Freedom of the Will* (ed., with critical introduction), Jonathan Edwards' *Works*, vol. 1. New Haven: Yale University Press.

1961A *Christian Ethics and the Sit-In*. New York: Association Press.

1961B *War and the Christian Conscience: How Shall Modern War Be Conducted Justly?* Durham, N. C.: Duke University Press. Published for the Lilly Endowment Research Program in Christianity and Politics.

1962A *Nine Modern Moralists*. Englewood Cliffs, N. J.: Prentice-Hall.

1963A *The Limits of Nuclear War: Thinking about the Do-Able and the Un-Do-Able*. New York: Council on Religion and International Affairs. An Occasional Paper in the Ethics and Foreign Policy Series.

1965A *Again, the Justice of Deterrence*. New York: Council on Religion and International Affairs. An Occasional Paper in the Ethics and Foreign Policy Series.

1965B *Deeds and Rules in Christian Ethics.* Edinburgh and London: Oliver and Boyd. *Scottish Journal of Theology* Occasional Papers, No. 11.

1965C *Nueve Moralistas Modernos.* Mexico, D. F.: Herrero Hermanos Sucesores, S. A.

1965D *Religion* (ed.). *The Princeton Studies: Humanistic Scholarship in America.* Englewood Cliffs, N. J.: Prentice-Hall.

1967A *Deeds and Rules in Christian Ethics.* New York: Charles Scribner's Sons.

1967B *Who Speaks for the Church? A Critique of the 1966 Geneva Conference on Church and Society.* Nashville and New York: Abingdon Press.

1968A *The Just War: Force and Political Responsibility.* New York: Charles Scribner's Sons.

1968B *Norm and Context in Christian Ethics* (ed. with Gene H. Outka). New York: Charles Scribner's Sons.

1970A *Fabricated Man: The Ethics of Genetic Control.* New Haven: Yale University Press.

1970B *The Patient as Person: Explorations in Medical Ethics.* New Haven: Yale University Press.

1970C *The Study of Religion in Colleges and Universities* (ed. with John F. Wilson). Princeton: Princeton University Press.

1970D *Gendaiteki Jitsuzon to Rinri* (*Nine Modern Moralists*, tr. by Kuniyasu Take). Kyoto, Japan: Sekai Shiso sha.

1970E *Who Speaks for the Church?* Edinburgh: St. Andrew's Press.

1973A *El Hombre Fabricado.* Translated by Julian Rubio. Madrid: Guadarrama.

ARTICLES AND CHAPTERS*

1935a "Christianity and War." *The Christian Advocate* 110/4 (February 15): 202-203.

1943a "The Great Commandment." *Christianity and Society* 8/4 (Fall).

1943b "The Manger, the Cross, and the Resurrection." *Christianity and Crisis* 3/6 (April 16): 2-5.

1944a "Natural Law and the Nature of Man." *Christendom* 9/3 (Summer): 371-381.

1944b "A Social Policy for Liberal Religion." *Religion in Life* 13/4 (Autumn): 495-507.

1946a "The Idealistic View of Moral Evil: Josiah Royce and Bernard Bosanquet." *Philosophy and Phenomenological Research* 6/4 (June): 554-589.

1946b "Religious Instruction Problematically Christian." *Journal of Religion* 26/4 (October): 243-262.

1946c "A Theology of Social Action." *Social Action* 23/2 (October 15): 4-34.

1946d "The Theory of Democracy: Idealistic or Christian?" *Ethics* 56/4 (July): 251-266.

1947a "Beyond the Confusion of Tongues." *Theology Today* 3/4 (January): 446-458.

1947b "Religion at Princeton." *Religious Education* 42/2 (March-April): 65-69.

1947c "A Theory of Virtue According to the Principles of the Reformation." *Journal of Religion* 27/3 (July): 178-196.

1948a "*Existenz* and the Existence of God: A Study of Kierkegaard and Hegel." *Journal of Religion* 28/3 (July): 157-176.

1949a "Elements of a Biblical Political Theory." *Journal of Religion* 29/4 (October): 258-283.

1949b "Non Solum in Memoriam Sed in Intentionem: A Tribute to the Late Rev. John W. Ramsey." *The Mississippi Methodist Advocate*, March 23: 8, 9, 12.

1950a "In This Is Love. . . ." *Motive* 11/1 (October): 21-23.

1951a "God's Grace and Man's Guilt." *Journal of Religion* 31/1 (January): 21-37.

1951b "The Revealer of Many Hearts." *Adult Teacher* (General Board of Education of the Methodist Church) 4/6 (June): 7-9.

1952a "God and the Family." Sunday School Lesson for May 18. *Crossroads* (Board of Christian Education of the Presbyterian Church in the U. S. A.), April-June: 59-61.

*References to periodicals are by name, volume, number, date, and page(s).

1952b "God's Estimate of Human Life." Sunday School Lesson for May 25. *Crossroads* (Board of Christian Education of the Presbyterian Church in the U. S. A.), April-June: 62-64.

1953a "Paul and Some of His Letters." A series of seven Sunday School lessons for adult classes, May 17-June 28. *Crossroads* (Board of Christian Education of the Presbyterian Church in the U. S. A.), April-June: 77-79; together with the exegesis of scripture and instruction for teachers, *Westminster Teacher*, April-June.

1955a "God and the Family." A series of five adult lessons. *Crossroads* (Presbyterian Board of Publications), July: 13-30; together with instructions to teachers, *Westminster Teacher*, July-September: 5-14.

1956a "Freedom and Responsibility in Medical and Sex Ethics: A Protestant View." *New York University Law Review* 31/7 (November): 1189-1204.

1956b "Love and Law." Pp. 80-123 in Charles W. Kegley and Robert W. Bretall (eds.), *Reinhold Niebuhr: His Religious, Social and Political Thought*. New York: Macmillan.

1956c "Marriage and the Kingdom of God." *Crossroads* (Presbyterian Board of Publications), January: 13-16, 19.

1956d "No Morality without Immortality: Dostoevsky and the Meaning of Atheism." *Journal of Religion* 36/2 (April): 90-108.

1957a "Christian Ethics." P. 227 in *Collier's Encyclopedia*, vol. 5. New York: P. F. Collier and Son Corporation.

1957b "The Church Is You." *Growing* (Presbyterian Board of Education), October-December: 14-16; also in *Victory* (Presbyterian Church of Canada), October-December: 4-6.

1957c "Mysticism." P. 343 in *Collier's Encyclopedia*, vol. 14. New York: P. F. Collier and Son Corporation.

1958a "A Fable." *The Chaplain* 15/5 (October): 27-28; reprinted in *Motive* 18/7 (April, 1959): cover, and *The Christian Advocate* 136/1 (January 5, 1961): 11.

1959a "Freedom and Responsibility in Medical and Sex Ethics: A Protestant View." Pp. 284-299 in Burke Shartel and B. J. George, Jr. (eds.), *Readings in Legal Methods*. Ann Arbor, Michigan: Overbeck.

1959b "The Legal Imputation of Religion to an Infant in Adoption Proceedings." *New York University Law Review* 34/4 (April): 649-690.

1959c "Religious Aspects of Marxism." *Canadian Journal of Theology* 5/3 (July): 143-155.

1959d "Right and Wrong Calculation." *Worldview* 2/12 (December): 6-9.

1960a "Faith Effective through In-Principled Love." *Christianity and Crisis* 20/9 (May 30): 76-78.

1960b "Male and Female He Created Them." *Victory* (Presbyterian Church of Canada), January-March: 1-4.

1960c "Reinhold Niebuhr: Leader in Social, Political and Religious Thought." *The New York Herald Tribune Book Review*, June 19: 4.

1960d "Sex and People: A.Critical Review." *Religion in Life* 30/1 (Winter): 53-70.

1960e "Theological Studies in College and Seminary." *Theology Today* 17/4 (January): 466-484.

1961a "The Case for Just or Counterforces Warfare." *Pittsburgh* [*Theological Seminary*] *Perspective* 2/3 (September): 7-20.

1961b "Dream and Reality in Deterrence and Defense." *Christianity and Crisis* 21/22 (December): 228-232.

1961c "The New Papal Encyclical—I." *The Christian Century* 78/36 (September 6): 1047-1050.

1961d "The New Papal Encyclical—II." *The Christian Century* 78/37 (September 13): 1077-1079.

1961e "The Nuclear Dilemma." Pp. 108-134 in U. S. Allers and W. V. O'Brien (eds.), *Christian Ethics and Nuclear Warfare*. Washington: Georgetown University Institute of World Polity.

1961f "Preface." Pp. xiii-xxix in Gabriel Vahanian, *The Death of God: The Culture of Our Post-Christian Era.* New York: George Braziller.

1961g "Right and Wrong Calculation." Pp. 47-54 in William Clancy (ed.), *The Moral Dilemma of Nuclear Weapons.* New York: The Church Peace Union.

1961h "Shelter Morality." *Presbyterian Life*, November 15: 7-8, 41-42; discussion, January 1, 1962: 4-5, 42.

1962a "The Case for Making 'Just War' Possible." Pp. 143-170 in John C. Bennett (ed.), *Nuclear Weapons and the Conflict of Conscience.* New York: Charles Scribner's Sons.

1962b "Community of Two." *Crossroads* (Presbyterian Board of Education) 12/3 (April-June): 92-94.

1962c "Death's Duel." *Motive* 22/7 (April): 2-5; also available from the Office of the University Chaplain, Pennsylvania State University, University Park, Pennsylvania.

1962d "Life, Death and the Law." *Journal of Public Law 11* (1962): 377-393.

1962e "Porcupines in Winter." *Motive* 22/8 (May): 6-11.

1962f "Princeton University's Graduate Program in Religion." *Journal of Bible and Religion* 30/4 (October): 291-298.

1962g "Turn toward Just War." *Worldview* 5/7-8 (July-August): 8-13.

1962h "U. S. Military Policy and 'Shelter Morality.' " *Worldview* 5/1 (January): 6-9; discussion 5/3 (March): 6-9.

1963a "Church and Academy: A Tension in Theological Education." *The Garrett Tower* 39/1 (December): 8-15.

1963b "The Just War Theory on Trial." *Cross Currents* 13/4 (Fall): 477-490.

1963c "Morgenthau on Nuclear War." *Commonweal* 78/21 (September 20): 554-557.

1963d "On Taking Sex Seriously Enough." *Christianity and Crisis* 23/19 (November 11): 204-206.

1963e *"Pacem in Terris." Religion in Life* 33/1 (Winter): 116-135.

1963f "Protestant Casuistry Today." *Christianity and Crisis* 23/5 (March 4): 24-28.

1963g "Toward a Test-Ban Treaty: Is Nothing Better than On-Site Inspection?" *Worldview* 6/7-8 (July-August): 4-10.

1964a "How Shall We Sing the Lord's Song in a Pluralistic Land? The Prayer Decisions." *Journal of Public Law* 13/2 (1964): 353-400.

1964b "Is God Mute in the Goldwater Candidacy?" *Christianity and Crisis* 24/15 (September 21): 175-178.

1964c "Justice in War." *New Wine, A Christian Journal of Opinion* 2 (Spring): 21-25.

1964d "Marriage Law and Biblical Covenant." Pp. 41-77 in D. A. Giannella (ed.), *Religion and the Public Order.* Chicago: University of Chicago Press.

1964e "Morals and Nuclear Weapons." Pp. 23-41 in *A Study of Morals and the Nuclear Program.* Albuquerque, N. M.: Headquarters Field Command, Defense Atomic Support Agency, Sandria Base.

1964f "On Taking Sexual Responsibility Seriously Enough." *Christianity and Crisis* 23/23 (January 6): 247-251.

1964g "The Status and Advancement of Theological Scholarship in America." *The Christian Scholar* 47 (Spring): 7-23.

1964h "Teaching 'Virtue' in the Public Schools." Pp. 336-339 in D. A. Giannella (ed.), *Religion and the Public Order.* Chicago: University of Chicago Press.

1964i "Theological Studies in College and Seminary." Pp. 21-114 in K. R. Bridgston and D. W. Culver (eds.), *The Making of Ministers.* Minneapolis: Augsburg Press.

1964j "The Uses of Power." *Perkins*[School of Theology]*Journal* 18/1 (Fall): 13-24.

1965a "A Christian Approach to the Question of Sexual Relations Outside Marriage." *Journal of Religion* 45/2 (April): 100-118.

1965b "The Church and the Magistrate." *Christianity and Crisis* 25/11 (June 28): 136-140.

1965c "The Ethics of Intervention." *Review of Politics* 27/3 (July): 287-310.

1965d "Lehmann's Contextual Ethics and the Problem of Truth-Telling." *Theology Today* 21/4 (January): 466-475.

1965e “Modern Papal Social Teachings.” Pp. 202-238 in Robert E. Cushman and Egil Grislis (eds.), *The Heritage of Christian Thought* (*Festschrift* for R. L. Calhoun). New York: Harper and Brothers.

1965f “More Unsolicited Advice to Vatican Council II.” Pp. 37-66 in James Finn (ed.), *Peace, the Churches and the Bomb*. New York: Council on Religion and International Affairs.

1965g “The Uses of Power.” *Catholic Mind* 63/1196 (October): 11-23.

1966a “Farewell to Christian Realism.” *America* 114/18 (April 30): 618-622.

1966b “A Letter from Canon Rhymes to John of Patmos.” *Religion in Life* 35/2 (Spring): 218-229.

1966c “Living with Yourself.” *The Pulpit* 37/7 (July-August): 4-8.

1966d “Moral and Religious Implications of Genetic Control.” Pp. 107-169 in John D. Roslansky (ed.), *Genetics and the Future of Man*. Amsterdam: North-Holland Publishing Co. (distributed in U. S. by Appleton-Century-Crofts).

1966e “Nuclear War and Vatican Council II.” *Theology Today* 23/2 (July): 244-263.

1966f “Responsible Parenthood: A Response to Fr. Bernard Haering.” In *The Vatican Council and the World of Today*. Providence, R. I.: Office of the Secretary, Brown University.

1966g “Tucker's *Bellum contra Bellum Justum*.” Pp. 67-101 in Robert W. Tucker, *Just War and Vatican Council II: A Critique*. New York: Council on Religion and International Affairs.

1966h “Two Concepts of General Rules in Christian Ethics.” *Ethics* 76/3 (April): 192-207.

1966i “The Vatican Council on Modern War.” *Theological Studies* 27/2 (June): 179-203; *Theology Today* 23/2 (July): 244-263.

1966j “Vietnam: Dissent from Dissent.” *The Christian Century* 33/29 (July 20): 909-913.

1967a “Counting the Costs.” Pp. 24-44 in Michael B. Hamilton (ed.), *The Vietnam War: Christian Perspectives*. Grand Rapids, Michigan: William B. Eerdmans Publishing Co.

1967b “Death's Duel.” *The Pulpit* 38/3 (March): 16-19.

1967c “Discretionary Armed Service.” *Worldview* 10/2 (February): 8-11.

1967d “From Princeton, with Love.” *Reflection* (Yale Divinity School) 64/1 (January): 5-6.

1967e “Is Vietnam a Just War?” *Dialog* 6/1 (Winter): 19-29.

1967f “On Sexual Responsibility.” *The Catholic World* 205/1228 (July): 210-216.

1967g “Over the Slope to Total War?” *The Catholic World* 205/1225 (June): 166-168.

1967h “Responsible Parenthood: An Essay in Ecumenical Ethics.” *Religion in Life* 26/3 (Autumn): 343-354.

1967i “The Sanctity of Life—In the First of It.” *The Dublin Review* 511 (Spring): 1-21.

1967j “Two Extremes.” *Dialog* 6/3 (Summer): 218-219.

1968a “The Case of the Curious Exception.” Pp. 67-135 in Gene H. Outka and Paul Ramsey (eds.), *Norm and Context in Christian Ethics*. New York: Charles Scribner's Sons.

1968b “Christian Ethics Today.” *Rockford College Alumni Magazine*, Spring: 3-6, 23.

1968c “Christianity and Modern War.” *Theology Digest* 16/1 (Spring): 47-53.

1968d “Dissent, Democracy and Foreign Policy: A Symposium.” *Headline Series* 190 (August): 40-44. New York: Foreign Policy Association.

1968e “Election Issues 1968.” *Social Action/Social Progress* 35/2//59/1 (September-October): 18-28.

1968f “Election 1968, and Beyond.” *Worldview* 11/12 (December): 16-19.

1968g “The Morality of Abortion.” Pp. 60-93 in Daniel Labby (ed.), *Life or Death: Ethics and Options*. Seattle: University of Washington Press.

1968h “Naturrecht und Christliche Ethik bei N. H. Søe.” *Zeitschrift für Evangelische Ethik* 12/2 (March): 80-98.

1968i “On Taking Sexual Responsibility Seriously Enough.” Pp. 44-54 in Gibson Winter (ed.), *Social Ethics*. New York: Harper and Row; London: S. C. M. Press.

1968j “Political Repentance Now.” *Christianity and Crisis* 28/18 (October 28): 247-252.

1968k “Politics as Science, Not Prophecy.” *Worldview* 11/1 (January): 18-21.

1968l "A Proposal to the New Moralists." *Motive* 28/7 (April): 38-44.

1968m "A Reaction to 'Black Power and the Shock of Recognition' by James Luther Adams." *Action/Reaction* (San Francisco Theological Seminary), Summer: 5-6.

1968n "Selective Conscientious Objection: Warrants and Reservations in the Just War Doctrine." Pp. 31-77 in James Finn (ed.), *Conflict of Loyalties: Selective Conscientious Objection.* New York: Pegasus, Western Publishing Co.

1968o "War and the New Morality." *Reformed Journal* 18/2 (February): 25-28, with subsequent discussion.

1969a "Introduction." Pp. xi-xvii in William V. O'Brien, *War and/or Survival.* Garden City, N. Y.: Doubleday and Co.

1969b "Medical Ethics: A Joint Venture." *Reflection* (Yale Divinity School) 66/3 (March): 4-5.

1969c "On Up-Dating Death." Pp. 253-275 in Donald R. Cutler (ed.), *The Religious Situation.* Boston: Beacon Press. Also (as "On Updating Death") pp. 31-54 in Donald R. Cutler (ed.), *Updating Life and Death: Essays in Ethics and Medicine.* Boston: Beacon Press.

1970a "Abortion: A Theologian's View." *AORN* (Journal of the Association of Operating Room Nurses), November: 55-62. Also in Valerie Vance Dillon (ed.), *In Defense of Life.* Trenton, N. J.: New Jersey Right to Life Committee.

1970b "The Biblical Norm of Righteousness." *Interpretation* 24/4 (October): 419-429.

1970c "Christian Love in Search of a Social Policy." Pp. 184-196 in Harmon L. Smith and Louis W. Hodges (eds.), *The Christian and His Decisions.* Nashville and New York: Abingdon Press.

1970d "Christianity and Modern War." Pp. 275-285 in Everett J. Morgan, S. J. (ed.), *Christian Witness in the Secular City.* Chicago: Loyola University Press.

1970e "Feticide/Infanticide Upon Request." *Child and Family* 9/3 (Fall): 257-272; *Religion in Life* 39/2 (Summer): 170-186.

1970f "Panel Discussion." *Annals of the New York Academy of Sciences* 169/2 (January 21): 576-583.

1970g "Reference Points in Deciding about Abortion." Pp. 60-100 in John T. Noonan, Jr. (ed.), *The Morality of Abortion: Legal and Historical Perspectives.* Cambridge, Mass.: Harvard University Press.

1970h "Shall We Clone a Man?" Pp. 79-113 in Kenneth Vaux (ed.), *Who Shall Live? Medicine, Technology, Ethics.* Philadelphia: Fortress Press.

1971a "The Betrayal of Language." *Worldview* 14/2 (February): 7-10.

1971b "Christian Ethics and the Future of Humanism." Pp. 83-91 in Carl W. Grindell (ed.), *God, Man and Philosophy.* New York: St. John's University Press.

1971c "Church Stand Should Be Withdrawn." *The Christian Advocate*, 15/21 (November 11): 11-12.

1971d "The Ethics of a Cottage Industry in an Age of Community and Research Medicine." *New England Journal of Medicine* 284/13 (April 1): 700-706.

1971e "The Morality of Abortion." Pp. 1-27 in James Rachels (ed.), *Moral Problems: A Collection of Philosophical Essays.* New York: Harper and Row.

1971f "A Proposal to the New Moralists." Pp. 47-54 in Paul T. Jersild and Dale A. Johnson (eds.), *Moral Issues and Christian Responses.* New York: Holt, Rinehart and Winston, Inc.

1971g "Some Moral Problems Arising in Genetic Medicine." *Linacre Quarterly* 38/1 (February): 15-20.

1971h "The Wedge: Not So Simple." *The Hastings Center Report*, No. 3 (December): 11-12.

1971i "Who Speaks for the Church?" Pp. 117-125 in Paul T. Jersild and Dale A. Johnson (eds.), *Moral Issues and Christian Responses.* New York: Holt, Rinehart and Winston, Inc.

1972a "Author-Reviewer Symposia." *Philosophy Forum* 12: 149-164.

1972b "Does the Church Have Any Political Wisdom for the 70's? *Perkins* [School of Theology] *Journal* 26/1 (Fall): 29-40.

1972c "Force and Political Responsibility." Pp. 43-73 in Ernest W. Lefever (ed.), *Ethics and World Politics.* Baltimore: Johns Hopkins Press.

1972d "Genetic Engineering." *Bulletin of the Atomic Scientists*, 28/10 (December): 14-17.

1972e "Genetic Therapy: A Theologian's Response." Pp. 157-175 in Michael Hamilton (ed.), *The New Genetics and the Future of Man.* Grand Rapids, Mich.: William B. Eerdmans Publishing Co.

1972f "The MAD Nuclear Policy." *Worldview* 15/11 (November): 16-20.

1972g "The Morality of Manipulation." *Worcester Polytechnic Institute Journal* 76/1 (August): 11-13.

1972h "Shall We 'Reproduce'? I. The Medical Ethics of *In Vitro* Fertilization." *Journal of the American Medical Association* 220/10 (June 5): 1346-1350.

1972i "Shall We 'Reproduce'? II. Rejoinders and Future Forecast." *Journal of the American Medical Association* 220/11 (June 12): 1480-1485.

1973a "Abortion: A Review Article." *The Thomist* 37/1 (January): 174-226.

1973b "The Abstractness of Concrete Advice." Pp. 335-345 in Norbert Brockman and Nicholas Piediscalzi (eds.), *Contemporary Religion and Social Responsibility.* New York: Alba House.

1973c "The Just Revolution." *Worldview* 16/10 (October): 37-40.

1973d "Medical Progress and Canons of Loyalty to Experimental Subjects." *Proceedings* (Institute for Theological Encounter with Science and Technology), 51-77.

1973e "Military Service as a Moral System." *Military Chaplains' Review* 2/1 (January): 8-21.

1973f "The Moral and Religious Implications of Genetic Control." Pp. 364-382 in Adela S. Baer (ed.), *Heredity and Society: Readings in Social Genetics.* New York: The Macmillan Co.

1973g "Morals and the Practice of Genetic Medicine." Pp. 71-84 in Joseph Papin (ed.), *The Pilgrim People: A Vision with Hope.* Villanova, Pa.: Villanova University Press.

1973h "The Nature of Medical Ethics." Pp. 14-27 in Robert M. Veatch, Willard Gaylin and Councilman Morgan (eds.), *The Teaching of Medical Ethics.* Hastings-on-Hudson, N. Y.: The Hastings Center, Institute of Society, Ethics and the Life Sciences.

1973i "Should Medicine Today Be Taught without Medical Ethics?" *Connecticut Medicine* 37/8 (August): 420-421.

1973j "A Political Ethics Context for Strategic Thinking." Pp. 101-147 in Morton A. Kaplan (ed.), *Strategic Thinking and Its Moral Implications.* Chicago: University of Chicago Center for Policy Study.

1973k "Screening: An Ethicist's View." Pp. 147-167 in Bruce Hilton, Daniel Callahan, Maureen Harris, Peter Condliff and Burton Berkley (eds.), *Ethical Issues in Human Genetics: Genetic Counseling and the Use of Genetic Knowledge.* New York: Plenum Publishing Corp.

1973l "Shall We 'Reproduce'?" Pp. 87-120 in Martin E. Marty and Dean G. Peerman (eds.), *New Theology No. 10.* New York: The Macmillan Co.

1974a "Conceptual Foundations for an Ethics of Medical Care: A Response." In *Ethics and Health Care: Proceedings of the Conference on Health Care and Changing Values.* Washington, D. C.: National Academy of Sciences.

1974b "The Indignity of 'Death with Dignity'." With Response by Leon R. Kass and Robert Morison. *Hastings Center Studies* 2/2 (May): 47-62.